BIBLICAL ETHICS

BIBLICAL ETHICS

A Guide to
the Ethical Message of the Scriptures
from Genesis through Revelation

T. B. MASTON

Mercer
University
Press

Biblical Ethics copyright © 1967 by T. B. Maston
A Mercer University Press Reprint . . . May 1982,
January 1988, July 1989, and July 1991
Originally published by World Pub. Co., 1967.
Published by Word Books, Publishers,
September 1969; eighth printing, March 1979.

The paper used in this publication meets
the minimum requirements of American National Standard
for Information Sciences—Permanence of Paper
for Printed Library Materials, ANSI Z39.48-1984

Except when otherwise indicated, Scripture quotations are from the Revised
Standard Version of the Bible (RSV), copyrighted 1946, 1952, © 1971, 1973
by the Division of Christian Education of the National Council of Churches of
Christ in the U.S.A., and are used by permission.

Library of Congress Cataloging in Publication Data

Maston, T. B. (Thomas Bufford), 1897-
    Biblical ethics.

    Reprint. Originally published: Cleveland: World Pub. Co., 1967.
    Includes bibliographical references and index.
    1. Ethics in the Bible.   I. Title.
[BS680.E84M3   1982]   241   82-6470
ISBN 0-86554-312-7   AACR2

CONTENTS

To
former students
who majored in Christian ethics
and particularly
to the memory
of
Charles P. Johnson

PREFACE

The Bible is the most important possession of the Christian churches, far more important than all of their buildings, institutions, and endowments. Protestants who give to it a "unique and unrivaled place of authority"[1] need in a special way to be acquainted with it and to see the relevance of its basic concepts and principles to the life of the individual and the world in which he lives. The present volume attempts to set forth the central moral concepts and the basic ethical principles of the Bible, many of which are abidingly relevant.

This book has resulted from a deepening sense of need for a survey of biblical ethics. Some good books on New Testament ethics have been published in recent years, but, with one or two exceptions, no comparable books have been published on Old Testament ethics. Also, so far as is known, no book has been published for many years that covers the ethics of both Testaments. This book is an attempt to meet that need.

The writing of this book has also stemmed from a conviction that an outstanding weakness, if not *the* outstanding weakness, of contemporary Christianity is ethical or moral. There are many factors contributing to this weakness, but a major one is the tendency to separate faith from daily living, theology from ethics. In turn, this tendency stems to a considerable degree from a failure on the part of many ministers and Christians in general to understand the significant place of the ethical in the biblical revelation.

The book was not written for scholars, but for ministers, laymen, and particularly college, university, and seminary students. It is hoped that many teachers will find the book useful as a text

1 Floyd V. Filson, *Which Books Belong in the Bible?* (Philadelphia: Westminster Press, 1957), p. 11.

or as required or supplementary reading, not only in courses in Christian social ethics, but also in courses in Old Testament, New Testament, and theology. There are some suggestions for additional study that may be used for assignments or as ideas for supplemental lectures. Pastors may find these suggestions useful for study purposes and as sources for possible talks or sermons.

The organization or outline of the chapters varies considerably, depending on the nature of the material covered. In some chapters a book-by-book sequence is followed. In others a topical outline dominates. It has been considered wise to insert between the chapters on the Old Testament and those on the New Testament a chapter on the Apocrypha, Pseudepigrapha, and the Dead Sea Scrolls.

In preparation for the writing of the book, the Old Testament and New Testament were re-read and studied in their entirety, with tentative outlines being worked out at that time. Also, R. H. Charles' translation of the Apocrypha and Pseudepigrapha was read along with T. H. Gaster's translation of the Dead Sea Scrolls. Concordances and standard reference books, such as Kittel's *Bible Key Words* (Harper), Alan Richardson's *A Theological Word Book of the Bible* (Macmillan), and *A Companion to the Bible* (Oxford) edited by J. J. Von Allmen, were utilized. Commentaries, particularly those with an exegetical approach, and other books, such as introductions and theologies of the Old Testament and New Testament, have been used to check personal conclusions and to enrich the material in various ways.

An attempt has been made to set forth in a systematic way the ethical content of the various books of the Bible. The study is really a *survey* of biblical ethics. This explains the inclusion of "miscellaneous" headings in some of the chapters and also the inclusion of some books that have less significance than others for the study. The survey would not be complete without them. An effort has been made to let the Scriptures largely speak for themselves. There has been no attempt to force the material into an arbitrary organization. While there are recurring and, to a degree, continuous themes, there is no one single unifying motif. There is, however, a central unifying Person—God. The ethical content of the Bible naturally evolves from the nature of the God that is revealed there. The basic concern throughout the Bible is not with man, but with God. This is as true in the ethics of the Bible as it is in its theology, which may explain the fact that theology and ethics are so closely related in the Scriptures.

There has been a conscious effort in this study to refrain from excessive evaluation of the material. Interpretation has been given in some places in an effort to allow the Scriptures to speak more clearly. It is hoped that the general approach which has been used will give maximum opportunity for readers to feel the impact of the total ethical content of the Scriptures. There are sections of the material that will be much more meaningful if studied with an open Bible. It will be discovered that the emphasis throughout has been on the positive rather than the negative and on the basic ethic rather than the applied ethic, whether individual or social. There are a few exceptions to the latter, such as Proverbs and some of the apocryphal and pseudepigraphic writings where the content is so largely applied or social. It is recognized that there is needed another book or a series of books on the social problems and issues of the Scriptures.

Occasional footnotes for supplemental reading and study are provided. This is particularly true regarding some of the major critical problems. An effort has been made in most cases to suggest books that will represent differing perspectives. These are intended particularly for teachers and other serious students of the Bible who want to do some background reading.

Since this is a book on biblical ethics, some statement should be made about the relation of biblical ethics to Christian ethics and the general place that the Bible has in Christian ethics and in the Christian life in general. The Bible occupies a peculiarly significant and authoritative position for Protestants. Otto Piper correctly suggests that "Protestant ethics must be based upon the Bible." He also says that "the authority of the Bible rests upon the fact that notwithstanding its historical origin it presents a view of life that is of lasting truth."[2] Students of Christian ethics and of the Christian life may differ widely in the ways they use the Bible and in their interpretation of *how* it is authoritative,

[2] Otto A. Piper, *The Biblical View of Sex and Marriage* (New York: Scribner's, 1960), p. 13.

but they generally agree that it *is* authoritative. Some scholars and Christians in general would cite particular laws or specific rules as authoritative in the Christian life. Those who take this position turn to the commandments of the Bible which they claim are found in both Testaments.[3]

There are others who place the emphasis on the principles or ideals of the Bible instead of on laws or specific precepts. Those who take this approach do not necessarily turn to the Bible for specific answers for every question or as a solution for every problem. They suggest that more important than the commandments are the principles or ideals that may be expressed through the commandments and may be the source of the commandments. Also, some would say that more important than any specific principle or ideal is the spirit or attitude revealed by and through the ideal.

Whether it is believed that the authority of the Bible rests primarily in its laws or in its principles and ideals, some would suggest that many of the specific teachings of the New Testament, as well as of the Old Testament, were historically conditioned. This implies, among other things, that some of the specific teachings are irrelevant and hence not authoritative for the contemporary Christian community. This does not necessarily mean that the prescriptive element is entirely lacking. It may be that behind the particular prescription or law there lies some principle or principles that are continually relevant and, hence, abidingly valid and authoritative. To use Piper's term, there is at least, revealed in the Scriptures "a view of life" that is relevant and authoritative.

In the contemporary period there is a particular emphasis on what is variously called a contextual, relational, or situational ethic. Those who hold this position maintain a distinctive approach in their analysis of the Bible and in its use, with emphasis not on laws or precepts nor on principles or ideals, but on relationships. For example, when the Bible is applied, their concern is with relations within the context of the contemporary scene.

[3] An article by Edward Leroy Long, Jr., "The Use of the Bible in Christian Ethics," *Interpretation*, XIX, No. 2 (April, 1965), 149–62, has been unusually helpful in this discussion of the relation of biblical ethics and Christian ethics.

Paul Lehmann, whose approach is contextual, says that "an analysis of Christian ethics involves a kind of running conversation between the New Testament, on the one hand, and our situation, as heirs of the New Testament, on the other."[4] The movement tends to be from the present situation to the Bible rather than from the Bible to the present. Lehmann also says: "A *koinonia* ethic is concerned with relations and functions, not with principles and precepts."[5] This statement, it seems to me, goes too far. It may be that the Christian ethic is *primarily* an ethic of community or a relational ethic, but there are at least certain principles and even precepts that are applicable to, and operative within, the framework of "relations and functions." In other words, as is so frequently true, the option should not be an "either-or" but a "both-and." A *koinonia* ethic may be concerned primarily with relations, but it should also be concerned with principles. There are precepts and particularly principles that govern relations within the covenant community.

It may be well to suggest that there is not so much difference between laws and principles as is sometimes supposed. For example, the basic principles found in the teachings of Jesus are in harmony with the fundamental law of God. By using the term "fundamental law" we would make a distinction between legal requirements—Old Testament and otherwise—and basic law. The latter is in harmony with our natures and the nature of the world in which we live. The basic law, and the laws that conform to and are expressive of it, are for our good. It was Jesus who said that man was not made for the Sabbath, but the Sabbath was made for man. This perspective concerning law will help to save us from legalism.

A strict choice does not have to be made between law, principle, and relationship. All have their proper place in biblical ethics and in the Christian life. One would do violence to the material found in the Bible if one sought to make everything in the Scriptures fit into a particular mold: law, principle, or relationship. It is a question of emphasis or primary concern. There is clearly a major

[4] *Ethics in a Christian Context* (New York: Harper and Row, 1963), p. 29.
[5] *Ibid.*, p. 124.

emphasis in the Bible on the matter of relationship. In the Old Testament it is the relation of God to His covenant people, but also, in turn, their relation to Him and to one another within the covenant and even to people outside of the covenant. The relational element is also common in the New Testament; the Church becomes the people of the New Covenant. Much of the ethical content of the New Testament is directed to those within the covenant relationship. Present in the Old Testament, but much more evident in the New Testament, is a relationship on a more personal basis. This reaches its climax in the writings of Paul and John with their emphasis on the union of the child of God with the resurrected Christ. Whether the relation is primarily individual or group, there are enumerated certain precepts and principles that evolve from that relationship and, in turn, become the test of the reality of the relationship itself.

The preceding discussion means, among other things, that the ethical teachings of the Bible should be of major concern to any Christian, regardless of his theory about Christian ethics. It is hoped that this study will be helpful to teachers, pastors, and others with varying theological perspectives and with differing theories regarding the relation of biblical ethics to Christian ethics and to the Christian life in general.

The book has been written with some hesitation, for I do not claim to be a technical biblical scholar. I have sought to make up for my deficiency by utilizing the writings of recognized scholars. I acknowledge my indebtedness to a number of them, without whose work the production of this volume would have been an extremely difficult, if not impossible, task. In addition to the authors who are cited in footnotes, there are many other persons who helped in various ways. The following read portions or all of the manuscript and made suggestions for its improvement: Clyde Francisco, Roy Honeycutt, Boyd Hunt, Bill Pinson, and C. W. Scudder. To two of my colleagues a special word of appreciation is due: Ralph Smith, in the area of the Old Testament; and J. W. MacGorman, in the area of the New Testament. Both men made many suggestions regarding sources and perspectives that contributed significantly to the final shape of the manuscript.

My son Gene was, as usual, particularly helpful in smoothing out construction and in improving writing style.

Among several secretaries who worked at various times on the manuscript, special appreciation should be expressed to Charles Meadows, Mrs. Ben Bledsoe, Mrs. Phil Perrin, and particularly to Mrs. Melvin Bridgford, who prepared the final copy. It has been a privilege to work with the staff of The World Publishing Company, who have made numerous suggestions that have strengthened the manuscript.

It is impossible to know how to express adequately my indebtedness to my companion of the years who contributes so much in ways that she can never know to all that I write and do.

T. B. MASTON

ABBREVIATIONS

Translations

ASV   American Standard Version (Thomas Nelson).

KJV   King James Version.

MOFFATT   James Moffatt, *A New Translation of the Bible* (Hodder and Stoughton).

NASB   New American Standard Bible (Broadman Press).

NEB   *New English Bible* (Oxford University Press; Cambridge University Press).

PHILLIPS   J. B. Phillips, *The New Testament in Modern English* (Macmillan).

RSV   Revised Standard Version.

SMITH   J. M. Powis Smith, Edgar J. Goodspeed, and others, *The Complete Bible: An American Translation* (University of Chicago Press).

WEYMOUTH   Richard Francis Weymouth, *The New Testament in Modern Speech* (Pilgrim Press).

WILLIAMS   Charles B. Williams, *The New Testament: A Private Translation in the Language of the People* (Moody Press).

Commentaries

Commentaries that follow a verse-by-verse format are referred to, in abbreviated form, in the body of the material, except when the reference is from the introduction.

CB   *The Cambridge Bible for Schools and Colleges* (Cambridge University Press).

Ex.G.   *The Expositor's Greek Testament* (Geo. H. Doran).

IB   *The Interpreter's Bible* (Abingdon Press).

ICC   *The International Critical Commentary.*

KD   C. F. Keil and F. Delitzsch, *Biblical Commentary on the Old Testament* (Eerdmans).

MC   *The Moffatt Commentary* (Hodder and Stoughton).

WC   *Westminster Commentaries* (Methuen).

WP   Archibald Thomas Robertson, *Word Pictures in the New Testament* (Broadman Press).

Other commentaries that are not volumes in a multi-volume series are referred to by the name of the author in the body of the material after an initial identifying footnote.

CHAPTER I

THE LAW

The Jews considered their Scriptures as essentially the Law (*Torah*) or the Pentateuch to which the other two major divisions of their Scriptures—the Prophets and the Writings—were subordinate. One Old Testament scholar claims that "the literature of the world contains no book to equal the Pentateuch in its importance and its effect."[1] The continuing importance of the Pentateuch stems, to a considerable degree, from its balanced emphasis on religion and life, theology and ethics.

The emphasis on the ethical is particularly prevalent in "The Covenant Code" (Exodus), "The Holiness Code" (Leviticus), and the book of Deuteronomy. Before studying these major areas, it will be helpful to explore some concepts that permeate and provide a general perspective for the Pentateuch and for the entire Old Testament.[2]

[1] Artur Weiser, *The Old Testament: Its Formation and Development,* trans. Dorothea M. Barton (New York: Association Press, 1961), p. 71.
[2] The following are a few of the many books, representing different perspectives, which will be helpful to those who want to study the critical problems of the Pentateuch: G. Charles Aalders, *A Short Introduction to the Pentateuch* (London: The Tyndale Press, 1949)—rejects the Wellhausen hypothesis and believes the Pentateuch is an anonymous work containing a great deal of Mosaic material; Oswald T. Allis, *The Five Books of Moses,* 2nd ed. (Philadelphia: The Presbyterian and Reformed Publishing Co., 1949)—rejects what he calls the "Development Hypothesis" of Graf-Wellhausen and defends the Mosaic authorship; Aage Bentzen, *Introduction to the Old Testament,* 2nd ed. (Copenhagen: G. E. C. Gad Publisher, 1952)—contains a very compact

Central Concepts[3]

No attempt is made here to study these concepts in detail. Attention is given chiefly to those aspects most directly related to a study of biblical ethics.

scholarly review of the literature on Pentateuchal criticism (II, 12–24), examines the documentary hypothesis (II, 24–60), concluding that there is widespread distrust of the theory (p. 60) and that it must be given up "in its purely literary form" (p. 61)—his emphasis is on form criticism; John Bright, *A History of Israel* (Philadelphia: The Westminster Press, 1959)—accepts the documentary hypothesis but considerably modifies it, believing that all the documents contain ancient material, and hence, they cannot be arranged in any neat order, and that one factor that necessitated a reappraisal of some of the claims of the Graf-Wellhausen school has been archaeological finds related to the age of Israel's origin (see particularly pp. 61–69); Samuel A. Cartledge, *A Conservative Introduction to the Old Testament* (Athens, Ga.: University of Georgia Press, 1944)—presents briefly, simply, and objectively the arguments for the Mosaic authorship, which he seems to accept in a modified form (pp. 44–49); Robert H. Pfeiffer, *Introduction to the Old Testament*, rev. ed. (New York: Harper, 1948)—accepts the Graf-Wellhausen theory with slight modifications that carry it further [There is an abridgment of this book under the title *The Books of the Old Testament* (Harper, 1957).]; H. H. Rowley, *The Growth of the Old Testament* (London: Hutchinson's University Library, 1950)—accepts the documentary hypothesis but discusses at some length "The Sources behind the Sources" (pp. 37–42), contending that there were written sources dealing with the period covered by the Pentateuch; Artur Weiser, *The Old Testament: Its Formation and Development*, trans. Dorothea M. Barton (New York: Association Press, 1961)—accepts the documentary theory, spelling it out somewhat in detail (pp. 99–142), and includes a compact history of Pentateuchal criticism (pp. 74–81); G. Ernest Wright, *The Old Testament Against Its Environment* (Chicago: Henry Regnery Co., 1950)—accepts the documentary theory but does not let it interfere with the presentation of the message of the Old Testament in general and the Pentateuch in particular—quite similar in perspective to Bright and Rowley; and Edward J. Young, *An Introduction to the Old Testament* (Grand Rapids: Eerdmans, 1949)—defends the Mosaic authorship and hence the unity of the Pentateuch, more thorough but not as objective as Cartledge. The books by Bentzen, Bright, Cartledge, Pfeiffer, Rowley, Weiser, and Young would provide material on the other major critical problems of the Old Testament, such as the dating and authorship of Deuteronomy, the nature of Job and Jonah, the unity of Isaiah, and other problems of lesser significance.

For a brief, thoroughly documented summary of Old Testament criticism, see John Bright's chapter entitled "Modern Study of Old Testament Literature," *The Bible and the Near East*, ed. G. Ernest Wright (Garden City, N. Y.: Doubleday, 1961).

[3] The concept of the covenant and the idea of holiness, both of which are very important in the Pentateuch and in the Old Testament in general, will be discussed later rather than in this section.

1. Concerning God.[4]

As Muilenburg says, there is "no unified and coherent body of ethical principles" in the Old Testament, but as he also says, the Hebrew "knew that he had been addressed, that he had been told what was required of him . . . and who it was who had exacted of him such demands." Furthermore, the Hebrew knew that "what is good is what God requires; what is evil is what God forbids."[5] Without any systematized formulation of their ethic "no other people had anything which remotely approached Israel in the profundity and vitality of the ethical foundations of its life."[6] This profundity and particularly the vitality resulted from Israel's relation to her God. He is the central point of reference in the Old Testament for both theology and ethics. The ethical content of the Old Testament was based upon and derived from the nature and will of God.

This theocentric approach is evident in the first questions of the Bible, all of which have considerable significance for biblical ethics. God's question to Adam was: "Where are you?" (Gen. 3:9); to Eve and again to Cain, it was: "What is this that you have done?" (Gen. 3:13; cf. 4:10), and to Cain: "Where is Abel your brother?" Cain's question to God was: "Am I my brother's keeper?" (Gen. 4:9). These questions were the beginning of a continuing dialogue between God and man, climaxed when God's Word became flesh and dwelt among us (John 1:14). In the Word, God's "invitation to conversation became an invitation to companionship."[7]

God is revealed in the Pentateuch as the Creator and as creatively active in the world. He is the sovereign God. All the nations of the world, as well as His own people Israel, are re-

---

[4] Edmond Jacob's *Theology of the Old Testament,* trans. Arthur W. Heathcote and Philip J. Allcock (New York: Harper and Row, 1958), is a particularly helpful source for a study of God in the Old Testament. The entire volume is organized around the work and character of God.

[5] James Muilenburg, *The Way of Israel: Biblical Faith and Ethics* (New York: Harper, 1961), p. 15.

[6] *Ibid.,* p. 76.

[7] D. T. Niles, *Reading the Bible To-day* (London: Lutterworth Press, 1955), p. 33.

sponsible to Him. He is concerned with the totality of the life of the individual, the nation, and the world.

This One who is the sovereign God is also the *Father* of His people (Ex. 4:22; Deut. 1:31; 32:36), a concept that is found elsewhere in Old Testament writings (see Ps. 89:26; Isa. 63:16; 64:8; Jer. 3:19) but is especially prominent in the life and teachings of Jesus. As a father, God loved Israel, an idea particularly prevalent in Deuteronomy. Because of His love He had brought Israel out of Egypt and had chosen her to fulfill His purpose (Deut. 4:37; 7:7–8). His love was an expression of His grace and sovereignty. He had "set his heart in love" upon Israel "above all peoples," although "heaven and the heaven of heavens, the earth with all that is in it" belonged to Him (Deut. 10:14–15). His love even included the sojourner in their midst (Deut. 10:18). God was no respecter of persons or showed no partiality, a truth that is deeply embedded in both the Old and the New Testaments and a truth which has great and abiding significance for human relations.

God's love expresses itself in *hesed,* a word which "has no exact equivalent in our modern languages."[8] It is variously translated as "mercy," "loving-kindness," or "steadfast love" (the latter being used largely, though not exclusively, in the Revised Standard Version). The great Jewish scholar, Moses Maimonides, says that *hesed* denotes "an excess of moral quality" and that "it is especially used of extra-ordinary kindness," of "kindness to those who have no claim whatever," and "is employed to express the good bestowed upon us by God."[9] Baab says that it "is predominantly a word for the outreaching love of God."[10]

Although the word "hesed" is found far more frequently in the Psalms than elsewhere in the Old Testament, the idea is expressed several times in the books of the Pentateuch. For example, it is said that "the Lord is slow to anger, and abounding in steadfast

---

[8] Jacob, p. 103.

[9] Jacob S. Minkin, *The World of Moses Maimonides, with Selections from His Writings* (New York: Thomas Yoseloff, 1957), p. 368.

[10] Otto J. Baab, *The Theology of the Old Testament* (New York: Abingdon Press, 1949), p. 128. For additional definitions of and statements regarding *hesed* see pp. 74–75.

love" (Num. 14:18). The servant of Abraham, in his search for a wife for Isaac, used the word three times (Gen. 24:12, 14, 27), the last time linking it with faithfulness (cf. Gen. 32:10; Ex. 34:6). Moses reminded the children of Israel that their Lord was "the faithful God who keeps covenant and steadfast love (*hesed*) with those who love him and keep his commandments, to a thousand generations" (Deut. 7:9; cf. Ex. 20:6; Deut. 5:10). The latter correctly suggests that *hesed* is closely related to the covenant idea (*berith*). (See I Sam. 20:8 for a good illustration—Jonathan and David.)

Another quality of God, which has major significance for biblical ethics, is His righteousness (*tsedeq, tsedaqah*). While there are very few specific references to the righteousness of God, the idea permeates the books of the Law. What is meant by "righteousness"? One is righteous when he fulfills the demands of a relationship. God's righteousness is known by His fulfillment of His covenant with His people. He, in turn, expects His people to be righteous or to fulfill the demands of the covenant. The righteousness He expects of His people covers the widest possible field—it covers "social, ethical, and religious behaviour,"[11] and not only behavior but also disposition.

This sketch of the nature of God would not be complete without a brief statement concerning the moral problems of the Pentateuch and of the Old Testament in general. These problems stem primarily from God's part in acts and activities that do not accord with contemporary Christian standards of morality. The problem is deepened for the searching Christian mind because it finds revealed in the Old Testament that God was not only righteous, just, and loving, but that He was also the sovereign God of

---

11 Walther Eichrodt, *Theology of the Old Testament*, trans. J. A. Baker (Philadelphia: Westminster Press, 1961), I, 240. For helpful articles on "righteous" and "righteousness," see E. R. Achtemeier, "Righteousness in the OT," *The Interpreter's Dictionary of the Bible*, ed. George A. Buttrick (New York: Abingdon Press, 1962), and N. H. Snaith, "Righteous, Righteousness," *Theological Word Book of the Bible*, ed. Alan Richardson (New York: Macmillan, 1959). Snaith, in particular, gives an ethical emphasis in his definitions of *tsedeq* and *tsedaqah*. He says, "The idea conveyed by the words is certainly ethical." He suggests, however, that there was a gradual development in the meaning of the words which ultimately included the idea of benevolence and salvation.

the nations. In the light of the kind of God the Hebrews claimed to have worshipped, how can one explain His approval of (or did He really approve?) the savagery of the children of Israel in the prosecution of war, such as the slaying of women and children (Ex. 17:14; Deut. 2:31–36; 3:3–6; 7:2–5)?

How can this and other moral difficulties in the Old Testament be explained?[12] Did God actually command the children of Israel to do these things or were they mistaken? Eichrodt, in a brief but helpful discussion, suggests, among other things, that God "reveals himself in different ways in the different periods of human history, and makes different claims on the obedience of his people in accordance with the general spiritual situation, without at the same time qualifying the reality of his fellowship." He further says, "What is required is to understand that those features which offend us are simply *the concomitants of a tremendous spiritual struggle* which was bound to burst into flame with the introduction into Israel of the religion of Yahweh."[13]

An educative process was at work. God had to begin with Israel and her neighbors where they were. To achieve His purposes with them, He had to adjust His acts and even His laws to the stage of their development. The statement by Jesus in response to the pressing question of the Pharisees regarding divorce throws considerable light on the proper evaluation and interpretation of the Old Testament. He said to them, "For your hardness of heart Moses allowed you to divorce your wives, but from the beginning it was not so" (Matt. 19:8). Here was something even in the law that was contrary to the original purpose and the ultimate ideal of God.

If we look carefully enough, however, we will discover in the Old Testament the original purpose of God or His ultimate ideal, which is always in harmony with the full revelation of God in Christ. For example, regarding divorce it is revealed that the

---

12 The cruelty of the wars of the Old Testament cannot be understood apart from the concept of "The Holy War," with the separation unto holy or sacred purposes of things and even people that had belonged to the profane. See Roland de Vaux, *Ancient Israel: Its Life and Institutions*, trans. John McHugh (New York: McGraw-Hill, 1961), pp. 258–61, for an excellent brief discussion of "The Holy War."

13 Eichrodt, I, 284.

priest was not to marry one who had been divorced "for the priest is holy to his God," which implies that there is something unholy about divorce (Lev. 21:7; cf. v. 14 and Ezek. 44:22). It plainly says in Malachi that the Lord hates "putting away" or "divorce" (Mal. 2:16). Again, although God commanded His people to fight, there is evidence that He disapproved of war. For example, David was not permitted to build a house for the Lord because he had "shed much blood" and "waged great wars" (I Chron. 22:8; 28:3). Also, the ideal age of the future was always portrayed as a time of peace (Isa. 2:2–4; 9:5–7; Micah 4:1–3).

2. Concerning man.

While there is an important place for man in the Old Testament, he is not the center. The Old Testament approach to life in general and even to the problems of man is theocentric rather than anthropocentric. Man, from the biblical perspective, is important primarily because of his relation to God.

There are, however, several more or less prevalent concepts concerning man that have considerable significance for this study and for contemporary human relations. One is the unity of mankind. This unity is evident whether one goes back to Adam or only as far back as Noah. It is clearly revealed that God "made from one every nation of men" (Acts 17:26), or "created every race of men of one stock" (NEB).

It is also plainly stated that God created man in His image, which is one of the most significant concepts in the Bible and one of the most formative factors in our Western way of life. The record says, "Let us make man in our image, after our likeness. . . . So God created man in his own image, in the image of God he created him; male and female he created them" (Gen. 1:26–27; cf. 5:1–2; 9:5–6).[14] Is any distinction to be made between "image" (*tselem*), which alone is used in Genesis 9:6, and "likeness" (*demuth*), which alone is used in Genesis 5:1 (see Gen. 5:3 for the use of both words)? There may be some etymological difference,

---

[14] Helmut Thielicke's *How the World Began*, trans. John W. Doberstein (Philadelphia: Muhlenberg Press, 1961), has a chapter entitled "Man—the Risk of God." The entire book is a series of sermons on the first chapters of Genesis with the subtitle: *Man in the First Chapters of the Bible.*

but it seems here that the use of the two words represents the Jewish proneness to parallelism.

Much more important for this study than any possible distinction between *tselem* and *demuth* is the meaning and significance of the fact that man was created in the image of God. The record of the Creation clearly reveals that man is related to the animal world, being created on the same day. However, he stands apart from the animal creation.

What is it that sets man apart? In other words, what does "the image of God" mean? God is a person, man is a person. There is no person without other persons. The most distinctive thing about a person is not only his capability for communication but the necessity of communication. This means, among other things, that man was created for fellowship. God Himself said, "It is not good that the man should be alone" (Gen. 2:18). He needs to have some one with whom he can share life, some one with whom he can communicate. On the human level the highest expression of this sharing is between a husband and wife. The highest level of communication is attained, however, only when man communicates with God.

It may be that the basic idea of the image is that man is created as God's representative in the world. Earthly monarchs have a habit of erecting images of themselves. God has created man as His image, the sign or symbol of His authority in the world. Man's authority or dominion over creation will be effective only in proportion to the reality of his relationship with and dependence upon God. If man is God's representative in the world he is to participate with God in His work in the world. This involves, at least to a degree, the "imitation" of God. God specifically says to His people: "You shall be holy; for I the Lord your God am holy" (Lev. 19:2; cf. 11:44).

Man is also represented in the Pentateuch as the sinner, as a rebel against God. It is revealed that sin separates God and man. Its evil consequences are seen in human relations (Cain and Abel) as well as in human-divine relations. The story of the Fall clearly shows that sin is social as well as spiritual—no man can sin unto himself. Inevitably others are involved in and affected by his sin (Gen. 3:8, 23–24; 4:14). Particularly significant is the fact that the image of God in man was not completely destroyed in the Fall (see Gen. 5:1–2). This is clearly seen in a statement made after the Flood. God said to Noah, "Whoever sheds the blood of man, by man shall his blood be shed; for God made man in his own image" (Gen. 9:6). Here is the basis for the dignity and worth of man, a dignity that belongs to all men. This is another truth that is abidingly relevant for the relation of peoples of various colors and cultures.

Still another concept, which is quite central and significant in Hebrew thought, is the close relation of the individual and the group or community. The sense of solidarity was unusually strong. The group was punished for the sins of the individual. Rewards were likewise shared by all. For example, not only was Noah, the just man, saved but also his family. There is evidence for what has been called "a corporate personality." A whole group composed not only of the present members but also of those who had been and would be members of the group were thought of as a single individual.

3. Concerning the Law.

The word *torah* (law) is derived from a root that means "to cast" or "to teach." One author contends that in the pre-exilic period, the word, in most cases, should be rendered "instruction or teaching" rather than "law."[15] The word *torah* is found only once in Genesis (26:5) and six times in the first chapters of Exodus (12:49; 13:9; 16:4; 28; 18:16, 20). Beginning with the Code of the Covenant, the word is quite prevalent, being found with some variation in use and meaning in most of the books of the Old Testament.[16] When used in its collective sense, *torah* refers to all the regulations or teachings regarding man's relation to God and to his fellow man. The word came to refer to the first five books of the Bible, which are frequently called the *Torah* or Law of Moses.

[15] Muilenburg, p. 25.

[16] For an excellent article from the perspective of a Jewish scholar, see Richard L. Rubenstein, "The Meaning of Torah in Contemporary Jewish Theology," *The Journal of Bible and Religion,* XXXII, 2 (April, 1964), 115–24.

In recent years, scholars have distinguished two general types or styles of laws: casuistic and apodictic. The former, usually quite specific, are frequently introduced with an "if" or "supposing that," and usually have a definite solution or punishment attached (see Ex. 21–23). These laws, in the main, were a common possession with other Semitic peoples. These laws which belonged primarily in the secular area became sacred to the children of Israel, since God as the sovereign God of the universe was, for them, the source for and the authority behind all law. In contrast, apodictic laws are rather general and operate as categorical imperatives; they are usually quite brief and lay down prohibitions in the second person future. Their requirements are unconditional. Apodictic laws in the Pentateuch are frequently found in short verses, the Ten Commandments being the best examples (for other examples see Ex. 23:1–3, 6–9; Lev. 18:6–23). The apodictic form of the law was largely, though not exclusively, the creation of Israel.

From the perspective of the Hebrews, as suggested previously, all laws ultimately came from God. They did not make a sharp distinction on the one hand between apodictic and casuistic laws, or on the other hand between ritualistic and ethical or moral laws. The intermingling of the secular and the sacred, of religion and morality resulted from "a disciplined determination to relate the whole of life to the one all-ruling will of God."[17]

It is true, however, that the ethical was quite prominent in the Israelite conception of law. Even ritualistic regulations frequently contained moral overtones. For example, the Law provided ritual acts as a means for the cleansing of moral sin, but those acts must be accompanied by penitence and restitution where the latter was possible (see Lev. 5:5b, but especially Num. 5:7b).

The Law also contained a great pedagogic purpose which was basically ethical or moral. Through the Law, God sought to reveal Himself and His will to Israel. One evident purpose of that revelation was the development of a responsive and responsible people, a people who would be more sensitive to the needs of others because they were more conscious of the nature and character of God. This moral purpose helps to explain the developmental

[17] Eichrodt, I, 75.

nature of the Law. There are some things in the Law, such as the divorce clause (Deut. 24:1–4; cf. Matt. 19:3–12), which do not measure up to the high requirements of the perfect revelation of God in Christ. The Law, however, represented progress for the people to whom it was addressed. God, through the Law, kept His people moving in the right direction, challenged by the Law to face toward the open road of a fuller revelation.

This means, among other things, that the Law was given to man for his good. It was an expression of God's grace and goodness and of His love for Israel. Ultimately written on the hearts of His people, the Law did not infringe on their freedom; rather, it provided for the fulfillment of their freedom. The Law also brought into the world new respect for human life. Special provisions were made for the socially disinherited, such as the widow, the orphan, the poor, the stranger or sojourner (Ex. 22:21–27), the slave (Deut. 23:15–16), and even the enemy (Ex. 23:4–5). The law of retaliation, or *lex talionis* (Ex. 21:23–25; Lev. 24:19–20; Deut. 19:21; Matt. 5:38), seemingly was intended primarily as a limitation of punishment—proportionate compensation. The fact that it was not as harsh as it sounds is seen particularly when it is examined in its context in Exodus (21:18–27). The Israelites could properly say, "What great nation is there, that has statutes and ordinances so righteous as all this law" (Deut. 4:8).

4. Concerning history.

In the Old Testament "history is the most characteristic channel through which thought is expressed."[18] The concern of the Israelites for history so pervades all the Old Testament that it ties its various parts into a cohesive whole. There is evident in and through the historical process the evolving will and purpose of God.

An integral aspect of the general perspective of the writers of Old Testament history was their faith that a force outside of

---

[18] Jacob, p. 197. Gerhard von Rad's *Old Testament Theology*, trans. D. M. G. Stalker (New York: Harper, 1962), is largely a theology of "historical traditions." For him Israel's faith is grounded in a theology of history. Also "the Old Testament writings confine themselves to representing Jahweh's relationship to Israel and the world in one aspect only, namely as a continuing divine activity in history" (I, 106).

history determined the course of history. That force was God. He was central in all that they wrote. History for them was a record of the acts of God in His world. He was revealed primarily by what He did in history rather than through theoretical theological propositions concerning Him. He was the hero of every Bible story. The writers had a more clearly defined theology of history than a philosophy of history.

The writers' theology of history explains their approach to history. History for them was based on facts, but they were not primarily concerned with the recording of facts. They were more interested in the interpretation of history, particularly of God's part in the historical process. Their main question was not "What has happened?" but "What is God seeking to do through what has happened?" Because of their consuming concern with the purposes of God, there is an element of faith in the Old Testament conception of history that is foreign to secular history. While historical events are used to disclose the glory and purpose of God, such events are never confused with Him. He works in and through them but He also stands above and beyond them.

Israel's historians believed that God was not only creatively active among His chosen people but also among other nations and peoples. They "drew the whole of creation into history." History for them was "reality in its totality."[19] They believed that Israel was elected through the grace and goodness of God and was destined by Him "to become the light and leaven of the nations." In other words, Israel was His chosen people but chosen to accomplish His redemptive purposes in the world.

The preceding means, among other things, that history in the Old Testament is "salvation-history" (*Heilsgeschichte*). This *Heilsgeschichte* is a history of movement from promise to fulfillment. Reality is understood "as a linear history moving toward a goal . . . . History is event so suspended in tension between promise and fulfillment that through the promise it is irreversibly pointed toward the goal of future fulfillment."[20]

[19] Wolfhart Pannenberg, "Redemptive Event and History," in *Essays on Old Testament Hermeneutics*, ed. Claus Westermann, trans. James Luther Mays, 2nd ed. (Richmond: John Knox Press, 1964), p. 319.
[20] Westermann, p. 317.

In harmony with their general perspective, the historians of the Old Testament sought to use history as a teaching instrument. It was used to teach great moral and religious truths. This helps to explain the selective nature of biblical history. The writers selected the events that could be used most effectively for teaching purposes. They were interested in the lessons of history, many of which are as relevant for the contemporary world as for the days of the Old Testament.

In addition to some lessons previously suggested, such as the divine control and the purposive nature of history, there are a number of other abiding lessons that naturally evolve from Old Testament history. These lessons are evident to some degree in the Pentateuch but are more clearly revealed in later Old Testament history. Among the more significant of these lessons are the following: (1) The kind of God a nation worships will mold the life of the nation; (2) God holds nations as well as individuals responsible; (3) righteousness exalts a nation but sin is a reproach to any people; (4) a nation will be held accountable by God for the treatment of its citizens by other citizens. This is particularly true of the treatment of the disinherited and the underprivileged.

5. *Concerning the morals of the narratives.*

Great moral truths are woven into the fabric of the stories in the Pentateuch, particularly in Genesis. Many of these stories might properly be labeled "didactic narratives." There is the generosity of Abram in dealing with Lot and the implied approval of God (13:2-18); the beautiful story of the choice of Rebekah as a wife for Isaac, strange in customs but relevant in basic principles and in spirit (24:1-67); the deception of the aged Isaac by his son Jacob and the clear demonstration in Jacob's life that the wages of sin is separation and that whatever a man sows he will also reap (27:1-45; 29:15-30); the purity of Joseph as an example for young men (39:6-10) and his magnanimity as an example for all men (45:1-28), all of which is explained by the fact that God was with him (39:2, 21, 23.)

The Covenant Code

Since the discovery of the Hammurabi Code in 1902, which supposedly dates back to 1700 b.c., it has been generally acknowledged that the Covenant Code or the Book of the Covenant (Ex. 20:22–23:33) is similar in form and content to the laws of ancient Mesopotamia.[21] While this is correct, there are some significant differences. The laws of the various countries of the East were believed to be received by the kings from the gods and promulgated and enforced by the kings. In contrast, for Israel "Moses is the mediator of the covenant, and in that role receives laws for Israel. It is not to Moses or to a king or to a legislative body that Israel is responsible, but to God."[22] And the God to whom they were responsible was the only true God, the sovereign God of the nations, a God of righteousness, justice, and holiness.

1. The source and significance of the covenant concept.

The word *berith,* translated "covenant," is used extensively in the Old Testament to describe agreements of various kinds: between individuals (Gen. 21:27; 26:28; I Sam. 18:3), between a husband and a wife (Mal. 2:14), between tribes (Ex. 23:32; Judg. 2:2; I Sam. 11:1), between monarchs (I Kings 20:34), and between a monarch and his people (II Kings 11:4). The deepest and most important meaning of *berith* is reached, however, when it refers to the covenant of God with His people. In turn, the covenant of God with His people takes on new beauty and depth if we accept Vriezen's idea that *berith* "means as it were a circle enclosing both partners, not so much a 'limitation' (Buber) as a being brought together into an intimate relationship."[23]

The historical background for the covenant concept is generally considered to be the suzerainty treaties between a king and his

21 See De Vaux (p. 143f.) for a discussion of other Eastern laws and codes.

22 Muilenburg, p. 64.

23 T. C. Vriezen, *An Outline of Old Testament Theology,* trans. S. Neuijen (Oxford: Basil Blackwell, 1958), p. 141.

vassals. Such treaties were quite common in the ancient Near East.[24] God is "the Great King." He promises to protect and provide for His people (vassals) if they in turn will be obedient and faithful to Him.

The covenant idea is not only an Old Testament but also a New Testament concept. Jesus, in instituting the Lord's Supper, referred to the cup as the "blood of the covenant" (Matt. 26:28). This was the New Covenant spoken of by Jeremiah (Jer. 31:31–34) and by the author of the Hebrews (Heb. 8:6–13). In this New Covenant Christians are the New Israel. They are the people of God. He has entered into covenant with them. The New Covenant, as was true of the Old, is a work of grace, yet the response of faith to that grace involves obedience to the One who is the source of the grace. Here is a solid basis for a continuing sense of obligation by the child of God. The biblical ethic in both Old and New Testaments might properly be called "a covenant ethic."

2. *The centrality of the concept.*

The idea of the covenant is not only central in the Covenant Code but in all of the Bible, the word *berith* being found in twenty-eight of the books of the Old Testament. One Old Testament scholar says that "no more fruitful inquiry can be made than to search the Scriptures for light on the covenant idea,"[25] while another writer considers the covenant concept the most influential idea in the Old Testament.[26] Eichrodt builds his entire monumental work on Old Testament theology on the concept of the covenant, an idea that extends well beyond the use of the word *berith.* For him the concept of the covenant "enshrines Israel's most fundamental conviction, namely, its sense of a unique relationship with God."[27] Eichrodt also suggests that it epitomizes "God's action in history," and although it "began at a

---

[24] See particularly George E. Mendenhall's booklet entitled *Law and Covenant in Israel and the Ancient Near East* (Pittsburgh: The Biblical Colloquium, 1955), and Meredith G. Kline, *Treaty of the Great King* (Grand Rapids: Eerdmans, 1963). The latter is not as technical as the former.

[25] Baab, p. 136.

[26] Vriezen, p. 139.

[27] Eichrodt, I, 17.

particular time and place" it is a "living process."[28] The particular time and place for the major covenant in the Old Testament was when the Israelites were encamped at Mount Sinai. All subsequent covenants, such as the one at Moab, recorded in Deuteronomy, were renewals or extensions of the covenant at Sinai. Here at Sinai, in a sense, was the beginning of Hebrew history.

3. The nature of the covenant.

God entered into covenant with Noah (Gen. 9) and with Abraham (Gen. 17), but at Sinai He entered into covenant with His people (Ex. 19:2–6; 24:7). The covenant at Sinai was significantly different from God's earlier covenants with Noah and Abraham. In the covenants with the latter individuals, God obligated Himself to carry out certain promises. No specific obligations were imposed on Noah and Abraham. The rainbow for Noah and circumcision for Abraham were signs of the covenant. In contrast, God's covenant with His people at Sinai laid specific obligations on the people. They were expected to obey the rules of the covenant, and it was assumed that God would protect them if they obeyed.

God is always the initiator of the covenant; it is not a contract between two people of equal or near-equal standing. This means that although there are two partners in the covenant—God and Israel—it was really unilateral rather than bilateral. God alone stated the conditions of the covenant; the people could not negotiate with God regarding the covenant nor change its conditions. They could either accept or reject it. Once they accepted it they could not annul it, although they could violate its conditions or break it. God alone had the power to dissolve the covenant, a power He never used. He is revealed not only as a covenant-giving God but also as a covenant-keeping God.

To return to Vriezen's idea, God offered at Sinai to enter into communion or into a circle or sphere with Israel. He drew up the rules or regulations that were in effect within the circle. By accepting those rules or conditions Israel was admitted to God's sphere of life, and by association with Him she was set apart unto His purposes or became sanctified or holy.

28 *Ibid.*, I, 18.

The fact that Israel entered voluntarily into covenant with God made the relationship a moral one. The Israelites had accepted certain obligations that they were morally bound to keep. The "free character of the covenant is the condition of its moral aspect."[29] An examination of the obligations of the covenant will reveal that they were both ritualistic and moral, without a clear distinction at times between the two, but with the emphasis on the moral. We can properly conclude that the covenant at Sinai called "into being a new moral entity: the people Israel," and that for both the Law and the Prophets morality was "a covenant between God and man."[30] Muilenburg suggests that "the ethical terminology of the Old Testament is derived in large part from the covenant relationship."[31]

The value of the covenant depended primarily upon the nature of the Initiator of the covenant and the purposes He had in mind for the covenant. The God revealed at Sinai, and elsewhere in the Old Testament, was a God of love and mercy. The requirements of the covenant were not arbitrary. They were best for Israel, as is true of every basic requirement of God. The fundamental idea back of the covenant was not legal obligation but divine grace, a grace not only expressed to and for Israel but also a grace that was reaching out to all men through Israel. God's covenant people were to be the instruments of His redemptive purpose.

4. The Ten Commandments and the covenant.

The commandments are referred to as "the words of the covenant" (Ex. 34:28). The two tables on which they were written are called "the tables of testimony" (Ex. 31:18; 32:15; 34:29) or later in Deuteronomy "the tables of the covenant" (Deut. 4:13; 9:9, 11, 15). They were placed (Ex. 25:16, 21; 40:20) in the "ark of testimony" (Ex. 25:22; 26:33–34; 30:26; 31:7; etc.), also referred to as "the ark of the covenant" (Num. 10:33; Deut. 10:8; Josh. 3:3;

[29] Jacob, p. 211.

[30] Yehezkel Kaufmann, *The Religion of Israel*, translated and abridged by Moshe Greenberg (Chicago: University of Chicago Press, 1960), p. 328.

[31] Muilenburg, p. 59.

etc.), which in turn was placed in "the tabernacle of testimony" (Ex. 38:21).

The Ten Commandments have been variously described as "an epitome of the covenant,"[32] as "the text of the covenant,"[33] and as "the deed of the Sinaitic covenant."[34] If the covenant at Sinai followed the pattern of suzerainty treaties of that time, then it is possible that the two tables or tablets were duplicates, with each one containing all of the commandments. It was customary in suzerainty treaties to have two copies of the treaty, one for the king and the other for his subjects or vassals.

The commandments are introduced with the striking words, "I am the Lord your God, who brought you out of the land of Egypt, out of the house of bondage." The expression is repeated in an abbreviated form four times in the commandments (Ex. 20:5, 7, 10, 12). Yahweh, their God, had the right to command; out of gratitude they should obey. Furthermore, God is the only proper beginning point for a biblically oriented religion or ethic. In the light of the significance of this introductory statement, it is understandable that Jews, in the main, have considered it the first of the commandments.

Regardless of the proper numbering of the commandments, there are two major divisions. The first deals with right relation to God, and the second with right relation to the human community or to one's fellow man. Here, as is so frequently true elsewhere in the Bible, there is a balancing of the vertical and the horizontal. It should be noted that right relation to God or the vertical comes first, followed by right relation to one's fellow man —an order which is typical of the Bible. It should never be forgotten, however, that these two belong together: to be right with God means to be right with one's neighbor. There are no duties to God that relieve man of his duties to his neighbor. There can be no compartmentalizing of the life of one who has entered into covenant with God. Just as there is oneness in the God of the

---

32 Kline, p. 17.
33 Mendenhall, p. 37.
34 de Vaux, p. 147. This book would be unusually helpful for a study of the social ethic or morality of the Old Testament.

covenant, so there is to be oneness or wholeness in the life of His people.

It is possible, of course, that too sharp a division of the commandments into a twofold pattern will not bear close scrutiny. The first four and last six of the commandments express two complimentary aspects of human responsibility. Certainly the provisions of the second division have a religious base. On the other hand, such a command as "You shall not take the name of the Lord your God in vain" may be "a matter of morality, that had its center in an attitude of heart, not a use of the tongue."[35] Similarly, the commandment regarding the Sabbath is an "ethical law of humanity"—the Sabbath was made for man, for his benefit (Mark 2:23–28). The fifth commandment (honor of parents), which applies to adults as well as children, has a definitely God-ward connotation and has been frequently grouped with the first four. From the Hebrew viewpoint, for example, parents stood in relation to their children as God's representatives.

Commandments six through nine have been aptly called "a moral bill of rights," giving expression to "certain inalienable moral rights": life (killing), integrity (adultery), property (stealing), and justice (bearing false witness).[36]

This "moral bill of rights" is followed by the tenth commandment, "You shall not covet what belongs to your neighbor." This commandment, in a sense, summarizes all the others relating to one's fellow man. On the other hand, it more than doubles the demands of the Decalogue by moving from the letter to the spirit, by including the inner as well as the outer life, the hidden desire as well as the overt act, thought and intent as well as outward conduct. The tenth commandment approaches most closely the inner emphasis of Jesus and evidently played a significant role in the moral and spiritual history of Paul (Rom. 7:7).

The commandments as a whole summarize, to a considerable degree, the basic requirements of the moral law of the Old Testament. "They are the rudimentary principles of morality, the

[35] Edwin McNeill Poteat, *Mandate to Humanity* (New York: Abingdon-Cokesbury Press, 1953), p. 113.
[36] *Ibid.*, p. 149.

germs of ethics, the . . . *seed-plot,* of religion."[37] If they can properly be considered laws at all they are apodictic or categorical in form. They are guideposts or basic principles for God's covenant people. They represent obligations that Israel had to accept if she came into the circle or sphere of the covenant with God. The "you" of the commandments is addressed to Israel as well as to the individual. "It is the form of address and the conceptual form belonging to a time when the individual standing in independence over against a group was still unknown."[38] The fact that the commandments stand at the beginning of the revelation at Sinai suggests that the religion of Israel was primarily prophetic and ethical rather than cultic and ritualistic.

5. The laws of the Covenant Code.

Many of the laws in the Covenant Code, as well as elsewhere in the Old Testament, may have had their origin in ancient legal traditions more or less common to all of the peoples of that time. But at least Israel gave to them her own peculiar stamp. For example, the blending of the civil or judicial, the moral and the strictly religious or cultic was, to a large degree, peculiar to Israel. All laws for the Israelites originated with God and all were equally binding upon His covenant people. All authority rested in God; there was no such thing as secular legislative authority.

There are other ways that the Covenant Code and Israelite law in general differed from the codes of surrounding peoples. Eichrodt suggests at least three distinctive emphases: (1) *"A higher value is placed on human life* than on any materialistic values." (2) *"The abolition of gross brutality* in the punishment of the guilty." (3) *"The rejection of any class-distinction in the administration of justice."* He further suggests that "the Book of the Covenant bears witness to the real growth of a deepened moral sensibility," which he says grows "out of the religious vitality that pulses through it."[39]

This "deepened moral sensibility" is seen, to a considerable de-

---

37 George Dana Boardman, *The Ten Commandments* (Philadelphia: Judson Press, 1946), p. 21.
38 Von Rad, I, 192.
39 Eichrodt, I, 77–79.

gree, in the civil and criminal laws in Exodus 21 and 22, which form the central part of the Covenant Code or the Book of the Covenant. C. F. Kent some years ago suggested that these laws could be arranged as four decalogues with two pentads each, or a total of eight pentads. H. Wheeler Robinson, in a more recent book, similarly suggests eight pentads but without the decalogue structure.[40] Using Kent, in the main, the outline of the structure with each subhead a pentad is as follows:

First decalogue: the rights of slaves
        (1) Male slaves (21:2–6)
        (2) Female slaves (21:7–11)
Second decalogue: assaults
        (1) Capital offenses ("acts of violence," Robinson) (21:12–17)
        (2) Minor offenses ("personal injuries," Robinson) (21:18–21, 26–27). Robinson gives the reference as 21:18–27.
Third decalogue: laws regarding domestic animals
        (1) Injuries by animals (21:28–32)
        (2) Injuries to animals (21:33—22:1, 3b, 4; cf. KJV and RSV for a difference in the order of the verses)
Fourth decalogue: responsibility for property
        (1) Property in general (22:5–9)
        (2) Property in cattle (22:10–15). Robinson gives as the last two pentads: deposits (22:7–13) and loans (22:14–17)

The rights of a male slave will serve as an illustration of the pentad structure. The word of Moses for God to the people was:

When you buy a Hebrew slave,
        (1) he shall serve six years, and in the seventh he shall go out free, for nothing.
        (2) If he comes in single, he shall go out single.
        (3) If he comes in married, then his wife shall go out with him.
        (4) If his master gives him a wife and she bears him sons or daughters, the wife and her children shall be her master's and he shall go out alone.

40 H. Wheeler Robinson, *The Old Testament: Its Making and Meaning* (New York: Abingdon-Cokesbury Press, 1937), p. 173; cf. Charles Foster Kent, *Israel's Laws and Legal Precedents* (New York: Scribner's, 1907), pp. 287–91.

> (5) But if the slave plainly says, "I love my master, my wife, and my children; I will not go out free," then his master shall bring him to God, and he shall bring him to the door or the doorpost; and his master shall bore his ear through with an awl; and he shall serve him for life.

In addition to the laws and judgments included in the pentad schematic plan, there are a number of other emphases in the Covenant Code. Among these are laws such as the following with the punishment for their violation specifically stated: cursing of parents, punished by death (21:17); causing a woman with child to have a miscarriage, punishable by fine if "no harm follows," otherwise the *lex talionis*—life for life, etc.—applies (21:22–25).[41]

There are also some admonitions with attendant motives or reasons for heeding them, such as: the proper treatment of the stranger, the widow, the orphan—if they cry, God will hear and His judgment would come upon their oppressors (22:21–24); the lending of money without interest to the poor of God's people and the restoring of a pledge before the sun goes down—God is compassionate and will hear their cry and, by implication, will send His judgment (22:25–27).

In addition, there are a number of brief apodictic laws or categorical statements. Among the more relevant of these, from the ethical perspective, are the exhortations not to "curse a ruler" (22:28) nor to "utter a false report," not to be "a malicious witness" (23:1) nor to "pervert justice" (23:2), or "be partial to a poor man in his suit" (23:3; cf. v. 6). They were not to take a bribe (23:8) nor "oppress a stranger" (23:9). (For casuistic or case laws, some of which have already been mentioned, which are frequently introduced with an "if" and have specific punishments attached, see 22:1, 2, 7, 10, 14, 16, 25; 23:4.)

---

[41] In Leviticus (24:19–20) the *lex talionis* is related directly to the "disfigurement" of a neighbor but indirectly to murder (see Lev. 24:17, 21); in Deuteronomy (19:21) it is related to false witnessing. In contrast, Jesus enunciated a principle of non-retaliation (Matt. 5:38–42). Mendenhall (p. 17) considers the *lex talionis* "a statement of policy rather than a binding law."

The Holiness Code

Most of the significant ethical-content material in the Book of Leviticus is found in the Law of Holiness or the Holiness Code (chaps. 17–26). While the idea of holiness is particularly prevalent in the Holiness Code, it is also quite prevalent in the entire Old Testament. The words "holy" or "holiness" are found in approximately three-fourths of the books of the Old Testament, being especially evident (other than in Leviticus) in Exodus, the Psalms, Isaiah, and Ezekiel. One author goes so far as to say that "the root *qds*" as found in various nouns, adjectives, and verb forms might be considered "the grammatical centre of the Old Testament just as the idea which it expresses is the theological centre."[42] The words derived from *qds,* such as *qados* and *qodes,* are practically always translated "holy," although they are used on occasion to refer to the "saints" or holy ones and to the "sanctuary" or the holy place.

1. The meaning of holiness.

The ethical content of the concept of holiness, in the Holiness Code and elsewhere, cannot be properly understood or evaluated apart from some idea of the etymology of the word. Scholars do not all agree, but most of them believe that the root meaning of the Hebrew words translated "holiness" is "to cut" and hence the central idea in the concept is "separation" or withdrawal from the ordinary. The term indicates more a relationship than a quality. The ethical was evidently not an integral part of the original idea.

A word cannot be properly defined, however, entirely on the basis of its etymology. This is particularly true of words found in the Bible. In the case of "holy" and "holiness" the Hebrews, as they frequently did, placed their particular stamp upon the words. Over a period of time new content was given to *qados* and *qodes.* This new content was derived primarily from the nature of

42 Jacob, p. 87.

their God, and "holiness" occupied "a position of unique importance" among the qualities attributed to Him.[43]

In the Holiness Code and elsewhere it is revealed that God the Holy One wished to share His holiness with His people. To use the concept of the covenant, He wanted to bring them into the circle or sphere of the covenant with Him. When they came into covenant with Him they were separated unto Him, and through their association with, and dedication to, the purposes of a Holy God, they became holy. Similarly, days, places, and things could be made holy (see Lev. 22:2–3; 23:2–4, 21) because of their association with and dedication to God. The priests in a particular way were to be holy to God (Lev. 21:6–7) and also to the people (Lev. 21:8).

Somewhat typical of the biblical emphasis in general, there was a negative as well as a positive aspect to the concept of holiness. It not only involved a separation unto God but also a separation from the world and the peoples of the world. Nowhere is this twofold nature of holiness stated more clearly than in the following: "You shall be holy to me; for I the Lord am holy, and have separated you from the peoples, that you should be mine" (Lev. 20:26). Notice particularly "to me" and "from the peoples."

God, for the Israelites, was the source of all holiness. He was the one who set apart, sanctified, or made holy the high priest (Lev. 21:15), the sanctuaries (Lev. 21:23), things such as food (Lev. 21:16), and in particular the children of Israel (Lev. 22:32). The obligation to be holy for Israel as a nation and as individuals derived from the fact that their God was holy (Lev. 19:2; 20:7; 21:8; 22:9).

2. *The ethical nature of holiness.*

The children of Israel usually adapted and put new content into words and concepts that they took over from their neighbors. This was definitely true regarding "holy" and "holiness." The latter stemmed, to a considerable degree, from the fact that whereas their neighbors emphasized the holiness of things, the Israelites emphasized the holiness of God. This, in turn, intro-

---

[43] Eichrodt, I, 270.

duced "*a personal element into the theory of holiness.*"[44] This was a link or a step in the direction of the moralization of the concept of holiness. This was particularly true since God the Holy One was also the Righteous or Just One and the God of love. In other words, He was a moral Being, and it was more or less inevitable that moral qualities would pervade the idea of His holiness. After all, if He was separated from the created world, He was also separated from the evil world. He, the Holy One, was also the Perfect One.

There is no sharp distinction, however, in Leviticus and the other books of the Law, between the cultic and the ethical aspects of holiness. They frequently lie side by side and at times are, from our perspective, rather curiously intertwined. The prophets brought to sharpest focus the moral requirements of a holy God. The moral aspect is rather prominent, however, in the Holiness Code. This stems, to some degree, from the nature of the law revealed there. Being separated unto God entailed obedience to His commands. The power and authority inherent in the Holy One were attached to His laws or commandments. Many of them were ethical, but even obedience to the cultic requirements involved a moral obligation, an obligation to obey God. The combining of a separation unto God and obedience to His commandments is underscored, in a particular way, in the following: "Consecrate yourselves therefore, and be holy; for I am the Lord your God. Keep my statutes, and do them; I am the Lord who sanctify you" (Lev. 20:7–8; cf. 18:5 and 22:3).

In the Holiness Code, as Eichrodt suggests, "the divine holiness as defined in purely religious terms is combined with the idea of *spotless purity.*" He also says that the crucial test is Leviticus 19:2: "You shall be holy; for I the Lord your God am holy." He concludes that the injunctions that follow this exhortation "make it clear that this holiness which is required of the people because of the holy nature of Yahweh implies moral purity and blamelessness."[45]

[44] *Ibid.*, I, 272.
[45] *Ibid.*, I, 278.

3. A study of Leviticus 19:1–18.

The verse just referred to (19:2) might be regarded as the keynote of the Holiness Code. One Jewish author considers it the central and culminating idea of the Jewish law,[46] while another Jewish scholar, in an old but standard work, says that it "sums up all morality in one comprehensive expression."[47] What are the evidences that "holiness" in Leviticus 19:2 has ethical or moral connotations or content? The main immediate evidence is what follows it. Following immediately the command to be holy (19:2) is the exhortation or command to reverence mother and father and to keep God's sabbaths. Then after a few verses (5–8) that deal with the more ceremonial or ritualistic, there follows a series of commands or exhortations concerning the relation of God's people to their fellow men. This section (vss. 9–18) is climaxed with that great statement: "You shall love your neighbor as yourself" (v. 18). This statement sums up all that had gone before. It also figures prominently in the ethical thought of the New Testament (Matt. 22:34–40; Rom. 13:8–10; Gal. 5:14; James 2:8). One Old Testament scholar says that this is "the highest expression of ethical and social feeling that may be imagined,"[48] while another suggests that it "is the climax of biblical morality."[49]

The exhortations in 19:9–18 are grouped into five pentads, which are divided into paragraphs in the Revised Standard Version. Each pentad contains five principles or statements, more or less clearly evident. Of real interest for this study is the fact that the statements or principles in all five pentads concern man's relation to his fellow man. In other words, they emphasize the ethical, moral, or horizontal. If these pentads are an extension and an application of verse 2, then "holy" in that verse very definitely is ethical in its emphasis.

---

[46] K. Kohler, *Jewish Theology* (New York: Macmillan, 1918), p. 101.

[47] M. Lazarus, *The Ethics of Judaism*, trans. Henrietta Szold (Philadelphia: Jewish Publication Society of America, 1900), I, 112.

[48] Vriezen, p. 335.

[49] Kaufmann, p. 320.

Notice how the first pentad (vss. 9–10) divides into its component parts:

When you reap the harvest of your land,
>   (1) you shall not reap your field to its very border,
>   (2) neither shall you gather the gleanings after your harvest.
>   (3) And you shall not strip your vineyard bare,
>   (4) neither shall you gather the fallen grapes of your vineyard;
>   (5) you shall leave them for the poor and for the sojourner:
I am the Lord your God.

Number five above concludes or gives the reason for the preceding exhortations. Notice in a particular way the closing words, "I am the Lord your God," which seem to be a refrain for this chapter and for the entire Holiness Code. The expression is found in some form approximately fifty times in chapters 17–26 and eight times in Leviticus 19:1–18 alone, being, in its shortened form, the concluding words for each of the five pentads. Throughout the Holiness Code the expression is evidently an abbreviation of "I the Lord your God am holy." If this is correct it considerably strengthens the evidence for the ethical content of holiness. The holiness of God provides the motive, the example, and possibly the authority for the exhortations for the children of Israel to be right in their relations with and treatment of their fellow men.

The close relation of this great passage (19:1–18) to the Ten Commandments strengthens the argument for the ethical content of holiness. Some scholars consider the passage a commentary on the Decalogue. Vriezen makes the interesting suggestion that 19:3f. combined with 19:12f. is a shortened form of the Decalogue and "seems to have been drawn up for children." He cites as one reason for this conclusion the fact that verse 3 begins with a demand for reverence or honor for parents and mentions the mother first.[50]

50 Vriezen, p. 336.

Deuteronomy[51]

A general survey will be made of some of the major ethical emphases of the entire book rather than restricting the study to the Deuteronomic Code (chaps. 12–26). This is being done primarily because much of the most significant ethical content material is not found in the so-called Code.

The book of Deuteronomy has been called "one of the most beautiful and profoundly ethical books of the Bible"[52] and "one of the decisive books of history."[53] It is one of the books of the Old Testament most frequently cited by New Testament writers. It contains "a matchless code of morals" as well as "a unique expression of true religion,"[54] has "a bigger, richer heart than any of its fellows in the Pentateuch,"[55] and breathes as nowhere else in the Old Testament "an atmosphere of generous devotion to God, and of large-hearted benevolence towards man."[56]

[51] The dating of Deuteronomy, along with the problem of authorship, is one of the major critical problems of the Old Testament. The whole documentary hypothesis is closely related to and dependent upon the dating of the last book of the Pentateuch. For representative viewpoints, see Pfeiffer (*Introduction to the Old Testament*), who says the author was a priest in Jerusalem (p. 179), that the author "contrived" to have his book "discovered in 621 B.D." (p. 181), and that the bulk of the book provided the background for Josiah's religious reformation (2 Kings 22:3—23:25); Rowley (*The Growth of the Old Testament*), who rejects the idea that the book was written immediately before Josiah's reform (p. 31) and suggests that it was written between the reform of Hezekiah and the reform of Josiah, had lain in the Temple for many years and was genuinely found; Weiser (*The Old Testament: Its Formation and Development*), who identifies "Josiah's book of reforms" and the "original Deuteronomy" (p. 128), but says the latter went "back to older sources" (p. 130); and Young (*Introduction to the Old Testament*), who accepts and defends the Mosaic authorship (pp. 97–108).

[52] Philip Birnbaum, comp. and ed., *A Treasury of Judaism* (New York: Hebrew Publishing Co., 1957), p. 63.

[53] G. Ernest Wright, "The Book of Deuteronomy," *The Interpreter's Bible*, ed. George A. Buttrick (New York: Abingdon Press, 1953), II, 331.

[54] Charles R. Erdman, *The Book of Deuteronomy* (Westwood, N. J.: Fleming H. Revell, 1953), p. 7.

[55] George Adam Smith, *The Book of Deuteronomy* in *The Cambridge Bible for Schools and Colleges*, ed. A. F. Kirkpatrick (Cambridge: University Press, 1918), p. xxviii.

[56] S. R. Driver, *An Introduction to the Literature of the Old Testament*, rev. ed. (New York: Scribner's, 1914), p. 79.

1. The covenant concept.

While Deuteronomy is quite distinctive, it is also rather closely related in some of its basic concepts to other books of the Pentateuch. For example, the covenant as the source of morality, so central in Exodus, is also found in Deuteronomy. There are references to the covenant made at Sinai or Horeb (4:13; 5:2). The people were warned not to forget the covenant "for the Lord your God is a devouring fire, a jealous God" (4:23–24). They can be assured that God will not forget His covenant with their fathers (4:31), which He made not only with their fathers but also with them (5:3). There was a sense in which they were present in their fathers when God entered into covenant with them. They are also assured that God will not only keep His covenant but also His "steadfast love (*hesed*) with those who love him and keep his commandments" (7:9; cf. 7:12–13). Here is revealed an ethical basis or condition for the keeping of the covenant. The people must love God and that love will express itself in obedience to His commandments (cf. John 14:15, 21, 23–24).

There is recorded in Deuteronomy a covenant that God made with the children of Israel in Moab (29:1). God's people must keep this covenant if they are to prosper (29:9), and if God is to be their God (29:13). If they forsake God's covenant, His judgment will come upon them (29:21–25). This covenant at Moab may have been simply a renewal of the covenant at Sinai or Horeb. Kline claims that Deuteronomy, in harmony with the pattern of suzerainty treaties, is a covenant renewal document.[57] In such documents the stipulations of the covenant were brought up to date.

Eichrodt suggests that a slight shift in the concept of *berith* (covenant) "can be detected in the Deuteronomic writings." He says that the word is used "to designate the once-for-all establishment of the covenant in history" but that there is also present the idea of an enduring relationship, and that it is used at times to refer to the obligations of the relationship, "the conditions of the covenant." "The legal basis of the covenant is brought into prominence," and on the human side there is a stress on keeping the

[57] Kline, p. 20.

covenant, with warnings against transgressing or breaking the covenant.[58] All of the preceding tends to heighten the ethical content of the covenant concept.

2. The idea of holiness.

This concept, closely related to the idea of the covenant and so prevalent in Leviticus, is also found in Deuteronomy. The main emphasis in the latter is on the holiness of the people as a nation. They were a people holy to the Lord their God; He had chosen them to be "a people for his own possession, out of all the peoples that are on the face of the earth" (7:6; cf. 14:2; 26:18). Notice the joining together of the negative and positive aspects of holiness. There was a separation from the peoples of the world coupled with a separation unto God. The Lord's promise to make Israel "a people holy to himself" is conditioned upon their keeping His commandments and walking in His ways (28:9). This condition underscores the ethical requirements of holiness. Walking in the ways of God meant the purging of evil from the midst of them (13:5; cf. 17:7, 12; 19:19). From the perspective of Deuteronomy, it also meant, in a special way, walking in the way of love (19:9).

3. Love.

The word "love" and love for God as a motive for ethical living are more prevalent in Deuteronomy than in the other books of the Pentateuch. Just as "covenant" is the key idea in Exodus and "holiness" in Leviticus, so "love" is the distinctive theme, motif, or concept in Deuteronomy.

The relation of man's love for God and God's love for man is not generally worked out in the Old Testament. "Deuteronomy alone makes attempts of that sort, basing the appeal for love to Yahweh on Yahweh's love to the patriarchs (x, 14–16), and promising Yahweh's love as a reward for loyalty to the law."[59] Love of

---

58 Eichrodt, I, 53–54.

59 Gottfried Quell and Gottlob Schrenk, "Love," *Kittel's Bible Key Words,* trans. and ed. J. R. Coates (New York: Harper, 1951), I, 11. In the same article Quell says that "the whole Covenant theory is based on the idea of love" (p. 11), and that "the thought of love is mainly used in Deuteronomy to support that of election and the Covenant" (p. 21). See Jacob (pp. 108–12) for a brief discussion of "The love of God," with considerable emphasis on its relation to the covenant.

God is revealed as the basic motive for obedience to the commandments of God, which again points up the ethical nature of the central concepts of the books of the Law.

Because God had increased the Israelites from seventy souls when they went into Egypt to a multitude "as the stars of the heaven" (10:22), they should love the Lord their God "and keep his charge, his statutes, his ordinances, and his commandments always" (11:1). One of the commandments of God was that the children of Israel should love and serve Him with all their heart and soul (11:13; 3:3), "walking in all his ways, and cleaving to him" (11:22; cf. 13:4). Since His commands are always commands of mercy and grace, His command for them to love and be obedient to Him was for their good (10:13; cf. I John 5:3). To be obedient meant they would be blessed of God; if disobedient they would be cursed of God. In the concluding address a choice is sharply set forth for the people: "I have set before you this day life and good, death and evil" (30:15). The way to life and the good was through obedience to the commandments of God and the first commandment was to love God (30:16), love being "the essential principle of the fulfillment of the commandments" (KD).[60]

Let us sum up by turning to the marvelous passage in Chapter 6. The chapter opens with the commandment or charge to Israel given to Moses. The purpose of the statutes and commandments he was to teach the people was that they and their children might fear or reverence God—a reverence which would be evidenced by their obedience—and that as a result their days might be prolonged. Then comes the Shema (the Hebrew for "hear," the first word in v. 4) in verses 4–9, which was and is "the primary confession of faith" of Jews and is "to be recited twice daily" (IB.).

Standing logically at the beginning of the charge to Israel was the greatest and most basic of the commandments: "You shall love the Lord your God with all your heart, and with all your soul,[61] and with all your might" (6:5). This simply meant that the

---

[60] Commentaries that follow a verse-by-verse format will be referred to in the body of the material rather than in footnotes. See page xix for a list of abbreviations that will be used.

[61] For other uses in Deuteronomy of "with all your heart and with all your soul" see 4:29; 10:12; 11:13; 13:3; 26:16; 30:2, 6, 10.

Israelites were to love God with their total personalities. They were to love Him supremely. Jesus considered this "the greatest command . . . and . . . first in importance" (Matt. 22:38, Williams). We should remember, however, that man's love for God differs from his love for another human being. Love for God involves "a holy fear or reverence (v. 13), and it expresses itself in the devoted and single-minded loyalty which issues in wholehearted and obedient service" (IB). The latter is implied in what immediately follows this great commandment. Moses said to the children of Israel: "And these words which I command you this day shall be upon your heart; and you shall teach them diligently to your children" (6:6-7). Love moves in a threefold direction: from God to man, from man to God, and from man to man.

4. Laws of the Code.

In addition to the major ethical emphases or concepts previously discussed, there are a number of other laws, exhortations, or teachings on various moral and social problems in the Deuteronomic Code, particularly in chapters 19-25. Space will permit only a bare mention of the most significant of these.

There are some instructions concerning going "forth to war" which are peculiar to Deuteronomy (20:1-9). Those who went forth were encouraged to be brave "for the Lord your God is with you" (v. 1). Some were to be excused from going into battle: those who had built a new home and had not lived in it (v. 5), had planted a vineyard and had not "enjoyed its fruit" (v. 6), and had "betrothed a wife" and had not "taken her" (v. 7). In addition, all who were "fearful and fainthearted" were to return to their houses (v. 8).

The law of divorce, or better, the law regulating divorce, is found in Chapter 24 (vs. 1-4). The right of divorce belonged to the husband alone. He could send away his wife if he saw "some indecency in her," but he had to give her a bill of divorcement, which was evidently a legal document and was for her protection. If she became the wife of a second man, she could never return as the wife of her first husband. There were two conditions under which a man could not put away or divorce a wife: (1) if he falsely accused her of premarital sex relations (22:13-21), and

(2) if he seduced her when a virgin and unbetrothed and hence had to marry her (22:28–29).

If a man had relations with a married woman, both were to be put to death (22:22), as was also true of relations with a betrothed virgin in a city (22:23–24). In contrast, relations with a betrothed virgin "in a field" or in the country meant death for the man alone (22:25–27); it evidently was assumed that she might have cried for help and no one could hear.

There are two interesting laws concerning inheritance. The right of inheritance of the oldest son was to be respected (the law of primogeniture), even though he might be the offspring of a hated wife (21:15–17). The law of the levirate required that if a man died without a son his brother was to take the widow as his wife (25:5–10). The law evidently stemmed from the desire to keep the inheritance within the family. It provided the background for a question concerning the resurrection which the Sadducees once asked Jesus (Matt. 22:23–33).

There are a number of other subjects that are touched on, to some degree, such as: cities of refuge were provided to which any one who killed his neighbor unintentionally might flee and hence save his own life (19:4–13); a neighbor's boundary marks were not to be removed (19:14); two or three witnesses were necessary for a charge to be sustained (19:15); a false witness was to receive the same punishment as the one he had witnessed against would have received, which was the *lex talionis* (19:16–21); there was to be fairness or impartiality in judgment (24:17–18; 25:1–3) and honesty in weights that were used (25:13–16). There was to be no lending for interest to a brother Hebrew although there could be to a foreigner (23:19–20). One's means of livelihood such as "a mill or an upper millstone" was not to be taken in pledge for a debt (24:6), nor was one to go into a house to collect a pledge (24:10–11). If the debtor was a poor man the pledge was to be returned when the sun went down—"you shall not sleep in his pledge" but return it to him "that he may sleep in his cloak and bless you" (24:12–13). Animals that had strayed were to be returned (22:1), but an escaped servant was not to be returned (23:15–16). A captive woman who had been taken as a wife could be sent away but she could not be sold as a slave (21:10–14).

There was to be no sacred prostitution among the children of Israel (23:17–18). When passing through a field or a vineyard, one was free to eat what he wanted (23:24–25).

This study of the ethical content of the Law has revealed that the Law is basic to any adequate understanding of the ethical teachings of the Scriptures in general. In the Law are found the foundational principles for practically everything that will be discussed later in the chapters on the Prophets and the Writings and even the chapters on the New Testament. There is a sense in which this chapter on the Law is introductory to our entire study.

An attempt has been made in the chapter to concentrate on the more abidingly relevant portions of the Law. For this reason more attention has been given to apodictic than to casuistic laws. We have concentrated largely on three basic concepts: the covenant, holiness, and love. These concepts are closely related to, if they do not evolve from, the nature and character of God. They, along with the moral nature of God, are the most central emphases in the Pentateuch, particularly in the sections with the most significant ethical material. These concepts are also central emphases throughout the Scriptures: the Prophets, the Writings, and the New Testament.

There is also a continuing stress that God expects His people to be like Him. He is a covenant-keeping God; He expects them to keep His covenant with them. He is holy; they are to be holy. He loves them; they are to love Him and one another. This idea of likeness to God is more basic and more pervasive than any other moral concept in the Law and elsewhere in the Scriptures. It may not be as evident on the surface as some other concepts or ideas, but it lies underneath and tends to give depth and meaning to God's expectations of His people.

CHAPTER II

THE PROPHETS

The Prophets were more closely related to the Law, particularly to apodictic in contrast to casuistic law, than is frequently supposed. There is an essential unity of the Law and the Prophets in perspective and over-all purpose. For example, the perspective is as God-centered in the Prophets as in the Law. Also, the covenant concept is a unifying factor in the Prophets as in the Law. This concept so prominent in both Old and New Testaments underlies much of the preaching of all the prophets, but it is particularly evident in Isaiah and Hosea of the eighth century and in Jeremiah and Ezekiel of a later century. The prophets in general preached against the sins of the people. Those sins were the violation of God's covenant with them and their mistreatment of those within the covenant community.

The content of the messages of the prophets was derived largely from their understanding of the character of the God of the covenant. It was this God who had called them and sought to speak through them to the people. They spelled out God's expectations of His people more specifically than the Law in certain areas, such as the political and the economic. There was a sense, however, in which the main burden of their preaching was an effort to call the people back to a proper understanding of and obedience to the Law.

This close relation of the prophets to the Law is as evident in their ethics as anywhere else. As Rowley says, "The seeds of ethical religion were planted at Sinai, and were later watered by prophetic teaching."[1] Or as Kaufmann says, "Prophetic morality is rooted in that of the Torah and is its culmination."[2] The ethical, however, is more central in the Prophets than in the Law. In the latter the distinction between the ritual and the moral is not as clearly drawn as it is in the Prophets. Furthermore, the Law does not as specifically place the ethical above the ritual as did the Prophets.[3]

Introduction

1. The meaning of "prophet."

The concept of the prophet and his function developed over a long period of time. The word "prophet" (*nabi'*)[4] is applied to individuals, such as Abraham (Gen. 20:7), Moses (Deut. 18:15, 18; 34:10; Hos. 12:13), and possibly Gideon (Judg. 6:8). Also, Miriam (Ex. 15:20), Deborah (Judg. 4:4), and others (II Kings 22:14; II Chron. 34:22; Neh. 6:14) are referred to as "prophetesses" (*nebi'ah*).

The meaning of the word "prophet" is revealed rather clearly by a reference to Aaron in his relation to Moses. Aaron is called the "prophet (*nabi'*) of Moses" (Ex. 7:1). Earlier in Exodus the meaning of this statement is revealed. When Moses at the burning bush protested that he could not speak, the Lord told him that He

---

[1] H. H. Rowley, *The Faith of Israel* (Philadelphia: Westminster Press, 1956), p. 60.

[2] Kaufmann, *The Religion of Israel*, p. 316.

[3] See H. H. Rowley, *From Moses to Qumran: Studies in the Old Testament* (New York: Association Press, 1963) for a chapter entitled "Ritual and the Hebrew Prophets."

[4] For a discussion of "nabism" in general and "classical prophecy," with the relation of the latter to the former, see Eichrodt, *Theology of the Old Testament*, I, 309–91. Another book that gives considerable attention to the background for the classical or canonical prophets is J. Lindblom's *Prophecy in Ancient Israel* (Oxford: Basil Blackwell, 1962).

would give him Aaron as his spokesman. God said to Moses: "You shall speak to him and put the words in his mouth. . . . He shall speak for you to the people; and he shall be a mouth for you, and you shall be to him as God" (Ex. 4:15–16). A prophet is one who speaks for another. In this sense, Abraham, Moses, and others were prophets of God.

2. *The work of the prophets.*

The classical or canonical prophets were not philosophers or even primarily theologians. They were the messengers of God at times of crisis in the life of the people of God. They were interpreters of God, but interpreters of Him in relation to world events.[5] They were caught in the tragic occurrences of their day and spoke of God's word and His will concerning those occurrences. They "carried on their criticism of society with a moral insight and a radical consistency never known before."[6]

The prophets, however, were not primarily social reformers, although they were deeply concerned with the social and moral problems of their day. The real source of their social passion and effectiveness was their concern for the will of God rather than for the welfare of men[7] or the preservation of the nation. They were primarily motivated, if not driven, by a deep sense of the reality of God. They brought the impact of this *"divine reality directly to bear on the sphere of moral conduct."*[8] For them, as for the Old Testament in general, what was good was what God required; what was evil was what He forbade or disapproved. Their point of reference was God and not man. They perceived what God was like and, hence, what men must become to be acceptable to God.

The God-centered approach gave to the prophets a deeper in-

---

[5] Abraham J. Heschel (*The Prophets* [New York: Harper & Row, 1962], p. xvii) says that prophecy "may be described as *exegesis of existence from a divine perspective.*" There is a distinctive emphasis in Heschel's book on "pathos," which is a recurring theme throughout the book and to which the author devotes a brief appendix.

[6] John Bright, *Jeremiah* (Garden City, N.Y.: Doubleday, 1965), p. xxiii. This volume is in the Anchor Bible series.

[7] Heschel says, "The prophet cannot say Man without thinking God" (p. 24).

[8] Eichrodt, I, 362.

sight into the moral and social conditions of their day than they otherwise would have had. They saw beyond the external appearance to the real cause for social inequalities and injustices. They believed that men and nations needed above all else to be right in their relations to God. They were also convinced that if men understood the nature of God and were right in their relations to Him, they would be right in their relations with one another.

The prophetic emphasis on ethical monotheism tended to universalize God, making Him the God of all peoples. "The point of emphasis in prophetic religion is the little word 'all': *all* men should bring *all* of their lives under the whole will of God."[9] Here is a solid basis for universal morality which is strengthened by the fact that God is revealed as a moral person.

Although the prophets were not primarily reformers, they "were a reforming political force which has never been surpassed and perhaps never equalled in subsequent world history."[10] The main reason for this fact was their deep consciousness of God's concern for and participation in the affairs of the children of Israel and of surrounding nations.

Early Prophets

The great eighth-century prophets crystallized the ethical monotheistic tendencies and represented the golden age of Hebrew prophecy. But before discussing them, some consideration should be given to the prophets who preceded them. The work of these prophets is recorded primarily in I and II Samuel and I and II Kings, books that were classified along with Joshua and Judges, as "The Early Prophets" by the Jews. These books record the history of God's people from the death of Moses to the fall of Jerusalem. Not only because of the Jewish classification, but also because the books are so closely related to the prophetic movement, it has been considered wise to discuss these books here rather than later

9 J. Philip Hyatt, *Prophetic Religion* (New York: Abingdon-Cokesbury Press, 1947), p. 51.
10 W. F. Albright as quoted by G. Ernest Wright, *The Old Testament against Its Environment* (Chicago: Henry Regnery, 1950), p. 46.

in connection with other historical books such as I and II Chronicles, Ezra, and Nehemiah.

1. The books.

What is there in these books, apart from the ministry of the prophets, that has some ethical significance? They are historical books, but history for the Hebrews was not a mere recording of events. For them, God was the chief factor in history. They were concerned with His will and purpose for them and for all men, and, for them, His will was inclusive of all of life.

The place of God in history is clearly seen in Joshua, the first of the books of "The Early Prophets," which some scholars believe was originally attached to the Pentateuch, making the latter the Hexateuch. One emphasis found in Joshua is that victory for the children of God comes from God, but not without their obedience and cooperation. This is pointed up with particular clarity in the victory at Jericho and the defeat at Ai. The latter also reveals the common Hebrew conception of group solidarity and corporate responsibility.

A continuing emphasis in the book is the call for obedience to the commandments of God. To be obedient to the commandments of the Law was to do the will of God, which in turn not only involved worshipping Him and Him alone but also walking in His way, and His way was the way of justice, righteousness, mercy, and holiness. The ethical content of this obedience is spelled out rather specifically in the latter part of Joshua. The people were to love the Lord their God and walk in all His ways and keep His commandments, serving Him with all their hearts and souls (22:5). The expression "to walk in all his ways" is a common Old Testament term for obedience to the instructions of God or the commandments found in His Law (see Deut. 8:6; 10:12; Jer. 7:23). Muilenburg says that "the primary image to express conduct or behavior in the Old Testament is the 'way' or 'road' (*derek*)."[11]

On the basis of obedience to the commandments of God, Joshua appealed to the people to avoid mixed marriages (23:6–7, 12–13). The covenant of the Lord with, and his blessings upon,

[11] Muilenburg, *The Way of Israel*, p. 33.

the people were also used by Joshua to appeal to them to serve the Lord, and Him only. The climax of that appeal comes in Joshua's challenging statement: "As for me and my house, we will serve the Lord" (24:15). In response the people said: "The Lord our God we will serve, and his voice we will obey" (24:24).

The book of Judges reveals over and over again a fourfold pattern or procedure: (1) Israel sinned by turning to other gods, by doing evil; (2) punishment or the judgment of God came upon them; (3) the people repented and cried unto the Lord for deliverance; and (4) He heard them and sent a deliverer. Then after a while they sinned again and the whole procedure was repeated. This pattern is rather descriptive of the experience of the child of God and of the people of God in general.

Among the deliverers was Samson, who was to be "a Nazarite to God from birth to the day of his death" (13:7; cf. Num. 6:2–21). Among other things, he was not to drink any strong drink as was also true of his mother (13:14).

In the books of Samuel and Kings, as is true of the Old Testament in general, God stands out as the central figure. He gave Samuel to Hannah in response to prayer. In turn, she "lent" Samuel to the Lord to serve in the temple as long as he lived (I Sam. 1:28). "The boy Samuel grew in the presence of the Lord" (I Sam. 2:21), growing "both in stature and in favor with God and with man" (2:26), which sounds strikingly similar to the statement about the boy Jesus (Luke 2:52).

The mature Samuel "administered justice to Israel" (I Sam. 7:17). When Israel demanded a king, God through Samuel selected Saul (I Sam. 10:1), and it was God's prophet who announced to Israel the conditions, ethical and religious, under which God would bless them and their king. His statement was:

> If you will fear the Lord and serve Him and hearken to His voice and not rebel against the commandment of the Lord, and if both you and the king who reigns over you will follow the Lord your God, it will be well; but if you will not hearken to the voice of the Lord, but rebel against the commandment of the Lord, then the hand of the Lord will be against you and your king [I Sam. 12:14–15].

The books of Kings (considered one book by the Jews) paint an increasingly dark picture of the sins of the kings and of the people. What might be considered the theme of the books is the charge of David to Solomon as his successor, which includes the following: "Be strong, and show yourself a man, and keep the charge of the Lord your God, walking in his ways and keeping his statutes, his commandments, his ordinances, and his testimonies" (I Kings 2:2–3). Notice again "walking in his ways," which is the way of obedience.

The author of Kings does not deal with the social crimes so prevalent in the writings of the prophets. "He was dealing with the history of the people as a whole. He painted on a broad canvas and with a large brush."[12] There was, however, a consistently "stern opposition to all those things in worship which detract from the highest and purest conception of morality."[13] Since Israel's God was a moral being, He had to be worshipped with clean hands and with a pure heart.

Although the emphasis in Kings is not primarily on the ethical or moral, God is revealed as strongly condemning injustice. This condemnation is revealed in the glimpses that we have into the lives and ministry of some of God's prophets, such as Elijah (I Kings 17–19, 21 and II Kings 1, 2) and Micaiah, the son of Imlah (I Kings 22). The climax is reached in II Kings when Isaiah appears on the scene as the advisor of King Hezekiah.

2. The prophets.

While there were men who could be described as prophets as far back as Abraham, the prophetic movement as such flourished from the time of Samuel, who was the last of an old order and the first of a new. It was Samuel who asked Saul that searching question followed by a statement that has been called the theme of the prophets:

12 Norman H. Snaith, "The First and Second Books of Kings," *The Interpreter's Bible*, III, 8.
13 *Ibid.*, p. 15.

Has the Lord as great delight in
    burnt offerings and sacrifices,
    as in obeying the voice of the Lord?
Behold, to obey is better than sacrifice,
    and to hearken than the fat of rams [I Sam. 15:22].

Other prophets, previous to the great eighth-century prophets, who stood in the line of the true prophetic tradition, were Nathan and Elijah. Both of them revealed that their God demanded righteousness even of the king.

Concerning Nathan the record says, "The Lord sent Nathan to David" (II Sam. 12:1). He was sent to rebuke David for having Uriah killed and taking his wife. Nathan told David a story about a rich man who took a poor man's one ewe lamb and killed and prepared it for a traveller who came to visit him. In anger David said, "As the Lord lives, the man who has done this deserves to die" (v. 5). The courageous prophet of God pointedly said to David, "You are the man" (v. 7). He also asked David a searching question, "Why have you despised the word of the Lord, to do what is evil in his sight?" (v. 9). Notice that the evil was primarily against God, or in the sight of God. Certainly David had sinned against Uriah and against the wife of Uriah, but his sin basically was against the fundamental law of God. David recognized the true nature of his sin when he said to Nathan, "I have sinned against the Lord" (v. 13; cf. Ps. 51). When Nathan rebuked David he was the forerunner of the great ethical prophets of later days.

Elijah was likewise a worthy predecessor of the great writing prophets. His stature is seen particularly in his encounter with Ahab in Naboth's vineyard. Through the scheming of Jezebel, Naboth had been put to death and Ahab had gone down to take possession of the vineyard of Naboth. In the meantime, the Lord had revealed himself to Elijah, saying, "Arise, go down to meet Ahab, King of Israel" (I Kings 21:18). After a rebuke from Elijah, Ahab complained to him, "Have you found me, oh my enemy?" Elijah's words were a typical prophetic reply, "I have found you, because you have sold yourself to do what is evil in the sight of the Lord" (v. 20). Ryder Smith says that the remarkable thing about this incident "is not that an eastern monarch should seize any piece of land that he liked, but that a prophet should be found to arraign him in the name of God."[14]

Both Nathan and Elijah, in speaking to the king in the name of their God, declared the ethical implications of Israel's religion. "They were not standing for the rights of man, but for the will of God, for in their view man's rights were sacred because they rested on the will of God."[15] This perspective was central in the work of the prophets in general. They defended the rights of the people, particularly the common people, but they did so basically because they considered such a defense to be the will of God and in harmony with His nature. Sins against the people were sins primarily against God Himself. They were violations of His will for the people.

Another incident in the life of Elijah has some ethical significance. In his experience with God at Mount Horeb (I Kings 19:9–18) he learned, among other things, that God was a God of history as well as a God of wonders. This lesson, which became increasingly clear to later prophets, was revealed to Elijah by God's instructions for him to go back and anoint not only Elisha to be his successor but also to anoint Jehu to be king of Israel and Hazael to be king over Syria. God was not only interested in the man who would be His prophet, but also in those who would be kings. His concern here was not only with Israel but also with Syria. The latter meant that God was not a mere national deity.

Another prophet who is not as well known as Nathan and Elijah, but who is worthy to be associated with them as examples of courageous moral action, is Micaiah, the son of Imlah. There is only one reference to his life, but it portrays a glorious incident (I Kings 22, cf. II Chron. 18). What a contrast between the four hundred false prophets who told Ahab to go up against Ramoth-Gilead "for the Lord will give it unto the hand of the king" (v. 6) and Micaiah who said, "What the Lord says to me, that I will speak" (v. 14), and as a result, he revealed the lying spirit of Ahab's prophets and predicted the defeat and death of Ahab.

14 C. Ryder Smith, *What Is the Old Testament?*, rev. ed. (London: Epworth Press, 1946), p. 105.

15 H. H. Rowley, *Moses and the Decalogue* (Manchester: Manchester University Press, 1951), p. 95.

For his honesty and courage he was slapped by one of the king's prophets. Furthermore, Ahab ordered: "Put this fellow in prison, and feed him with scant fare of bread and water, until I come in peace" (v. 27). Micaiah's parting words to Ahab were: "If you return in peace, the Lord has not spoken by me" (v. 28). Here was a true prophet of God and a worthy forerunner of the great prophets of succeeding centuries. God had spoken to him; he would speak the word of God whatever the cost.

Eighth-Century Prophets: Common Elements

The increasingly ethical tone of the prophets can be traced in the work of Nathan, Elijah, and Micaiah, and to a lesser degree in the ministry of Elisha. This ethical tone or emphasis was climaxed, however, in the great writing prophets who came a few years later. It was the eighth-century poet-prophets—Amos, Hosea, Isaiah, and Micah—who conceived "the doctrine of the primacy of morality"; it was they who regarded morality "as decisive for the destiny of Israel."[16] The "primacy of morality" is seen in both the common and distinctive elements or emphases in each of these prophets. There are at least three common elements that are of major importance for this study and are quite as relevant to the contemporary world as to the days of the prophets.

1. The proper relation of religion and ethics.

These great prophets brought morality and religion into a unique relationship. This was not the mere interfusion of the two; rather, it was "the integration of both into a new unity as when hydrogen and oxygen combine to produce water."[17] The two, religion and ethics, were interwoven in their messages. Morality for them had no basis outside of religion, and religion was vindicated by morality.

Beginning with Amos, there was an almost complete moraliza-

[16] Kaufmann, p. 345.
[17] H. Wheeler Robinson, *Inspiration and Revelation in the Old Testament* (Oxford: Clarendon Press, 1946), p. 79.

tion of the idea of God and, hence, of sin. Amos and the other eighth-century prophets greatly reduced, if they did not eliminate, the emphasis on the ceremonial law. They believed that what God basically required of men was not sacrifices but obedience to the moral law. Closely related to the preceding is the fact that the prophets were passionately religious, which in turn is the reason why they were so insistently ethical. They must be counted among the great moral pioneers of history. In them, ethical religion reached its peak in the Old Testament.

2. The balance between judgment and hope.

God's judgment, for the eighth-century prophets, was coming upon His people because they had been unfaithful to Him—they had played the harlot (Amos 5:2; Hosea 4:12; 5:7; 9:1; 11:7; 13:16; Isa. 1:21); and also because they were wrong in their relations to their fellow men. Kaufmann suggests that "the distinctive feature of classical prophecy is its vehement denunciation of social corruption."[18]

The sins of the children of Israel against their fellow men were spelled out quite specifically. These could be summed up, however, by saying that God looked for justice (*mishpat*) among them and found bloodshed (*mispah*), for righteousness (*tsedaqah*) and "behold, a cry (*tseaqah*)!"—a "play on words similar in sound but sharply contrasting in meaning" (IB) (Isa. 5:7). That cry frequently was the cry of the poor, the orphaned, the widowed, the stranger —special protégés of God and, hence, of special concern to the prophets of God (Amos 2:6–7; 5:11–12; 8:4, 6; Isa. 1:23; 3:14–15; 10:2–3). Heschel says that "prophecy is the voice that God has lent to the silent agony, a voice to the plundered poor."[19] This is true of the prophet of every age; he speaks in defense of the underprivileged and the oppressed.

Transgression after transgression, or rebellion after rebellion (Amos 2:6), made the judgment of God upon Israel inevitable (see Amos 4:12; 7:8; 8:2). The certainty of the judgment was based as much on the unchangeableness of the moral character of God as it was upon the sinfulness of the people. The judgment was God's,

18 Kaufmann, p. 347.
19 Heschel, p. 5.

although He would use a nation afar off as the instrument of His judgment. He would "whistle for it from the ends of the earth" (Isa. 5:26). Assyria, which was to be used as the rod of God's anger, the staff of His fury and indignation (Isa. 10:5), would in turn be punished because of its arrogance and haughty pride (Isa. 10:12). The prophets believed that God was the Lord of all history;[20] all nations were accountable to Him.

The idea of judgment in the Prophets is closely related to "the day of the Lord." There is little known about the origin of the term. It was "already an entrenched popular hope in the eighth century."[21] It seems clear that the people of Israel thought of "the day of the Lord" as a day of judgment upon their enemies and of triumph and exaltation for them. Amos injected "a distinctive ethical content" into the idea.[22] At least he reversed the commonly held view of "the day of the Lord." He said to the children of Israel, "Woe to you that desire the day of the Lord!" He then pointedly asked them, "Why would you have the day of the Lord?" Following this question, he gives the reason for his "woe." He says that the day of the Lord "is darkness, and not light" (5:18) and later added, "and gloom ["blackness," Smith] with no brightness in it" (5:20). Isaiah and Micah rather frequently spoke of "the day" or "that day," which evidently usually referred to the day of the Lord. They considered the day not only a day of punishment but also of discipline and purging. Bright suggests that for them it became "the prelude to promise," a promise, however, "to a new and obedient Israel which did not as yet exist."[23]

Bright also says that in Isaiah and Micah there was "an apparently inconsistent juxtaposition of uncompromising doom and unequivocal assurance."[24] This apparent inconsistency, which is

---

[20] See R. B. Y. Scott, *The Relevance of the Prophets* (New York: Macmillan, 1944), Chap. 7, for a discussion of the prophetic view of history. Norman K. Gottwald's *All the Kingdoms of the Earth* (New York: Harper & Row, 1964) is a thoroughly documented and distinctive discussion of "Israelite Prophecy and International Relations in the Ancient Near East."

[21] Bright, *A History of Israel*, p. 243.

[22] Baab, *The Theology of the Old Testament*, p. 193.

[23] Bright, *A History of Israel*, p. 281.

[24] *Ibid.*, p. 278.

not a real inconsistency, is characteristic of the prophets in general. In their messages, even in Amos, there is a balancing of judgment and hope. The element of hope in Amos is found particularly in the last chapter (9:8–9, 11, 14–15). Even if a part of this chapter is a later addition, as some scholars contend,[25] the element of hope is found in Chapter 5, where, speaking for the Lord, he says, "Seek me and live" (v. 4), "Seek the Lord and live" —"obtain possession of a true life" (KD) (v. 6), and again, "Seek good, and not evil, that you may live" (v. 14). The "seek me" or "seek the Lord" is "a common phrase for the expression of religious desire implying worship and obedience" (ICC).

The element of hope, however, was more prevalent in the other eighth-century prophets than in Amos. In Hosea this element of hope was related to his experience with his faithless wife (2:19–20). As he had forgiven and restored his wife, so God in His love would forgive and restore Israel. He would love "the people of Israel, though they turned to other gods" (3:1). He would "heal their faithlessness," would "love them freely"—"with perfect spontaneity" (KD), His anger would turn from them (14:4).[26] In a passage full of ethical terminology the Lord speaks as follows to the people through the prophet:

> And I will betroth you to me for ever; I will betroth you to me in righteousness and in justice, in steadfast love, and in mercy. I will betroth you to me in faithfulness; and you shall know the Lord [2:19–20; cf. Mic. 7:18–20].

The threefold repetition of "betroth" portrays the solemnity of the promise and underscores the indissolubility of the new covenant. The moral qualities that are mentioned are attributes of God which assure the indissolubility of the covenant.

Isaiah, as optimistic as any of the eighth-century prophets, includes an element of hope in the midst of his description of the

---

[25] Pfeiffer (*Introduction to the Old Testament*) believes that 9:9–15 is "a post-exilic assurance" (p. 580) as is true of the last chapters of Hosea (p. 571), a position not acceptable to Young (*An Introduction to the Old Testament,* p. 251).

[26] Heschel, in a striking statement says, "Intense is His anger, but profound is His compassion. It is as if there were a dramatic tension in God" (p. 46).

terrible destruction by the wrath of God which is compared to a devouring fire. He asks the searching questions:

> Who among us can dwell with the devouring fire?
>> Who among us can dwell with everlasting burnings?
>>> [33:14].

Isaiah answers his questions as follows:

> He who walks righteously ["practices it continually," KD] and speaks
>> uprightly ["sincerely," Smith; his "words are in perfect agreement with his inward feelings and outward condition," KD];
>> who despises the gain of oppressions,
>> who shakes his hands, lest they hold a bribe,
>> who stops his ears from hearing of bloodshed,
>> and shuts his eyes from looking upon evil [33:15].

Notice that each of these qualities is ethical or moral and that the man who has these qualities need not fear God.

The prophets' hope for Israel is closely related to the idea of the remnant. It is clearly revealed that the remnant is the work of God's grace (Isa. 1:9). Also, the remnant idea, particularly in Hosea and Isaiah, contains the seeds of the new covenant, which is prevalent in the thought of some of the later prophets, such as Jeremiah and Ezekiel, and particularly in the New Testament.[27]

The real basis for the hope so prevalent in the prophets was their faith in God. Their doctrine of God would not let them believe that the failures and sins of God's people could ultimately frustrate His purposes for them or totally cancel His promises to them.

The confidence of the prophets in the ultimate triumph of God was closely related to their expectation of the coming of One who would be the

> ruler in Israel,
> whose origin is from of old,
> from ancient days [Mic. 5:2].

27 For a good brief discussion of the remnant, see A. Lelievre, "Remnant," *A Companion to the Bible,* ed. J. J. Von Allmen (New York: Oxford University Press, 1958), pp. 354–57.

Isaiah similarly said that there would come forth "a shoot from the stump ["stalk" or "trunk," IB] of Jesse" (Isa. 11:1) who would judge the poor with righteousness "and decide with equity for the meek of the earth" (Isa. 11:4)—"The poor and humble, or meek, are the peculiar objects of His royal care" (KD). Righteousness would "be the girdle of his waist, and faithfulness the girdle of his loins" (11:5). That day would be a day of peace:

> They shall not hurt or destroy in all my holy mountain;
>> for the earth shall be full of the knowledge of the Lord
>> ["experimental knowledge which consists in the fellowship of love" KD]
> as the waters cover the sea [11:9].

3. The exaltation of righteousness above ritual.

This is another significant common element in Amos, Hosea, Isaiah, and Micah. "To the ordinary Israelite sin was a neglect of ritual regulations; to the prophets it was a violation of the moral law."[28] Many of the rites and ceremonies of the people were no longer expressions of genuine worship. They were frequently used as substitutes for moral living. While the prophets were not critical of worship as such, they strongly contended that the substitution of the forms of worship for the reality of worship was an abomination to the God of Israel, who was an ethical being. Also for them a valid test of the reality of worship was the ethical results in the lives of the people. All four of the eighth-century prophets repeatedly reiterated "the fact that Jehovah by His very Nature demands right conduct from His worshippers and will be content with nothing less."[29] And by right conduct the prophets meant primarily right relations within the community of the people of God. For them, as for the law, the emphasis in the use of the word "righteousness" was on relationship.

Two or three of many illustrations from the prophets of their exaltation of righteousness above ritual will suffice. Amos paints

[28] W. O. E. Oesterley and Theodore H. Robinson, *Hebrew Religion: Its Origin and Development*, 2nd ed. rev. (London: Society for Promoting Christian Knowledge, 1937), p. 231.

[29] Norman H. Snaith, *The Distinctive Ideas of the Old Testament* (Philadelphia: Westminster Press, 1946), p. 65.

a rather dark picture of the moral conditions among the people and predicts that the day of the Lord would be darkness and not light. Then, speaking for the Lord, he says that the Lord hates their feasts, will not accept their offerings, and is not pleased with their music (5:21-23). Subsequently, he reveals to the people what the Lord really wants:

> But let justice [*mishpat*] roll down like waters,
>> and righteousness [*tsedaqah*] like an everflowing
>> stream [5:24].

Amos here and elsewhere clearly "distinguishes ritual from ethics, and declares that by itself the first is worthless, and that the second is the essential element in the religion of Jehovah. The ethical issue is clearly taken at last."[30]

Hosea in one brief statement sums up the matter as follows:

> For I desire steadfast love and not sacrifice,
>> the knowledge of God, rather than burnt offerings
>> [Hos. 6:6; cf. I Sam. 15:22].

But love for whom—for God? or for man? If it is love for God, then He is saying to the people that He wants their love and not their sacrifices devoid of their love. Even if this is the correct conception of the passage, there are deep ethical overtones. When one loves God, he loves those whom God loves. It seems more likely, however, that here is meant love for one's fellow man, a love which is the fruit of fellowship with God or results from the knowledge of God. In the two places where Christ quotes the verse, the context suggests an ethical connotation (Matt. 9:13; 12:7).

Isaiah in a number of places stresses righteousness rather than ritual but nowhere more pointedly than in the first chapter. Speaking to the rulers and the people, he says:

> What to me is the multitude of your sacrifices?
>> says the Lord;
> I have had enough of burnt offerings of rams
>> and the fat of fed beasts;

30 Smith, p. 117.

I do not delight in the blood of bulls,
    or of lambs, or of he-goats.
When you come to appear before me,
    who requires of you
    this trampling of my courts?
Bring no more vain offerings;
    incense is an abomination to me.
New moon and sabbath and the calling of assemblies—
    I cannot endure iniquity and solemn assembly.
Your new moons and your appointed feasts
    my soul hates;
they have become a burden to me,
    I am weary of bearing them.
When you spread forth your hands,
    I will hide my eyes from you;
even though you make many prayers,
    I will not listen;
    your hands are full of blood.
Wash yourselves; make yourselves clean;
    remove the evil of your doings
    from before my eyes;
cease to do evil,
    learn to do good;
seek justice,
    correct oppression;
defend the fatherless,
    plead for the widow [1:11–17].

In opposition to the false service of God, Yahweh "calls for moral reformation and enunciates the true conditions on which the restoration of His favour depends" (CB). "No splendor of worship can compensate for a complete disregard of the moral demands of God in social relationships" (IB).

This section would not be complete without at least quoting the great statement of the central message of the eighth-century prophets found in Micah, which will be referred to again later:

"With what shall I come before the Lord,
    and bow myself before God on high?
Shall I come before him with burnt offerings,
    with calves a year old?
Will the Lord be pleased with thousands of rams,
    with ten thousands of rivers of oil?

Shall I give my first-born for my transgression,
    the fruit of my body for the sin of my soul?"
He has showed you, O man, what is good;
    and what does the Lord require of you
but to do justice, and to love kindness
    and to walk humbly with your God? [Mic. 6:6–8].

Orelli says that the last two lines (v. 8) are "an epitome of the moral law."

Whether the prophets were attempting to eliminate the whole sacrificial system[31] or were simply attempting to correct the abuses of the system,[32] they certainly exalted righteousness above ritualistic forms and ceremonies. Such an emphasis was inevitable for men who spoke for an ethical God.

Eighth-Century Prophets: Distinctive Emphases

In addition to the preceding common elements, the messages of the eighth-century prophets contain some rather distinctive emphases.

1. Amos: prophet of justice.

Amos, a "rugged radical if there ever was one,"[33] lived at a time when Israel, on the surface at least, had reached the zenith of its prosperity and power. The prophet saw, however, beneath the surface where there was rottenness and sin. The foundations had become decadent. Collapse was inevitable. He predicted that God was about to bring an end to the nation.

The fact that the Israelites were the people of God did not guarantee their protection, as they seemed to think (5:14). Such could not be true if their God was a moral God, a God of law and

31 John Skinner, *Prophecy and Religion* (Cambridge: University Press, 1922), p. 181, and Hyatt, *Prophetic Religion,* pp. 127ff.

32 H. Wheeler Robinson, *Redemption and Revelation in the Actuality of History* (New York: Harper, 1942), p. 250, and H. H. Rowley, *The Re-discovery of the Old Testament* (Philadelphia: Westminster Press, 1946), pp. 154ff.

33 Baab, p. 252.

order rather than of caprice and favoritism. Actually, their additional privileges increased their responsibilities. The Lord, through Amos, stated this principle plainly:

You only have I known
    of all the families of the earth;
therefore I will punish you
    for all your iniquities (3:2).

Notice the use of the "therefore." This concept of the unique responsibility of Israel, which underlies the work of all the prophets, is clearly evident in Amos.

He attacked with vigor the social evils of his day, particularly the oppression of the poor, accompanied by luxurious living and idle self-indulgence (2:6–8; 4:1; 5:10–12; 6:4–6, 12; 8:4–6). From the positive standpoint justice, equity, and honesty were the qualities which God demanded of Israel. No one of these concepts was more central in the thought of Amos than justice. For him, God was a God of justice, who demanded this same quality in His people.

2. Hosea: prophet of love.

Like Amos, Hosea foresaw God's judgment coming upon Israel because of man's sin against his fellow man. While Hosea pointed out some specific sins of the people (4:1–2; 12:7), he was, in the main, more general than Amos. God's judgment was coming because of "their wicked deeds" (7:12), their wayward ways (10:10), or their sins (8:13; 9:9).

The most distinctive element in Hosea grew out of his experience with his unfaithful wife. In a sense, his grief became his gospel. At least, his experience with Gomer gave him "the richest and most profoundly developed understanding of the idea of love in the whole Old Testament."[34] In spite of the sins of Israel, God could not altogether desert her (11:8–9). She was His betrothed. His wrath against her was tempered with love, which was "Hosea's most significant contribution to the doctrine of God,"[35] and, we

[34] Eichrodt, I, 251.
[35] Knudson, p. 181.

might add, his most significant contribution to Old Testament ethics. For him, the love of God could not be defeated. "Never in the history of man's thought has the boundless optimism of love found more striking expression than in Hosea."[36] It is this love that would not let the children of Israel go that causes some to speak of Hosea as the first prophet of grace, although that grace was limited to Israel. Through his own agony, Hosea "reached deeper than any other of the Prophets into the secret of religion."[37] It may be this that has caused one author to call Hosea the Jeremiah of the Northern Kingdom and the John of the Old Testament.[38]

The figure of Yahweh as husband was used by later prophets (Jer. 2:2; 3:1; Ezek. 16:32). However, God is not only portrayed by Hosea as the husband of Israel but also as her father. One of the tenderest passages in the Old Testament is the opening verses of Chapter 11:

When Israel was a child, I loved him,
          and out of Egypt I called my son [cf. Ex. 4:22–23].

Yet it was I who taught Ephraim to walk,
          I took them up in my arms;
          but they did not know that I healed them
          ["cared for them," Smith].
I led them with cords of compassion,
          with the bands of love,
and I became to them as one
          who eases the yoke on their jaws,
          and I bent down to them and fed them [11:1, 3–4].

The wounded but surviving love of God was as central in Hosea as the offended righteousness of God was central in Amos. He was as definitely the prophet of love as Amos was the prophet of justice. While he did not originate the idea of the love of God, it is as basic in his message as in any book of the Old Testament.

---

[36] Oesterley and Robinson, p. 239.
[37] Theodore H. Robinson, *Prophecy and the Prophets*, 2nd ed. rev. (London: Gerald Duckworth and Co., 1953), p. 78.
[38] George L. Robinson, *The Twelve Minor Prophets* (Grand Rapids: Baker Book House, 1952), p. 16.

3. Isaiah: "the prophet of divine transcendence."[39]

No single concept can describe adequately the ministry and message of the one who is generally considered the greatest of the prophets. Possibly these words of Wheeler Robinson are as accurate and adequate as any. The transcendence of God, so predominant in Isaiah, was based upon and was an expression of His holiness. As justice is central in Amos, and love in Hosea, so holiness is uniquely emphasized in Isaiah. Knudson suggests that "the ethical conception of holiness is especially prominent in Isaiah."[40] God, for him, was separated to "absolute moral purity, free from spot or defilement."[41] The moral or ethical enaphasis is seen in the record of Isaiah's vision of the Lord in the Temple and his reactions to it (Isa. 6:1–9). He saw the Lord high and lifted up and heard the seraphim singing, possibly antiphonally, "Holy, holy, holy is the Lord of hosts." His first reaction was: "Woe is me! For I am lost; for I am a man of unclean lips." He gives the reason for this reaction: "For my eyes have seen the King, the Lord of hosts!" This strongly suggests that he gave some ethical significance to the holiness of God. The vision created within him a sense of moral unworthiness.

It was natural and almost inevitable, growing out of Isaiah's experience with the Lord, that the holiness of God would be prominent in his messages and ministry. This emphasis is more pronounced in Isaiah than in any of the other prophets, although some emphasis on holiness is found in Amos (4:2) and in Hosea (11:9). Isaiah's characteristic name for Yahweh was "the holy one of Israel" with the name being used approximately thirty times in the book. "Yahweh is the Holy One of Israel not because He

[39] Robinson, *The Old Testament: Its Making and Meaning*, p. 89. For a scholarly and relatively thorough discussion of Isaiah, see Gerhard von Rad, *Old Testament Theology* (New York: Harper and Row, 1965), II, 147–87. The author says that "the preaching of Isaiah represents the theological high water mark of the whole Old Testament" (p. 147). This volume would prove helpful background reading for the prophets in general.

[40] Knudson, p. 151.

[41] Robinson, *Prophecy and the Prophets*, p. 99.

is consecrated to Israel but because He has consecrated Israel to Himself."[42] Eichrodt says that Isaiah carries the name "the Holy One of Israel" before him "like some standard or oriflamme of his message."[43]

The prophet spells out rather specifically what it would mean for the children of Israel to be acceptable to "the Holy One of Israel" who "shows himself holy in righteousness" (Isa. 5:16)— righteousness for Isaiah is an essential element in holiness. It can be summed up by saying that God expects His people to be holy and righteous. To be holy meant to belong to God and hence to be separated from the evil in the world. The latter separation results from one's separation or dedication to God.

Righteousness for Isaiah, who expounded its nature at greater length than any other prophet, contained four chief elements: justice, mercy, truth, and peace. Truth for him meant more than speaking the truth: "It is a reliability that permeates character."[44] The first two of the four elements are prevalent in earlier prophets: justice in Amos, and mercy, or steadfast love, in Hosea.

Peace is another idea that is particularly prominent in Isaiah and closely related to the idea of transcendence. In Isaiah and in the other prophets, peace is also closely related to righteousness and truth. Isaiah speaks of a final or ultimate peace when wars will cease and Israel's messianic king will rule over the nations (Isa. 9:2–7). There will be "a paradisal existence in which all forms of strike will have been removed (Isa. 11:1ff.)."[45] Nowhere is this peace pictured more graphically than in that well-known passage in the second chapter, which is also found in Micah 4:3:

> He shall judge between the nations,
>   and shall decide for many peoples;
>   and they shall beat their swords into plowshares,
>   and their spears into pruning hooks;
> nation shall not lift up sword against nation,
>   neither shall they learn war any more [Isa. 2:4].

[42] Jacob, *Theology of the Old Testament*, p. 89.
[43] Eichrodt, I, 279.
[44] Smith, p. 124, fn.
[45] C. F. Evans, "Peace," *A Theological Word Book of the Bible*, ed. Alan Richardson, p. 165.

This peace will not be a reality until "the mountain of the house of the Lord shall be established" and "all the nations shall flow to it," until the God of Jacob shall teach the peoples of the nations His ways and they respond by walking in those ways, and until Zion shall be triumphant and the word of the Lord shall go forth from Jerusalem (2:2–3). The real secret of peace is the coming of the Prince of Peace, who will rule with justice and righteousness (9:6–7).

The emphasis on peace, as is true of holiness, is also found in the latter part of Isaiah (40–66), attributed by some scholars to another author.[46] Yahweh will make a covenant of peace with his people (54:10), which is related to his "steadfast love" (*hesed*) and "compassion" (*raham*). The peace of God is also related to obedience to the commandments of God (48:18), to righteousness (57:2; 60:17), and to justice (59:8). Conversely, "there is no peace . . . for the wicked" (48:22; 57:21).

4. Micah: preacher against the sins of the cities.

Micah, a contemporary of Isaiah in the Southern Kingdom, was from the country and was appalled by and preached against the sins of Jerusalem and the cities in general (1:5, 9, 12; 5:11, 14). This was his most distinctive emphasis.

Micah cried out against unworthy rulers (3:1–4, 9–11) and false prophets (3:5–7). In common with Amos, he condemned the idle and greedy rich (2:1–2; 6:12). He was one prophet whose messages made a rather lasting impression; a portion of at least one message was remembered approximately a century later (Jer. 26:16–19).

No statement, however brief, about the ethics of Micah would be complete without some reference to the great passage in Micah

---

46 Many scholars make either a twofold (1–39 and 40–66) or a threefold (1–39, 40–55, 56–66) division of Isaiah. The author of the second portion is known as Deutero-Isaiah and in the case of a threefold division it is said that the last chapters were written by Trito-Isaiah. See Rowley (*The Growth of the Old Testament*, pp. 89–100) for a very compact interpretation of the book based on the threefold division. For a commentary by one who makes a twofold division of the book, see James D. Smart's *History and Theology in Second Isaiah* (Philadelphia: Westminster Press, 1965). Typical of his general position, Young (*An Introduction to the Old Testament*) believes "that Isaiah himself wrote the entire prophecy" (p. 199).

6:6–8, quoted previously, which contains an epitome of the social teachings of all the prophets. One verse (6:8) sums up the teachings of the prophets. It is "the most comprehensive statement of the ethical teaching of the prophets"[47] and "the perfect ideal of religion." Here the prophet reveals that God's will for man is to do justice or justly, to love mercy or kindness, and to walk humbly or obediently with his God. "The supreme virtue of religion, as the Hebrew conceived it, is grouped with the two outstanding moral virtues. The religious virtue is that humility of bearing and of conduct, 'making modest the walking' before God, which alone answers properly to man's constant dependence upon Him."[48] The two moral virtues are *mishpat* (justice) and *hesed* (mercy, loving-kindness, or steadfast love). The latter (*hesed*) has been described as "one of the richest words in the whole vocabulary of the Old Testament."[49] In this verse is united the strictly religious (vertical) and the ethical (horizontal), which is typical not only of prophetic religion but also of the basic teachings of both the Old Testament and the New Testament.

Transitional Prophets

While prophecy reached its zenith at least from the ethical viewpoint in the eighth century, there were other great prophets, particularly in the seventh and sixth centuries. Three of these— Zephaniah, Nahum, and Habakkuk—might be called "prophets of transition." They ministered in the period between the great eighth-century prophets and the equally great Jeremiah and Ezekiel. These three transitional prophets along with Jeremiah, a younger contemporary, were active in the last forty years of the Kingdom of Judah.

[47] Knudson, p. 166. Von Rad says of the same verse, "This is the quintessence of the commandments as the prophets understood them" (II, 186–87).

[48] Robinson, *Inspiration and Revelation in the Old Testament*, p. 83.

[49] T. H. Robinson, "Epilogue: The Old Testament and the Modern World," *The Old Testament and Modern Study*, ed. H. H. Rowley (Oxford: Clarendon Press, 1951), p. 359.

1. Zephaniah: "the day of the Lord."

Zephaniah's message was largely a reflection of Amos. His major theme was the coming of the day of the Lord, an idea that Amos, approximately 150 years before, had lifted to a new level by making it a day of universal and moral judgment. For Zephaniah the day of the Lord was to be the consummation of the history of the world.

In language strikingly similar to the words of John the Baptist (Matt. 3:2) and Jesus (Matt. 4:17), Zephaniah saw the day of the Lord as at hand (1:7). It was hastening fast and the sound of it was bitter (1:14-15). In addition to specific references to the day of the Lord there are frequent references to "the day" or "that day" (1:9, 10, 15; 3:8, 11, 16). The idea permeates the whole book.

Zephaniah pronounced the judgment of God upon Jerusalem (3:1), whose sin was threefold: rebellion against God, inner defilement, and cruel or oppressive treatment of man. The judgment was directed particularly against those who should have provided moral and spiritual leadership for the people: the officials, judges, prophets, and priests (3:3-4).

He suggests a way of possible escape in the day of the wrath of the Lord. His suggestion sets forth the requirements of the good life:

Seek the Lord, all you humble of the land,
    who do his commands;
seek righteousness, seek humility;
    perhaps you may be hidden
    on the day of the wrath of the Lord [2:3].

The ultimate triumph of Jerusalem or Judah is beautifully stated in the closing verses of the brief book (3:19-20).

2. Nahum: prophet of vengeance.

The book of Nahum, by a contemporary of Zephaniah, is "an oracle" ("solemn utterance" or "burden") concerning Nineveh (1:1). He "is the prophet of vengeance, and of vengeance against the foreign oppressor."[50] The pertinent lessons of Nahum might be summarized as follows: (1) God is the God of the nations; His government is inclusive not only of His own people but also of their enemies. (2) His judgment is sure, swift, and terrible. (3) His grace is operative in and through His judgment:[51] "The Lord is good, a stronghold in the day of trouble" (1:7); He will afflict no more (1:12);

> Behold, on the mountains the feet of him
>   who brings good tidings,
>   who proclaims peace! (1:15)

3. Habakkuk: recurring and perplexing problems.

Habakkuk, the third of the poet-prophets of the seventh century, struggled with two closely related problems. The children of God through the centuries have continued to seek satisfactory answers to these problems. The first and possibly the most basic one, which is a moral as well as a religious problem, is why so frequently the righteous suffer and the evil prosper (cf. Job and Psalms 37, 49, and 73). The other question that plagued Habakkuk was: Why is an evil nation, the Chaldeans, used to punish God's people who are more righteous than the instruments of their punishment?

Habakkuk may not have found solutions for these perplexing problems, but he did discover something which will relieve the anxiety of the individual child of God and possibly of the nation regarding these problems. In one of the great statements of the Old Testament, Habakkuk says: "Behold, he whose soul is not upright in him shall fail, but the righteous shall live by his faith" ("by reason of his faithfulness," Smith) (2:4). This is one of the Old Testament passages that is most frequently quoted in the New Testament (*see* Rom. 1:17; Gal. 3:11; Heb. 10:38).

Of the five woes found in Habakkuk, Chapter 2, all but the last are clearly ethical or moral: (1) "Woe to him who heaps up what

[50] Robinson, *The Old Testament: Its Making and Meaning,* p. 103.

[51] Robinson, *The Old Testament: Its Making and Meaning, Ibid.,* p. 111.

is not his own" (2:6); (2) "Woe to him who gets evil gain for his house" (2:9); (3) "Woe to him who builds a town with blood, and founds a city on iniquity" (2:12); (4) "Woe to him who makes his neighbors drink of the cup of his wrath, and makes them drunk, to gaze on their shame!" (2:15); and (5) "Woe to him who says to a wooden thing, Awake; to a dumb thing, Arise!" (2:19)—a reference to idolatry.

Jeremiah and Ezekiel

These two prophets were contemporaries, although the place and the immediate occasion for their messages differed drastically. Jeremiah's long ministry of forty years began in the seventh century and extended into the sixth century. Ezekiel's ministry was entirely in the latter century. Jeremiah remained in Jerusalem even after its fall until he was forced to go to Egypt (Jer. 43:6–7). In contrast, Ezekiel was carried off as a captive to Babylon in 597 B.C., eleven years before the fall of Jerusalem. His entire ministry was during the Exile beginning some years before the fall of the city but also extending for many years after the fall of Jerusalem. This explains the nature of his messages. H. Wheeler Robinson suggests that Ezekiel was "a denunciatory prophet" until the fall of Jerusalem (chaps. 1–24) and "a consoling pastor" or "watchman" after that event. The latter chapters of the book could be divided into two main divisions: (1) messages of judgment upon foreign nations (chaps. 25–32), and messages of promise and hope for Judah and Jerusalem (chaps. 33–48). There is some material of considerable significance in all sections of the book, as well as in Jeremiah.

1. Emphases common with other prophets.

There are a number of these common emphases. For example, Jeremiah and Ezekiel sound like Amos when they defend the rights of the sojourner, the fatherless, the widow, and the needy (Jer. 5:28; Ezek. 22:7, 29). Similar to Amos, Jeremiah says that every one from the least to the greatest of the people was "greedy for unjust gain; and from prophet to priest," every one dealt

falsely (Jer. 6:13; 8:10). Their burnt offerings and their other
sacrifices were not pleasing to God (Jer. 6:20). Vows and sacrifices
could not avert their doom (Jer. 11:15). In language strikingly
similar to Amos, he says that the Lord delights in kindness, justice, and righteousness (Jer. 9:24). Ezekiel, like Amos, saw the
day of the Lord as near and foresaw that it would be "a day of
clouds, a time of doom for the nations" (Ezek. 30:3).

Jeremiah and Ezekiel, similar to Hosea, considered the unfaithfulness of the people as one reason for the impending judgment
of God. They had burned incense to other gods (Jer. 1:16), having
forsaken God (Jer. 2:13, 19). Jeremiah, whom Eichrodt says is
"the only man to have fully absorbed the preaching of Hosea,"[52]
similar to Hosea, speaks of God's relation to Israel as that of a
parent and a child (Jer. 31:9) and as of a husband and a wife
(Jer. 3:1ff.; cf. Ezek. 16:8). Israel, the wife, had been faithless (Jer.
3:20). She had played the harlot "with many lovers" (Jer. 3:1; cf.
Ezek. 16:15–63), "committing adultery with stone and tree" (Jer.
3:9).

In common with other prophets, both Jeremiah and Ezekiel
foresaw the judgment of God coming upon their people. Because
of sin the whole land would be laid waste (Jer. 4:20). One reason
for this was that the people were "skilled in doing evil, but how
to do good they know not" (Jer. 4:22). The Lord invited His
prophet to search through the streets of Jerusalem to see if he
could find a man "who does justice and seeks truth," with the
implication that God would pardon Jerusalem if the prophet
found one just or truthful man (Jer. 5:1). With judgment impending, God assured the people of Judah that there was still
hope for them if they would mend their ways, if they would
"truly execute justice one with another," if they would not oppress the alien, the fatherless, the widow, nor shed innocent blood
or go after foreign gods (Jer. 7:3–10; cf. 35:15). Other sins that
were specifically condemned were the getting of riches unjustly
(Jer. 17:11; 22:17; Ezek. 22:13), and the building of houses by
unrighteousness and injustice (Jer. 22:13). Because of their sins,
God had already taken away his peace (*shalom*), steadfast love
(*hesed*), and mercy (*rahamim*) (Jer. 16:5).

52 Eichrodt, I, 253.

Ezekiel points out in a specific way the sins of the princes, priests, and false prophets (Ezek. 22:25–28). In a striking statement he says that the prophets had "daubed . . . with whitewash" for the princes, "seeing false visions and divining lies for them" (Ezek. 22:28). In harmony with some of the other prophets, Jeremiah (chaps. 47–51) and Ezekiel (chaps. 25–32) portrayed the moral judgment of God as inclusive of nations other than Israel.

The idea of the restoration of at least a remnant of God's people, found in the messages of other prophets, is also prevalent in Jeremiah and Ezekiel. Both of the prophets related the restoration of the remnant to the messianic age, to a "righteous Branch" of the seed of David who would "reign as king and deal wisely" and "execute justice and righteousness in the land." His name would be "the Lord is our righteousness" (Jer. 23:5–6; cf. 33:15–16; Ezek. 37:24–25). The restoration was an expression of God's steadfast love, which endures forever (Jer. 33:11), a result of the grace of God (Jer. 24:6–7; Ezek. 11:17–19; 36:26), and was for His name's sake rather than for the sake of His people, who had been faithless (Ezek. 36:21–23, 32, 36; cf. 39:7, 21–29). His spirit, however, would breathe life into the dry bones (Ezek. 37:14), and would take His people from among the nations (Ezek. 37:21), and in the process He would save them from their backsliding (Ezek. 37:23). The restoration would involve an inner spiritual and moral change. The people of Judah were to circumcise the foreskin of their hearts (Jer. 4:4) and were to cleanse themselves from wickedness (Jer. 4:14).

2. Distinctive emphases.

The central emphasis on a new heart and the closely related idea of a new and inner covenant are unique contributions of Jeremiah and Ezekiel. The "new covenant" was not a totally different "covenant"; rather, it was a "renewed" covenant. Nowhere is the concept of the new or renewed covenant stated more clearly than in Jeremiah 31:31–34, which has been called "The Gospel before the Gospel" (IB). God, speaking through the prophet, said that the days were coming when He would make a new covenant with His people. (For some New Testament references to the new covenant concept, see I Cor. 11:25; Heb. 8:8–12; 10:16–17.)

The nature of the new covenant is stated in verse 33 as follows: "But this is the covenant which I will make with the house of Israel after those days, says the Lord: I will put my law within them, and I will write it upon their hearts; and I will be their God, and they shall be my people." The difference between the old covenant and the new "consists merely in this, that the will of God as expressed in the Law under the old covenant was presented externally to the people, while under the new covenant it is to become an internal principle of life" (KD). This covenant was to be an everlasting covenant (Jer. 32:38–40; 50:5; Ezek. 16:60, 62). The new spirit or heart, which was the work of God, would cause the people to walk in His statutes and observe His ordinances (Ezek. 36:27).

The new covenant idea has been called "the cornerstone of personal religion."[53] Although this new covenant was to be with the house of Israel and the house of Judah (Jer. 31:31), "the idea was bound to break its nationalistic limitations and become the Magna Charta of personal religion."[54]

The responsibility of the individual is emphasized in both Jeremiah and Ezekiel. While this emphasis was important in both of the prophets, it would be a mistake to consider them the originators of individualism among the people of Israel. There was always some consciousness of individual responsibility. This is seen, at least to some degree, in the Ten Commandments, in the Covenant Code in general, and pointedly in the work of earlier prophets, such as Nathan and Elijah, who faced their kings with the courageous statement: "You are the man." The emphasis on individual responsibility is more prominent, however, in Jeremiah and in Ezekiel than elsewhere in the Old Testament, being spelled out more fully in the latter than in the former.

---

[53] J. Philip Hyatt, *Jeremiah: Prophet of Courage and Hope* (New York: Abingdon Press, 1958), p. 87.

[54] Hyatt, *Prophetic Religion*, p. 25. The writer of the Epistle to the Hebrews quoted Jeremiah 31:31–34 when he explained the superiority of Christianity, with Christ as the high priest and the mediator of a better covenant (Heb. 8:1–13). It is possible that Christ had this idea of Jeremiah's in mind when He spoke at the last supper of "the covenant" (Matt. 26:28), and Paul when he spoke of "a new covenant, not in a written code but in the Spirit" (II Cor. 3:6).

Jeremiah's emphasis on the individual stems, to some degree, from his own personal experience. He was "driven in upon God by the isolation resulting from his unpopularity."[55] This would explain the fact that "Jeremiah's individualism centers in man's close relationship with God, and he is thus the earliest exponent of *personal religion.*" On the other hand, "Ezekiel's individualism emphasizes man's own responsibility for his deeds, and he is thus the first to teach *personal responsibility.*"[56] While this distinction is not entirely accurate, it does point out a difference in emphasis.

The idea of personal responsibility was a recurring theme in the messages of Ezekiel. In a rather striking passage he says that even if Noah, Daniel, and Job were in the land, all they could deliver would be their own lives by their righteousness (Ezek. 14:14, 20). He recognized that he, "a watchman for the house of Israel" (Ezek. 3:17), was responsible unto God. If he failed to warn the wicked, God would require the latter's blood at his hands (Ezek. 3:18). The prophet comes back to the idea of the watchman and his responsibility in Chapter 33. The watchman is responsible for the blowing of the trumpet; the people are responsible for hearing and taking heed (Ezek. 33: 2–6).

Both Jeremiah and Ezekiel rejected the common proverb by which the people tended to explain and excuse their troubles. The proverb was:

The fathers have eaten sour grapes,
    and the children's teeth are set on edge
        [blunted].

Jeremiah plainly said: "But every one shall die for his own sin, each man who eats sour grapes, his teeth shall be set on edge" (Jer. 31:30). Similarly, Ezekiel, in Chapter 18, emphasizes in a most pointed way the responsibility of the individual. The Lord, speaking through Ezekiel, said, "This proverb shall no more be used by you in Israel. Behold, all souls are mine; . . . the soul that sins shall die" (18:3–4). The sins for which they would be

[55] Robinson, *The Old Testament: Its Making and Meaning*, p. 105.

[56] Oesterley and Robinson, p. 293.

condemned are spelled out rather specifically: sins against God and against their fellow man, with the emphasis on the moral rather than the ceremonial. Some of the sins were stated negatively, others positively. The statement is as follows:

> If a man is righteous and does what is lawful and right—if he does not eat upon the mountains or lift up his eyes to the idols of the house of Israel, does not defile his neighbor's wife or approach a woman in her time of impurity, does not oppress anyone, but restores to the debtor his pledge, commits no robbery, gives his bread to the hungry and covers the naked with a garment, does not lend at interest or take any increase, withholds his hand from iniquity, executes true justice between man and man, walks in my statutes, and is careful to observe my ordinances—he is righteous, he shall surely live, says the Lord God (18:5–9; cf. 22:6–12).

In succeeding verses this general statement is repeated and applied to the son and to the father.

The conclusion of the entire passage is:

> The soul that sins shall die. The son shall not suffer for the iniquity of the father, nor the father suffer for the iniquity of the son; the righteousness of the righteous shall be upon himself, and the wickedness of the wicked shall be upon himself (18:20).

Here is both a glorious and a terrible truth. The truth is "the moral freedom of the individual" (ICC). It is glorious not to be responsible for anyone else's sins. It may be terrible to be responsible for one's own sins.

Other Prophets

In addition to the prophets previously discussed, there are a number of others that have not been mentioned.

1. Prophets of the restoration.

There were three of these prophets: Haggai, Zechariah, and Malachi. Haggai was concerned almost exclusively with the rebuilding of the temple. Zechariah was concerned to a considerable degree with the same problem, but in words strikingly similar to earlier prophets, he said to the people:

> These are the things that you shall do: Speak the truth to one an-
> other, render in your gates (places where courts of justice
> were held) judgments that are true and make for peace, do
> not devise evil in your hearts against one another, and love
> no false oath, for all these things I hate, says the Lord
> [Zech. 8:16–17].

Malachi, who evidently ministered after the temple had been rebuilt (1:10; 3:1, 10), touched on one matter of major social and ethical significance. Many of the Jews had put away their Jewish wives or "wives of their youth" and had taken foreign wives— daughters "of a foreign god." The Lord who had been a witness to the covenant (cf. Gen. 31:50) between them and their former wives (2:14; cf. Prov. 2:17), exhorts his people through the prophet not to be "faithless to the wife" of their youth (2:15). This is followed by the general statement: "For I hate divorce, says the Lord, the God of Israel," and one who divorces the wife of his youth covers his "garment with violence." The "soiled gar- ment is a symbol of uncleanness of heart (cf. Zech. iii. 4; Isa. lxiv. 5 [v. 6 in RSV]; Rev. iii. 4, vii. 14)" (KD). The entire emphasis is closed with the statement: "So take heed to yourselves and do not be faithless" (Mal. 2:16). Note the recurring emphasis on faith- lessness which serves as a refrain (vss. 10, 11, 14, 15, 16).

2. Miscellaneous prophets.

Other books usually listed with the prophetic books are: Dan- iel, Joel, Obadiah, and Jonah. The Jews listed Daniel[57] with The

---

[57] Rowley, who dates Daniel in the second century B.C., says that the stories in Daniel "are not historical" (*The Growth of the Old Testament*, p. 156) but that they do contain "a kernel of inexact historical traditions of the sixth century B.C." (p. 161). In another book, *The Servant of the Lord and Other Essays on the Old Testament* (London: Lutterworth Press, 1952), Rowley suggests that the materials the author "used were probably taken from various sources, oral and written" (p. 267) and adapted to the needs of his own day. Pfeiffer (*Introduction to the Old Testament*, pp. 764–66) agrees with Rowley about the dating of Daniel. In contrast, Young (*Introduction to the*

Writings rather than with The Prophets. Its viewpoint is apocalyptic rather than typically prophetic. Its most important contribution from the perspective of biblical ethics is its view of history:
that the power of God is greater than all the powers of earth, and
that His kingdom ultimately will triumph.

Scholars differ considerably about the dates for the writing of
the other prophetic books. They also differ about the nature of
Jonah—whether it is history or drama.[58] These matters do not
affect the content of the books. Jonah, which is sometimes listed
with the eighth-century prophets, has been called "a pearl among
the writings of the prophets."[59] It is not so much prophecy as a
story about a prophet. Its central message is God's inclusive love
and compassion for all men.

The preaching of Joel, except for the army of locusts, sounds
very much like Amos with his emphasis on the judgment of God
and the day of the Lord. The latter is revealed as near (1:15; 2:1),
as "a day of darkness and gloom" (2:2), and a great and terrible
day (2:11, 31). It is such a terrible day that the question is asked:
"Who can endure it?" (2:11), which sounds like Isaiah's question,
"Who among us can dwell with the devouring fire?" (Isa. 33:14).
Just as Isaiah says, there are some who can dwell with the devouring fire, Joel likewise implies that some can endure the "great and
terrible day" of the Lord. He says:

"Yet even now," says the Lord,
    "return to me with all your heart,
with fasting, with weeping, and
      with mourning;
    and rend your hearts and not
      your garments."

Old Testament, p. 351) dates the book in the sixth century B.C. and says that
it was written by Daniel who was living at the royal court of Babylon at the
time.

    [58] G. Ch. Aalders, in a booklet (*The Problem of the Book of
Jonah* [London: Tyndale Press, 1948]), after examining the evidence carefully
concludes that Jonah is historic narrative rather than a parable or an allegory.

    [59] Curt Kuhl, *The Old Testament: Its Origin and Composition*,
trans. C. T. M. Herriott (Edinburgh and London: Oliver and Boyd, 1961),
p. 210.

Return to the Lord, your God,
     for he is gracious and merciful,
slow to anger, and abounding in
       steadfast love,
     and repents of evil (2:12–13).

The brief book of Obadiah, similar to Nahum, is a message of vengeance.

There is no portion of the Old Testament that speaks more pointedly to the needs of our day than the prophets. The relevance of their messages stems from the fact that the problems they dealt with were human problems and those problems are basically the same from generation to generation. For example, many people in the days of the prophets thought they could be right in their relations with God simply by being faithful to the formalities of their religion. This has been a continuing problem that prophets of God have faced in every age. The word of the prophet is that no man is acceptable to God unless he treats his fellowman rightly, and to treat his fellowman rightly means to treat him as God treats him. The latter means among other things that he will have a particular concern for the underprivileged and the disinherited of society. This emphasis, so prominent in the prophets, speaks loudly to our class- and color-conscious churches in a day when the restless masses of the world are on the move.

The prophets' messages are just as applicable to nations as to individuals and churches. The prophets plainly say that all nations are accountable to God. Any special blessings that a nation receives from Him increase its responsibility to Him. God plays no favorites and shows no partiality even in relation to His chosen people. He has often used a people less righteous than His own as the instrument of His judgment against them. Peoples of the contemporary period should remember that what God has done in the past He may do again.

It is also plainly evident in the prophets that the health of a nation and a people cannot be determined by external appearances. A nation may be most decadent at the very time when it seems most prosperous. Material wealth and prosperity are not the real test of the vitality of a people.

The contemporary prophet of God should not forget that the Old Testament prophets not only proclaimed the judgment of God but also preached a message of hope. In other words, the way of salvation was still available. If the nation would repent of its sins, turn from evil and turn to God, He would forgive, receive, and restore. This, as well as every other aspect of the preaching of the prophets, is pertinent for the contemporary world.

CHAPTER III

THE WRITINGS

The Jews, as indicated previously, made a threefold division of their Scriptures: the Law, the Prophets, and the Writings. The Writings were the last to obtain canonical standing and were the least reverenced of their Scriptures. Vriezen suggests that with them "we have come to the borderland of the Old Testament books of revelation."[1] Filson even suggests that there is no proof that the Sadducees ever accepted the Writings as scripture. He also says that "the discovery of manuscript fragments at *Qumran* indicate that among the Essenes a number of the Writings, while known and used, may not have been accepted as fully canonical."[2] Some books in the Writings, however, are of major importance from the perspective of biblical ethics. Although their ethical content is not as well unified as it is in the Law and the Prophets, there is evident the same central emphasis on God and on His expectation that His people should be like Him.

1 Vriezen, *An Outline of Old Testament Theology*, p. 74.
2 Filson, *Which Books Belong in the Bible?*, p. 47.

Historical Books

In the broadest sense, the historical books of the Bible might be divided into three major groups: (1) the Pentateuch, in which history provides a background and framework for legislation; (2) the four books classified by the Jews as the early prophets: Joshua, Judges, I and II Samuel, and I and II Kings; and (3) the later historical books: I and II Chronicles, Ezra, and Nehemiah. These three major divisions provide in broad outline, with some gaps, the history of the world, with a particularly Jewish interpretation, from its beginning to about 400 B.C. The first two of these divisions have been discussed previously.

At least a brief statement should be made concerning the last of the predominantly historical books of the Old Testament. The Jews treated I and II Chronicles as one book and Ezra and Nehemiah as one book. Some scholars suggest that originally all four books formed a single work and were possibly written by the same author, frequently called "the Chronicler," who may have been Ezra.

1. The Chronicles.

Whoever the writer was, he selected and adapted much of the material for the Chronicles from Genesis, Samuel, and Kings. Nowhere is the selective nature of Old Testament history more evident. Certain historical events were chosen to be used as teaching instruments. One of the main emphases of the Chronicler, found in all Old Testament history, was the conviction that God was central in the historic process. This viewpoint might be summed up in the words of encouragement that King Hezekiah addressed to his people:

> Be strong and of good courage. Do not be afraid or dismayed before the king of Assyria and all the horde that is with him; for there is one greater with us than with him. With him is an arm of flesh; but with us is the Lord our God, to help us and to fight our battles (II Chron. 32:7–8).

The God who was central in the unfolding of history is portrayed as holy (I Chron. 16:10), as a covenant-keeping God (I Chron.

16:15), and as a God of mercy (I Chron. 21:13), in whom is no perversion of justice or partiality or taking of bribes (II Chron. 19:7). Also, it is stated that "his steadfast love endures forever" (I Chron. 16:34).[3]

There are other specific ethical teachings or implications in the Chronicles. It is recorded that Saul died for his unfaithfulness, "he did not keep the command of the Lord" (I Chron. 10:13). In contrast, David, a good king, "administered justice and equity to all his people" (I Chron. 18:14). David, however, was not permitted to build God's house because he was a warrior and had shed blood (I Chron. 22:6–8; 28:3). One of the most frequently quoted statements from the Chronicles is the word of the Lord to Solomon: "If my people who are called by my name humble themselves, and pray and seek my face, and turn from their wicked ways, then I will hear from heaven, and I will forgive their sin and heal their land" (II Chron. 7:14). The words "turn from their wicked ways" is an essential part of the admonition with its attendant promise.

2. Ezra and Nehemiah.

Two moral problems that are discussed, to some degree, in these books are the charging of interest to fellow Jews (Neh. 5:8–13; cf. Lev. 25:35–37) and the violation of the Sabbath (Neh. 13:15–22). The major moral and social problem, however, in Ezra and Nehemiah is the intermarriage of the Israelites with the surrounding peoples (Ezra 9:1; cf. Ex. 34:11–16; Deut. 7:1–8). The priests and the Levites as well as the people in general were guilty. There is a listing of the names of those who had taken foreign wives (Ezra 10:18–44). Nehemiah says that the mixing had become so serious that their children "could not speak the language of Judah" (Neh. 13:24). The problem of intermarriage was basically religious rather than political or racial. The priests, the Levites, and the people were challenged to make a covenant with their God (Ezra 10:3; cf. Neh. 13:25) and to separate themselves from the people and from their foreign wives (Ezra

---

3 For other places where the same expression is found in these historical books, see: II Chron. 5:13; 6:14, 42; 7:3, 6; 20:21; and Ezra 3:11. This is a favorite emphasis in the Psalms.

10:11) with their worship of foreign gods. Under the pressure of Ezra, the children of Israel took an oath that they would do as he had said (Ezra 10:5; cf. Neh. 10:30).

The Psalms

The book of Psalms, consisting of 150 poems, is divided into five books (1–41; 42–72; 73–89; 90–106; 107–150). In the Psalms "every mood of Israel's faith is reflected, and the voices of many generations are heard."[4] Those voices do not always speak the same language. There is considerable diversity in their moral and religious tone.

Since the Psalms were the songs of Israel, we should not expect a great deal of ethical material. Hymns are used primarily for worship; not for instruction. The Psalms contain, however, considerably more moral and ethical content material than is found in most contemporary hymnbooks. It is natural, since the Psalms were the songs of the people, that much of their ethical content would be derived from a description of the character of God.

1. God's steadfast love.

God is particularly portrayed as a God of kindness (Smith), loving-kindness (KJV, ASV), or steadfast love (RSV). This term "steadfast love" or "loving-kindness" is the usual translation of the Hebrew word *hesed*[5] which is found approximately 120 times in the Psalms and about 130 times elsewhere in the Old Testament. H. Wheeler Robinson says that *hesed* denotes something comparable to the New Testament term *agape* (love),[6] while Snaith suggests that its nearest New Testament equivalent is *charis* (grace).[7] Muilenburg says that it is "susceptible of many

4 Bernhard W. Anderson, *Understanding the Old Testament* (Englewood Cliffs, N. J.: Prentice-Hall, 1957), p. 444.

5 There are at least three places in the Old Testament where *hesed* or a closely related word is used in a bad sense (Lev. 20:17; Prov. 14:34; 25:10).

6 Robinson, *The Old Testament: Its Making and Meaning*, pp. 139–40.

7 Norman H. Snaith, "Loving-Kindness," *A Theological Wordbook of the Bible*, ed. Alan Richardson, p. 136.

renderings . . . depending upon the context" and that "it can mean kindness, covenant love, steadfast love, devotion, fidelity, even grace."[8] Whatever the meaning of *hesed*, "it belongs to the covenant circle of ideas."[9] It is frequently joined with other moral qualities of God such as mercy (25:6; 51:1; 103:4), justice (33:5; 119:149), righteousness (33:5; 85:10), forgiveness (86:5), redemption (130:7), and especially faithfulness (25:10; 40:10; 57:3, 10; 61:7; 85:10; 86:15; 89:1-2, 14, 24, 49; 98:3; 115:1; 117:2; 138:2).

The *hesed* or steadfast love of God, according to the Psalmist, is precious (36:7), better than life (63:3), good (69:16), and great (86:13; 117:2). The earth is full of God's steadfast love (33:5; 119:64). It extends to the heavens (36:5) and even above the heavens (108:4). It is better to trust God's steadfast love than to trust in riches (52:7-8).

Particularly prominent is the idea that God's *hesed* endures forever (100:5; 106:1; 138:8), existing from "everlasting to everlasting" (103:17). The fact that God's *hesed* or steadfast love endures seems to be the theme of at least four Psalms: (1) Psalm 89, where God's steadfast love is coupled with His faithfulness; (2) Psalm 107, where the term occurs six times and there is an exhortation that men consider and thank the Lord for his steadfast love (vv. 1, 8, 15, 21, 31, 43); (3) Psalm 118, where the emphasis in the first four verses that God's steadfast love endures is repeated in the last verse (29); and (4) Psalm 136, a wonderfully constructed poem in which the last line of all twenty-six verses end with the refrain, "for his steadfast love endures for ever." The first nine verses of this great psalm suggest that the creative work of God was an expression of His steadfast love.

2. Other moral qualities of God.

Although the major and, in many ways, the distinctive emphasis in the Psalms is on the loving kindness or steadfast love of God, there is considerable emphasis on other moral qualities of God. He is the righteous God (7:9; 129:4); "a righteous judge" (7:11; 9:4; 96:13; 119:75, 137), whose "righteousness is righteous for

---

8 Muilenburg, *The Way of Israel*, p. 59.
9 Gottfried Quell and Gottlob Schrenk, "Righteousness," *Kittel's Bible Key Words*, IV, 3, n. 3.

ever" (119:142; cf. 111:3) and who is revealed by his righteous acts (71:15–16). Even the heavens declare the righteousness of God (50:6; 97:6).

The righteousness of God is frequently joined with His justice (72:1; 89:14; cf. 33:5; 99:4), and His graciousness, goodness, and mercy (111:4; 112:4; 116:5).[10] There are a number of additional references to the goodness (25:8; 100:5; 119:68; 135:3), graciousness (103:8; 135:3; 145:13; 147:1), and mercy (103:4) of God. These qualities, along with justice, are included, to some degree, in the righteousness of God.

Since God is both righteous and just, He is also impartial, blessing both the small and the great alike (115:13). He judges people with equity (9:8; 67:4; 75:2; 96:10; 98:9). Consistent with the general Old Testament conception of God, however, He has a special concern for the underprivileged or the disinherited of the earth. He is a stronghold for the oppressed (9:9) and a refuge for the poor (14:6). He raises up the needy,[11] lifting them up from the ash heap (113:7). They stand at his right hand (109:31). He is the helper of the fatherless (10:14), being the source of justice for the fatherless (10:18) and the oppressed (76:9; 103:6). He is also the protector of widows (68:5; cf. 146:9). He "champions the rights of the forlorn and feeble" (140:12, Moffatt).

There are still other ethical qualities ascribed to God. He is holy (22:3; 99:3, 5, 9; 111:9), being the Holy One of Israel (71:22; 78:41; 89:18). He is also a covenant-keeping God (89:34), always mindful of His covenant with Israel (105:8; 111:5), which He considers an everlasting one (105:10).[12]

---

[10] Snaith ("Righteous, Righteousness," *A Theological Wordbook of the Bible,* ed. Alan Richardson, pp. 202–4) suggests that the words translated "righteous" and "righteousness" (*tsedeq* and *tsedaqah*) contain a considerable and even a primary ethical connotation, including the ideas of justice, mercy, and benevolence, particularly in relation to the helpless. The two words justice (*mishpat*) and righteousness (*tsedaqah*) are closely related. It does seem, however, that "justice" in general refers to a mode of action and righteousness to a quality of a person. Also, righteousness goes beyond justice.

[11] Some of the references to the needy in the Psalms evidently were not to the poor but to those who were oppressed in general or persecuted. The Psalmist himself on occasion would be in that category.

[12] Psalms 105 and 106 spell out in considerable detail God's dealings with Israel, which proved that He had been faithful to His part of the covenant.

While the idea that God was not only the God of Israel but also the God of all nations is not as prominent in the Psalms as in the prophets, it is present. He is "a great king over all the earth" (47:2), reigning "over the nations" (47:8; cf. 46:10). Several Psalms concentrate on God's moral government of the world (1, 34, 75, 77, 90, 92, 112).

There are some verses in Psalm 146 which have ethical significance and portions of which sound somewhat similar to Isaiah 61:1–2, which was read by Jesus at Nazareth at the time of the announcement of His messiahship. The words from the Psalm are as follows:

Happy is he whose help is the God of Jacob, . . .
    who executes justice for the oppressed;
    who gives food to the hungry.

The Lord sets the prisoners free;
    the Lord opens the eyes of the blind.
The Lord lifts up those who are bowed down;
    the Lord loves the righteous.
The Lord watches over the sojourners,
    he upholds the widow and the fatherless;
    but the way of the wicked he brings to ruin
          [146:5, 7–9].

This section on the ethical or moral qualities of God might be summarized in the following statement:

Men shall proclaim the might of thy terrible acts,
    and I will declare thy greatness.
They shall pour forth the fame of thy abundant
        goodness,
    and shall sing aloud of thy righteousness.

The Lord is gracious and merciful,
    slow to anger and abounding in steadfast love.
The Lord is good to all,
    and his compassion is over all that he has made. . . .

The Lord is faithful in all his words,
    and gracious in all his deeds.
The Lord upholds all who are failing,
    and raises up all who are bowed down
          [145:6–9, 13b–14].

3. Additional ethical teachings.

Although most of the ethical content of the Psalms is derived from the description of the nature and character of God, there are some additional ethical and social teachings of considerable importance. As an introduction to these teachings, possibly a brief statement should be made regarding the imprecatory psalms, where the Psalmist calls down the wrath of God on his enemies. Even in these Psalms there is frequently found ethical material of a rather high standard. For example, in the same Psalm where the Psalmist says,

> as wax melts before fire,
> let the wicked perish before God [68:2],

he also refers to God as the "father of the fatherless and protector of widows," who gives "the desolate a home to dwell in" and leads "the prisoners to prosperity" (68:5–6).

In another imprecatory psalm there is a hint of a redemptive motive or purpose. The Psalmist prayed to God to make his enemies "like whirling dust" and "like chaff before the wind" (83:13) and pleaded with God to consume them as a fire consumes a forest, to pursue them with His tempest and to terrify them with His hurricane (83:14–15). But, then, notice what follows this appeal for the wrath of God:

> Fill their faces with shame,
> that they may seek thy name, O Lord. . . .

> Let them know that thou alone,
> whose name is the Lord,
> art the Most High over all the earth [83:16, 18].

Let us consider now some more strictly positive emphases. The Psalmist prays that the Lord will teach him to walk in the truth or in the way of the Lord (86:11), since the one who walks in the way of the Lord is blessed or happy (128:1).[13] Walking in the way

---

13 The expression "to walk in the way of the Lord" or something comparable to it is found rather frequently in the Old Testament (Deut. 8:6; 10:12; 28:9; II Kings 21:22; Prov. 2:13; 14:2; 28:26; Isa. 33:15; 38:3). The idea is also prevalent in the New Testament (John 12:35; Col. 2:6; Gal. 5:16; cf. I John 1:7; Eph. 2:2; 5:2).

of the Lord or in obedience to or in harmony with His will and way is the outward expression of an inner relationship. The Psalmist, in a number of places, captures and expresses this inner emphasis, which is particularly prevalent in Jeremiah and Ezekiel. The man is blessed or happy who does not walk in the counsel of the wicked, stand in the way of sinners, nor sit in the seat of the scoffers, but delights in the law of the Lord, and meditates on the law day and night (1:1–2).

This inner emphasis is found in a number of other places. For example:

> The law of the Lord is perfect,
>   reviving the soul; . . .
> the precepts of the Lord are right,
>   rejoicing the heart [19:7–8a].

This psalm closes with a prayer which would be appropriate for a child of God every day:

> Let the words of my mouth and the meditation
>   of my heart
> be acceptable in thy sight,
> O Lord, my rock and my redeemer [19:14]

The great psalm of confession (51) likewise emphasizes the inner. This is seen especially in verse 6: "Behold, thou desirest truth in the inward being"; and in the petition in verse 10: "Create in me a clean heart, O God, and put a new and right [steadfast or constant] spirit within me." Then in language that sounds like the voice of the prophets, the Psalmist says,

> For thou hast no delight in sacrifice;
>   were I to give a burnt offering,
>   thou wouldst not be pleased.
> The sacrifice acceptable to God is
>   a broken spirit;
>   a broken and contrite heart, O God,
>   thou wilt not despise [vv. 16–17].

The Psalmist at times appealed to motives, at least by implication, that were not the highest when measured by contemporary

Christian standards. He uses the prudential or common sense appeal so prevalent in the Proverbs. For example, it is said that the man who delights in the commandments of God is blessed or happy (112:1; cf. 106:3): "wealth and riches are in his house" (112:3), the Lord will be gracious and merciful to him (112:4), he will never be moved (112:6), "he rises to high power and honour" (12:9, Moffatt). Again, the Psalmist says that "the righteous flourish like the palm tree" (92:12) and that "no good thing does the Lord withhold from those who walk uprightly" (84:11).

The customary Jewish viewpoint, which is prevalent in the Psalms, was that God punished the wicked and prospered the righteous. The bitter experience, however, of some of the righteous or pious and the evident prosperity of the wicked led to some serious questions concerning the validity of the old and orthodox dogma, questions similar to those that provided the background for the book of Job. These questions regarding the orthodox position are set forth rather clearly in several Psalms (34, 37, 49, 73). While there may not be an entire vindication of faith simply for the sake of faith, there is, in places at least, a spiritualizing of the blessings of God. Psalm 73 will serve as an example. When the Psalmist saw the prosperity of the wicked (v. 3) and beheld how their riches increased (v. 12), his first reaction was one of complaint and bitterness (vv. 13–14). An answer to the problem came to him when he went into the sanctuary, where the precarious existence of the wicked was revealed to him (vv. 16–20). In contrast, he says of himself:

> Nevertheless I am continually with thee;
> > thou dost hold my right hand.
> Thou dost guide me with thy counsel,
> > and afterward thou wilt receive me to glory
> > > [vv. 23–24].

There are some other miscellaneous ethical teachings in the Psalms. There are statements concerning the tongue (34:13; 39:1), admonitions regarding the proper treatment of the poor (41:1), and strong warnings concerning the dangers of riches. Men are warned not to place their trust in riches (49:6); they cannot ransom one's life (49:7–9). Since death is inevitable, one who has accumulated wealth will have to leave it to others (49:10), carrying nothing with him when death comes (49:17). The Psalmist says that all blessings come from God, including children, who are "a heritage from the Lord" (127:3). One psalm (79) deals with a continuing problem of the children of Israel, which was particularly acute for Habakkuk: the suffering of the children of Israel at the hands of nations worse than they.

4. Some particular psalms.

There are at least three or four psalms that deserve special attention from the perspective of this study. One of these is Psalm 37, an acrostic poem, which is as much a collection of proverbs as a Psalm. It deals with the perplexing problem of the frequent prosperity of the wicked, which is both a religious and an ethical problem. The initial word of the Psalm is, "Fret not yourself because of the wicked" (v. 1; cf. Prov. 24:19). The Psalmist gives negative and positive reasons for the non-fretful life. The wicked shall soon "fade like the grass" or "wither like the green herb" (v. 2). They shall be cut off (v. 9) or perish (v. 20); their plots to destroy others will be a boomerang to destroy them (vv. 14–15)—"the weapon of sin turns against the sinner himself."[14] In contrast, the Lord upholds the righteous (v. 17). They will "possess the land" (vv. 29, 34) and will have a posterity (v. 37). The Psalmist's admonition is:

Depart from evil, and do good;
    so shall you abide for ever.
For the Lord loves justice;
    he will not forsake his saints.
The righteous shall be preserved for ever,
    but the children of the wicked shall be cut
      off [vv. 27–28].

Here, as in the law and the prophets, "the ethical character of the covenant is thoroughly founded on religion; it is obedience springing from faith" (Weiser).

---

[14] Artur Weiser, *The Psalms: A Commentary*, trans. Herbert Hartwell (Philadelphia: Westminster Press, 1964), p. 319. Since this commentary follows a more or less verse-by-verse format, subsequent references will be in the body of the material.

Psalm 101 "is imbued with the intense moral earnestness of Old Testament religion" (Weiser). The Psalm describes the ideal Prince, who says that he "will give heed to the way that is blameless" or the way of integrity (v. 2), and then proceeds to describe that way. It is described in both negative and positive terms. The one who walks in the way that is blameless or in the way of integrity hates "the work of those who fall away" or loathes "the doing of transgression" (Smith; v. 3), will destroy him "who slanders his neighbor secretly," and will not endure "the man of haughty looks and arrogant heart" (v. 5). One who practices deceit will not be permitted to dwell in his house, and a man who utters lies cannot continue in his presence (v. 7). He will destroy the wicked or evildoers (v. 8). Perverseness of heart will be far from him (v. 4).

From the positive standpoint, the Prince says that he will "walk with integrity of heart" within his house (v. 2), will look with favor "on the faithful in the land" and promises that the one "who walks in the way that is blameless" will minister to him (v. 6).

Another psalm that is unusual in its construction and "a many colored mosaic of thoughts" (Weiser) is Psalm 119. It is too long to discuss in detail. It is arranged in twenty-two stanzas composed of eight verses each, a total of 176 verses. The eight verses within each stanza begin with the same letter of the Hebrew alphabet, starting with *Aleph,* the first letter in the alphabet.[15] In every verse except one (122) there is found one of ten expressions used to designate the law of God. This is the great psalm of the Law.

The Psalmist's idea of the law of God in Psalm 119 was considerably more inclusive than the Mosaic legislation. It seems to include all aspects of the divine revelation. This revelation is given to man for his guidance. Also, "the whole psalm is animated by a profound inwardness and spirituality, as far removed

---

15 There are other alphabetical or acrostic psalms, such as 9, 10, 25, 34, 37, 111, 112, and 145. There is some evidence of alphabetical construction elsewhere, such as in Lamentations 1, 2, 3, and 4 and Proverbs 31. Smith, in his translation, brings out the acrostic nature of these poems.

as possible from the superstitious literalism of a later age."[16]
For this inner emphasis, see such verses as 11, 14, 47, 48, 69, 78, 97,
113, 119, 127, 159, 167.

One of the greatest summaries of the basic requirements of
ethical religion found in the Old Testament is Psalm 15. This
psalm, from the viewpoint of ethics, ranks with Leviticus 19, Job
31, and the best in the prophets.

The searching question is asked,

> O Lord, who shall sojourn in thy tent?
> Who shall dwell on thy holy hill? [v. 1].

The Psalmist proceeds to describe the one who can sojourn, dwell,
or abide in the presence of the Lord (cf. Ps. 24:3–5; Isa. 33:14–16).
He describes the type of individual who can be received as a guest
by the Lord. And, it should be remembered that a guest in an
oriental home not only received the hospitality of the home but
also the protection of the host.

There are listed in Psalm 15 eleven qualities or requirements,
none ritualistic but all moral or ethical. These qualities are
divided into two main groups: the positive (vv. 2, 4) and the negative (vv. 3, 5).

The eleven requirements for one to abide in the presence of
God are as follows:

1. "He who walks blamelessly," uprightly, perfectly, or sincerely.
2. He who "does what is right"—always practices what is right.
3. He who "speaks truth from [or "with"] his heart"—his heart goes
   along with his speech; he is no flatterer. (The verbs in the preceding [walks, does, speaks] describe habitual or continuous action. These are three general qualities followed by eight specific
   qualities.)
4. He who "does not slander with his tongue" or "is not hasty with
   his tongue" (Smith)—does not wander about spying or snooping.
5. He who "does no evil to his friend"—does nothing to bring suffering or misfortune to his fellow man.

16 A. F. Kirkpatrick, "The Book of Psalms," *The Cambridge
Bible for Schools and Colleges*, ed. A. F. Kirkpatrick (Cambridge: Cambridge
University Press, 1902), p. 701.

6. He who does not "take up a reproach against his neighbor"—takes up in the sense that he receives from others and passes on to others any reproach or gossip concerning his neighbor, or takes up in the sense that he stoops down to pick it up so as to cast it on his neighbor or place it on his back.
7. The one "in whose eyes a reprobate ["bad man," Smith] is despised"—he judges wisely or estimates the true worth of men and does not judge them on the basis of what they may have. The reprobate is one who is stained or spotted as with smallpox.
8. The one "who honors those who fear the Lord"—his judgment of others reveals himself and his personal standards and ideals.
9. The one "who swears to his own hurt and does not change ["retract," Smith]"—his word is as good as his bond.
10. The one "who does not put out his money at interest"—the charging of interest or usury was forbidden to the Jews in the case of a fellow countryman (Lev. 25:35–37), but it was considered legitimate for foreigners (Deut. 23:19–20).
11. The one who "does not take a bribe against the innocent"—either as judge or witness. Bribery has always been one of the curses of oriental countries.

The conclusion of the Psalmist is, "He who does these things shall never be moved." Weiser suggests that "the spiritual grandeur of the psalm rests on the high level of its ethics."

The Proverbs

No books in the Writings are more important from the viewpoint of ethical content than those generally classified as wisdom literature. This wisdom literature, found in Proverbs, Ecclesiastes, Job, and in some of the Psalms (see Pss. 1, 37, 49, 73, 111) falls into two general classes: (1) Prudential—practical advice to the young, which is best illustrated by the book of Proverbs where moral living is usually portrayed as the way to happiness and success; (2) Reflective—consideration of some particular problem, which is best illustrated by the book of Job. Ethical content of considerable significance is found in both types or classes.

While prophecy was possibly the chief factor that shaped the moral ideas and ideals of Israel, it is in the wisdom literature that we find "the most ordered and complete statement of Hebrew ethics in general."[17] As Muilenburg says, "Here, if anywhere, we may speak with some propriety of ethics, at least in an elemental form."[18]

1. The general nature of Proverbs.

The book is a "collection of collections" with 1:1–6 introductory to the entire collection. Scholars differ somewhat about other divisions or collections but the rather generally accepted divisions are as follows: 1:7–9:18; 10:1–22:16; 22:17–24:22; 24:23-34; 25:1–29:27; 30:1-33; 31:1-9; and the acrostic poem (31:10-31) on the good wife. In addition to the poem on the good wife, there are some other unified or thematic sections of varying lengths (see 1:20-33 on wisdom), but in the main the book is composed of short, pithy, and more or less isolated sayings.

The interest throughout the book is on ethics or morals. It has been called a "handbook of Jewish morality."[19] There is little attention given to the ritualistic, the devotional, or the dogmatic. For example, in language strikingly similar to the prophets, the wise man says,

To do righteousness and justice
    is more acceptable to the Lord
        than sacrifice [21:3; cf. I Sam. 15:22; Hos.
        6:6; Mic. 6:6-8].

"The ethical conception of piety, announced by the prophets, lost none of its force with the sages" (ICC). The introductory verses of the book state an ethical or moral purpose for the first collection of proverbs and possibly for the entire book. A portion of that purpose was:

That men may know wisdom and
        instruction,
    understand words of insight,

[17] Robinson, *Inspiration and Revelation in the Old Testament,* p. 241.

[18] Muilenburg, p. 98.

[19] H. Wheeler Robinson, *The Religious Ideas of the Old Testament,* 2nd ed. (London: Gerald Duckworth and Co., 1956), p. 154.

receive instruction in wise dealing,
    righteousness, justice, and equity ["honesty,"
      Smith];
that prudence may be given to the simple,
    knowledge and discretion to the youth [1:2–4].

The book is so rich in moral and ethical content that all that can be done is to call attention to a few of the more significant emphases. It will be discovered that the ethics found in the Proverbs is practical rather than theoretical, largely individual or personal rather than social. Even when social institutions such as the home are discussed, the emphasis is on the personal and practical.

2. Perspective.

Toy says, "For the standard of right doing the appeal in *Proverbs* is to common sense or to the command of God."[20] We shall discuss these—common sense and God—in reverse order.

God occupies a central place in the book of Proverbs as He does in Hebrew life in general. However, the word "God," which is usually the translation of the closely related words *el, elah,* or *elohim* is found only seven times in the Revised Standard Version of the text of Proverbs. In contrast, the word "Lord," usually the translation of *Yahweh,* is found eighty-five times. It seems evident, however, that *Yahweh* in the Proverbs does not refer exclusively to a national deity but also to the supreme and only God.

It is *Yahweh* or the Lord who gives wisdom and "stores up sound wisdom for the upright," guards the "paths of justice" and preserves "the way of his saints" (2:6–8). As a father He reproves those He loves (3:12), He blesses the abode of the righteous (3:33), hears his prayer (15:29), and is a stronghold to the one "whose way is upright" (10:29). One who trusts in the Lord is happy (16:20) and safe (29:25). The Lord is a "shield to those who take refuge in him" (30:5). No wonder men are admonished to trust Him (3:5–6), to honor Him with their substance (3:9), and to commit their work to the Lord (16:3).

20 Crawford H. Toy, "A Critical and Exegetical Commentary on the Book of Proverbs," *The International Critical Commentary,* 4th impression (Edinburgh: T. & T. Clark, 1948), p. xiv.

There are frequent exhortations to fear or reverence the Lord. The sentiment expressed in the word "fear" gradually "advances from the form of mere dread of the divine anger to that of reverence for the divine law" (1:7, ICC). Such fear or reverence "is the beginning of knowledge" (1:7; cf. Ps. 111:10), which has been called "the motto, or keynote" of the entire book of Proverbs (CB). It is said that "fear of the Lord is instruction in wisdom" (15:33). It even seems that fear of the Lord is equated with wisdom (8:12–14). There are many blessings that come to those who fear or reverence the Lord. It prolongs life (10:27), "is a fountain of life" (14:27), and a source of life that satisfies (19:23). One who fears the Lord will avoid evil (16:6). No wonder it says in the Proverbs that the man "who walks in uprightness fears the Lord" (14:2), and that "the man who fears the Lord always" is blessed (28:14).

It is suggested in the Proverbs that there are a number of things that are an abomination to the Lord, they are incompatible with his nature. The word "abomination" was "originally ritualistic" but "later acquired an ethical meaning" (11:1, ICC). Some of the things that are an abomination to the Lord that carry ethical or moral connotations are false balances (11:1), diverse weights and measures (20:23; cf. 16:11), and lying lips (12:22). A man who is perverse or "crooked" (Smith) (3:32; cf. 11:20), arrogant or "proud-minded" (Smith) (16:5), or who condemns the righteous or justifies the wicked (17:15) is an abomination to the Lord. The sacrifice, the way, and even the thoughts of the wicked (15:8–9) are also an abomination to Him. In one place there are listed "six things which the Lord hates, seven which are an abomination to Him. The use of the words "six" and "seven" imply that the list is not exhaustive. The ones listed are as follows:

haughty eyes, a lying tongue
    and hands that shed innocent blood,
a heart that devises wicked plans,
    feet that make haste to run to evil,
a false witness who breathes out lies,
    and a man who sows discord among brothers
                [6:17–19].

In addition to the religious perspective, the prudential or common sense perspective is also quite prevalent in Proverbs. There is an attempt throughout to convince the individual that wrongdoing is foolish and that right living is wise. In other words, right conduct is presented as sane and sensible. While the negative and the positive are frequently joined together in antithetical parallelism, this brief statement will be restricted to the positive.

It is emphasized that "a man who is kind benefits himself" (11:17), that "a liberal man will be enriched" (11:25; cf. 12:14), and that riches, honor, and life are the reward for humility and the fear of the Lord (22:4). Those who keep the instructions or commandments of the wise man are promised "length of days and years of life and abundant welfare" (3:1–2; cf. 4:4; 7:2; 19:16).

3. General concepts.

As one would expect, *wisdom* is one of the basic concepts in Proverbs. The first stated purpose of the collection is "that men may know wisdom" (1:2). The use of the term "wisdom" in Proverbs, as in most Hebrew literature, differs somewhat from the Greek use. The emphasis is practical rather than theoretical. As such, it is closely related to prudence and understanding. It includes "knowledge of right living in the highest sense" and from this perspective it includes both "moral and religious intelligence," with the religious element "practically identical with the moral" (1:5, ICC). This close relation of the moral and the religious is a typical Hebraic concept. Oesterley suggests that "Wisdom, in the ethical-religious sense—which is the only sense in which it is understood by the wisdom writers—is confined to Israel" (14:34, WC).

A high value is placed on wisdom. It is "the crown of the wise" (14:24) and "a fountain of life" to one who has it (16:22). It is described as sweet to the taste (24:14). Naturally, the wise man would say "get wisdom" (4:5) or be attentive to it (2:2; 5:1). He also says that "a man of understanding sets his face toward wisdom" (17:24).

In spite of the high value placed on wisdom, it is kept in proper perspective. It is not considered the *summum bonum* as it is in much Greek thought. Typical of the Hebrew perspective, God and His will are supreme. Everything is subservient to Him and ultimately evolves from Him. He is the source of wisdom (8:22; cf. 2:6).

Wisdom is also kept in proper perspective by being vitally related to the Lord's moral expectations of His people. For example, wisdom in Proverbs is associated with such virtues as prudence or "good sense" (Smith) (8:12; 14:8), righteousness and justice (9:9; 8:20; 10:31), humility or modesty (Smith; 11:2), and truth (23:23) if the latter can be called a virtue.

Righteousness is a concept of considerable significance in The Proverbs. The emphasis, however, is on the righteousness of man rather than on the righteousness of God.

It may seem unusual that there are comparatively few exhortations for one to be righteous. Rather, in harmony with the prudential approach in The Proverbs, the emphasis is on the benefits that are promised to one who is righteous. For example, it is said that "the righteousness of the upright delivers them" (11:6), that "in the path of righteousness is life" (12:28; cf. 10:16; 21:21). It is also stated that the Lord "loves him who pursues ["follows after," Smith] righteousness" (15:9), and that the Lord's name is a strong tower to the righteous man (18:10). Naturally, it is said:

Better is a little with righteousness
    than great revenues with injustice [16:8].

There are many additional blessings promised to the righteous. Among these are the fact that he will be delivered from death (10:2), will not go hungry (10:3), his desire will be granted (10:24), and he will be established for ever (10:25; cf. 10:30). "The Lord is a stronghold to him whose way is upright" (10:29), he will be delivered from trouble (11:8, 21; 12:13, 21; 28:18), and he will find refuge through his integrity (14:32). The "root of the righteous stands firm" (12:12). Also,

  . . . a righteous man falls seven times
    and rises again;
  but the wicked are overthrown by
    calamity [24:16].

This does not refer to the righteous man falling into sin (*see* v. 15) but into trouble or calamity. As Toy says, the righteous "shall never be permanently cast down" (ICC) (cf. Ps. 37:24; Mic. 7:8). It is also said that the righteous will flourish like a green leaf (11:28; cf. 14:11) and in his house there will be "much treasure" (15:6).

Some of the characteristics of the righteous man are definitely and specifically ethical. His thoughts are just (12:5), he hates falsehood (13:5), he "ponders how to answer" (15:28)—he is careful about his speech. Also, he is liberal (21:26), is bold as a lion (28:1), "knows the rights of the poor" (29:7), and even "has regard for the life of his beast" (12:10). "The desire of the righteous ends only in good" (11:23).

The righteous and righteousness are a blessing to a nation.

Righteousness exalts a nation,
    but sin is a reproach to any people [14:34].

"The sentiment is substantially that of the prophets, that national prosperity accompanies obedience to divine law" (ICC). Also, it is said that the king's "throne is established by righteousness" (16:12), his justice "gives stability to the land" (29:4). The people in general rejoice "when the righteous are in authority" (29:2) and the city rejoices "when it goes well with the righteous" (11:10) and it is exalted "by the blessing of the upright" (11:11).

4. Specific teachings.

In addition to the teachings already discussed there are in The Proverbs a number of subjects that are touched on to some degree. Some of these are abidingly relevant. Some are rather closely related to things previously discussed, such as wisdom and righteousness. For example, it is said that "the mouth of the righteous is a fountain of life" (10:11) and *the tongue* "of the wise brings healing" (12:18).

It is suggested that "death and life are in the power of the tongue" (18:21). It is also said that

Pleasant words are like a honeycomb,
    sweetness to the soul and health to the body
                    [16:24].

There is the oft-quoted statement:

A soft ["gentle," Smith] answer turns away wrath,
but a harsh word stirs up anger [15:1].

A tale bearer reveals secrets (11:13), and alienates a friend (17:9).
Similarly, it is said that "a whisperer separates close friends"
(16:28). In contrast,

For lack of wood the fire goes out;
and where there is no whisperer,
quarreling ceases [26:20].

The conclusion is that one "who restrains his words has knowledge" (17:27) and will keep himself out of trouble (21:23). It is also suggested that there is more hope for a fool than for one who is "hasty in his words" (29:20).

There are frequent *warnings against the harlot, the strange or loose woman* (2:16). She is "one who is not bound to the man by legal ties, who is outside the circle of his proper relations, that is a harlot or an adulteress" (ICC). Such a woman says to those she seeks to entice: "Stolen water is sweet and bread eaten in secret is pleasant" (9:17). The wise man says:

. . . the lips of a loose woman drip honey,
and her speech is smoother than oil;
but in the end she is bitter as wormwood
["a symbol in OT of suffering," ICC],
sharp as a two-edged sword.
[5:3–4; cf. 7:5].

Her mouth is a deep pit (22:14), and she "lies in wait like a robber" (23:28). The young man should preserve his way from the evil woman, and "from the smooth tongue of the adventuress" (6:24). The wise man says,

Can a man carry fire in his bosom ["the lap
of the garment," ICC]
and his clothes not be burned?
Or can one walk upon hot coals
and his feet not be scorched?

So is he who goes in to his neighbor's wife;
    none who touches her will go unpunished
        [6:27-29].

The whole matter is summed up as follows:

He who commits adultery has no sense;
    he who does it destroys himself
        [16:32].

In contrast, a man should "drink water from his own cistern" (5:15)—"let thy own wife be thy source of enjoyment, as refreshing as water to a thirsty man" (ICC). A man should rejoice in the wife of his youth (5:18; cf. Mal. 2:14), should be "infatuated always with her love" (5:19), remembering that "a man's ways are before the eyes of the Lord" (5:21).

There are a number of other specific teachings concerning *the family and family relationships*. There are rather frequent references to the quarrelsome, contentious, or nagging wife. The wise man says that it is better to live in a corner of the housetop (21:9; 25:24) or in "a desert land" (21:19) than "in a house shared with a contentious woman." Again, it says:

A continual dripping on a rainy day
    and a contentious woman ["quarrelsome wife,"
    Smith] are alike [27:15; cf. 19:13].

To restrain her would be like restraining the wind or grasping oil in one's hand (27:16). Closely related to the preceding is the following:

Better is a dinner of herbs where love is
    than a fatted ox and hatred with it [15:17; cf. 17:1].

The other side of the picture concerning woman is also seen in the book of Proverbs. There is the familiar statement, "A good wife is the crown of her husband" (12:4), and the frequently referred to last chapter of the book, which contains the acrostic poem, "the alphabetic Ode or 'Golden ABC' of the perfect wife" (ICC). The ideal wife "is far more precious than jewels" (31:10); precious to her husband, to her family, and also to the com-

munity. She is industrious, providing for the needs of her family.
"Her husband is known in the gates" (31:23), and "her children
rise up and called her blessed" (31:28). Her helpfulness reaches
beyond her home:

> She opens her hand to the poor,
>> and reaches out her hands to the needy [31:20].

In addition to all of this:

> She opens her mouth with wisdom,
>> and the teaching of kindness is on her tongue [31:26].

The entire passage has been called "the most remarkable exposition in the Old Testament on the position of women" (31:31,
WC).

Proverbs also includes many specific instructions to parents and
children. Parents are admonished to "train up a child in the way
he should go" (22:6); literally, "according to his way"; or in the
way his natural bent would lead him; or, in the deepest sense, in
the way that God would have him to go. If the parents will do
this they can be assured that even when he is old he will not
depart from it. It will be the pattern of his life. According to the
wise man, an important aspect of that training was discipline
(13:24). A child who is left to himself unrestrained as an animal
to roam as he will "brings shame to his mother" (29:15). In contrast, it is said:

> Discipline your son, and he will give you rest;
>> he will give delight to your heart [29:17].

There are some instructions regarding *legal and political affairs*. One should not witness against his neighbor without cause
or in a spirit of revenge (24:28–29). A man who bears false witness
is compared to a war club or a maul that shatters and to "a sword,
or a sharp arrow" (25:18). The false witness will not go unpun-
ished (19:9). There was also counsel against standing surety for a
debt (22:26–27), and if surety had been given one should diligently seeks to be released (6:1–5).

There are words of wisdom for the king. In at least two places some requirements for an ideal king are set forth. He "does not sin in judgment" (16:10), his lips are righteous, and "he loves him who speaks what is right" (16:13).

The counsel to King Lemuel by his mother centers primarily on chastity, sobriety, and justice to the poor. He was not to give his strength, evidently his virility, to women (31:3). He was not to drink wine or strong drink, since rulers who drank tended to forget what had been decreed and to pervert the rights of the afflicted (31:4–5). King Lemuel was admonished to speak "for the rights of all who are left desolate," and to judge righteously and to maintain the rights of the poor and needy (31:8–9).

There is considerable material in the Proverbs on *justice, impartiality,* and, from the negative viewpoint, *bribery*. It is stated that it is not good to show partiality (28:21; cf. 18:5). The one who justifies the wicked and the one who condemns the righteous are "alike an abomination to the Lord" (17:15). A man is wicked who accepts a bribe "to pervert the ways of justice" (17:23). One who is thus "greedy for unjust gain makes trouble for his household" (15:27). A man should not rob the poor or "crush the afflicted ["the lowly," ICC] at the gate [the place of judgment]" (22:22);

> for the Lord will plead their cause
> and despoil of life those who despoil them [22:23].

There are some statements regarding *poverty and wealth*. In general, wealth is considered a reward for piety and uprightness. Many things, however, are said to be more precious than riches. Among these are a good name (22:1), righteousness (16:8), and the fear of the Lord (15:16). There is a particularly strong emphasis on wisdom as greater or more precious than riches (3:13–15; 8:11, 19; 16:16). One reason given for this is the fact that wisdom is the source of riches (3:16; 8:18, 21). Wisdom would also decree that one should not "toil to acquire wealth" (23:4) because

> When your eyes light upon it, it is gone;
> for suddenly it takes to itself wings,
> flying like an eagle toward heaven [23:5].

Although riches are of value, one is not to trust in them (11:28). On the other hand, there is no glorification of poverty in Proverbs. There is even some suggestion that one may bring poverty on himself through his slothfulness (12:27) or intemperance (23:21). Nevertheless, the Lord will plead the cause of the poor (22:22–23) and "he who mocks the poor insults his Maker" (17:5). Furthermore,

> He who is kind to the poor lends to the Lord,
>   and he will repay him for his deed [19:17].

The rich and poor should remember that God is the Maker of both (22:2) which implies impartiality. Any man, rich or poor, will get justice from the Lord (29:26).

The ideal of a golden mean between poverty and wealth is set forth in one place:

> Two things I ask of thee;
>   deny them not to me before I die;
> Remove far from me falsehood and lying;
>   give me neither poverty nor riches;
>   feed me with the food that is needful for me,
> lest I be full, and deny thee,
>   and say, "Who is the Lord?"
> or lest I be poor, and steal,
>   and profane the name of my God [30:7–9].

Job

The greatest of the wisdom books is Job,[21] which avoids the utilitarian morality of Proverbs which tends to relate righteousness to prosperity and evil to suffering. Job, by concentrating on a single theme, also differs in structure from most wisdom literature.

---

21 See Pfeiffer in *Introduction to the Old Testament* (pp. 667–83) for a scholarly statement of various perspectives concerning the major critical problems of the book such as its integrity, date, and authorship. Young (*Introduction to the Old Testament*, pp. 309–13), in a more compact and simpler way, gives a similar review of viewpoints but with a different personal conclusion.

1. *General appraisal.*

The book of Job has been acclaimed as one of the greatest books of all times. There are the oft-quoted statements by Tennyson that it is "the greatest poem of ancient and modern times," and by Carlyle that "there is nothing written, I think, in the Bible or out of it of equal merit." It has been described by biblical scholars as "the greatest work of genius in the Old Testament, and one of the world's artistic masterpieces";[22] "the incomparable literary masterpiece of our Bible. . . . Perhaps the most original work in the literature of mankind";[23] and "the noblest production of Hebrew poetry" the understanding of which "marks an epoch in a man's life."[24]

What is it that makes Job such a great book? H. Wheeler Robinson suggests that all great literature must have two essential features. First, it must deal with a subject of permanent interest, with "the concern of no single generation but of all the ages; it must touch the great things of our common humanity, which the changing years cannot touch." Second, he suggests that "great literature is always more or less closely related to the particular age of its production."[25] In other words, Robinson says that great literature grows out of a particular age but that its basic message is ageless—it speaks to every age. Job meets Robinson's requirements and hence should be included in the "great literature" of the world.

2. *An abiding moral problem.*

Suffering, and particularly the suffering of the innocent, which is a major if not the central problem of Job, has been, through the centuries, one of man's most perplexing problems. It has been and is very definitely a moral problem. Since the God revealed in the Bible is a moral Being and also the sovereign God of the universe, how can the suffering of the innocent be explained?

[22] Rowley, *The Growth of the Old Testament,* p. 143.
[23] Mary Ellen Chase, *The Bible and the Common Reader,* rev. ed. (New York: Macmillan, 1952), p. 244.
[24] H. Wheeler Robinson, *The Cross in the Old Testament* (Philadelphia: Westminster Press, 1955), p. 15.
[25] *Ibid.*

The cry of suffering humanity through the centuries has been and still is, "Why?" This cry helps to explain the abiding relevance and appeal of the book of Job. The book gives expression, to some degree, to the perplexities and the hurts of humanity. Its message reaches every soul that has suffered and thought.

While the suffering of the innocent may not be, as some scholars suggest,[26] the most basic problem dealt with in Job, it is the most immediately evident one. The Prologue of the book reveals that Job "was blameless and upright, one who feared God, and turned away from evil" (1:1). The suffering of Job came as a result of the challenge of Satan to God: "Does Job fear God for nought?" (1:9). Since Job did not know the reason for his troubles, it was natural that he and his friends would struggle with the problem of his suffering.

The arguments of his friends, which followed in general the orthodox Jewish position, were that men suffered because they had sinned. Job was suffering, hence he had sinned and should repent of his sins. This general position was the background for a question the disciples once asked Jesus, "Who sinned, this man or his parents, that he was born blind?" (John 9:2). Some suffering unquestionably comes as a result of sin, "but the Book of Job maintains that there is a large residue of unexplained suffering."[27]

Job's problem would have been largely solved for him if he could have given up his faith in God. He would have still suffered physically but he would have escaped the inner torture of his soul. But rather than give up his faith in God, "it is in God that he seeks the reason for his suffering."[28] Also, the problem was considerably deepened for Job since he had no clear-cut doctrine of immortality. For him there was no righting of the inequalities of life in the next world. Ultimately he was forced to the conclusion, which may be the main purpose of the author, "that there is

[26] For example, Samuel Terrien ("Job," *The Interpreter's Bible,* III, 897) suggests "the meaning of faith" as the main problem of Job, while Anderson (p. 491) similarly says that the main emphasis is on "the character of man's relationship to God."

[27] Robinson, *The Cross in the Old Testament,* p. 48.

[28] Terrien, *Interpreter's Bible,* III, p. 899.

a mystery in suffering which cannot be wholly understood by man, a mystery that goes back to God."[29]

At least Job and his friends never solved the problem theoretically. Even at the conclusion of his long struggle, Job was unable to explain the union of suffering and innocence in his case or in the case of others. His suffering was still a mystery to him. There is, however, in Job a practical conclusion if not a genuine solution to the problem of suffering. The conclusion is that "if there is such a thing as innocent suffering, then suffering is not necessarily the proof that a man is abandoned by God, and if the sufferer will have faith in God and be humbly submissive to Him, then he may enjoy the fellowship of God even in his suffering."[30] To use a great promise of the New Testament, one who suffers can conclude "that in everything God works for good with those who love him, who are called according to his purpose" (Rom. 8:28). The "good" may be their conformity "to the image of his Son" (Rom. 8:29), but that makes the promise the more glorious.

We may conclude, therefore, that the underlying purpose of Job's suffering was to prove that suffering need not alienate a believer from God. Looking at it from the perspective of the Prologue, "the purpose of Job's suffering is to vindicate God's trust in him."[31]

What Job's suffering did for him is of real significance. He came through all of his and his friends' questionings and accusations to a stronger faith in God. His closing words to God were:

"I had heard of thee by the hearing of the ear,
        but now my eye sees thee;
therefore I despise myself,
        and repent in dust and ashes" [42:5–6].

"Here he declares that the knowledge of God that had come to him in his suffering was as superior to anything he had before known as the knowledge of sight is to the knowledge of a rumour."[32] He had not discovered a solution to his problem but his doubts were dispelled when he came face to face with God.

29 Robinson, *The Cross in the Old Testament*, p. 16.
30 Rowley, *The Growth of the Old Testament*, p. 146.
31 *Ibid.*, p. 144.
32 *Ibid.*, p. 147.

Let us repeat that suffering may enrich one's fellowship with God. This is a practical although not a theoretical solution to the problem of suffering and to evil in general. The answer of Jesus to His disciples was, "It was not that this man sinned, or his parents, but that the works of God might be made manifest in him" (John 9:3).

3. The final monologue.

This monologue contains some of the richest and most exalted ethical material of the Old Testament.

> For grace and pathos, in charm of picturesque narrative, and pensive, tender, yet self-controlled emotion richly and variously expressed, it may be doubted whether Chapters xxix and xxxi have ever been surpassed. . . . He must be dull and hard indeed who can read these Chapters without being touched to the very heart.[33]

In Chapter 29 Job reviews his prosperous days of the past, when he was respected and honored by old and young. In those days he "delivered the poor . . . and the fatherless" (29:12) and "caused the widow's heart to sing for joy" (29:13). Righteousness was as a robe to him, he as a robe to it (29:14). He was eyes to the blind, feet to the lame, and a father to the poor and needy (29:15–16). Chapter 30 is an interlude and a description of his present plight.

In Chapter 31 he defends himself and in doing so sets forth some of the highest moral concepts to be found in the Old Testament. Most of the superlatives of the English language have been applied to the chapter. Lange calls it "incomparable," when "measured by the Old Testament standard,"[34] while another writer considers it the "high watermark of Old Testament ethics."[35] Still another author claims that the chapter expresses a

---

33 Samuel Cox, *A Commentary on the Book of Job,* 3rd ed. (London: Kegan Paul, Trench, Trubner, and Co., 1894), p. 366.

34 John Peter Lange, "Job," *Commentary on the Holy Scriptures,* translated and edited by Philip Schaff (Grand Rapids: Zondervan, n.d.) p. 546.

35 Julius A. Bewer, *The Literature of the Old Testament,* revised by Emil G. Kraeling, 3rd ed. (New York: Columbia University Press, 1962), p. 339.

higher ethical ideal than the Decalogue.[36] A contemporary Old
Testament scholar says that the chapter represents a level "otherwise unattained in the Old Testament," and that its spiritual-
ization of sinfulness, "reaching the most secret thoughts," is
unknown previously.[37] Paul Scherer says that "nowhere else in the
O. T. is there set such a lofty standard of ethical conduct" (IB).

In protesting his innocence, Job examines a number of hypo-
thetical sinful acts and introduces each of them with an "if" (vv.
5, 7, 9, 13, 16, 19, 20, 21, 24, 25, 26, 29, 31, 33, 38, 39). In each
case "he clears himself of any deed—or even intention—of religious or ethical turpitude, thereby revealing in exquisite terms
the highest moral conscience to be found in the O. T." (IB). The
word "intention" in the preceding quotation suggests the dis-
tinctively high moral quality of Job 31. Some emphasis on the
inwardness of moral conduct is found elsewhere in the Old
Testament, but nowhere is it spelled out more clearly than in
Job 31:1:

> I have made a covenant with my eyes;
>   how then could I look upon a virgin?

This verse approaches the spirit and motive found in the teachings of Jesus. The emphasis on inner motive is also evident in a
number of other verses of the chapter (vv. 7, 9, 25, 29, 33). Job
understood that out of the heart are the issues of life.

He claimed that he had not looked "upon a virgin" (v. 1), had
not "walked with falsehood" (v. 5), had not been "enticed to
["after," Smith] a woman" (v. 9), had not rejected the cause of a
manservant or a maidservant (v. 13), had not "withheld anything
that the poor desired" nor caused "the eyes of the widow to fail"
("grow dim," Smith; v. 16), had not eaten his bread alone but
had had the fatherless to eat with him (v. 17), had not seen anyone "perish for lack of clothing" (v. 19), had not trusted in (v. 24)
or rejoiced because of his wealth (v. 25), had not "rejoiced in the
ruin" ("calamity," Smith) of one who hated him (v. 29), had not

---

[36] T. H. Robinson, "Epilogue: The Old Testament and the Modern World," *The Old Testament and Modern Study,* ed. H. H. Rowley, p. 356.
[37] Pfeiffer, p. 701.

even concealed his transgressions from men (v. 33), and had not illegally or wrongfully taken any land or the produce of the land (vv. 38–40).

There is at least one of the preceding claims that should be spelled out more in detail. It reveals at least one motive for Job's high level of living. He says he had not rejected the cause of a servant when the latter had brought a complaint against him. He gives the reason for his action. It is derived from his relation and his understanding of God. He says,

> What then shall I do when God rises up?
>   When he makes inquiry, what shall I answer him? [34:14]

He adds:

> Did not he who made me in the womb make him?
>   And did not one fashion us in the womb? [31:15]

In the presence of God the master and the servant are on the same level. Terrien claims that "this awareness of the equality of birth among men is as high as the ethical level of the N. T." (IB).

The source of Job's social conscience was "his deep commitment to the will of God who cares for all men" (see vv. 2, 6, 15, 23, 28). "It was religion which justified, supported, explained, and made possible his morality" (IB). Here, as in the law and the prophets, is seen the close relationship of religion and ethics. Everywhere they are joined together.

The Five Rolls

The books in the Hebrew canon known as the Five Rolls or Megilloth were: Ruth, the Song of Solomon, Ecclesiastes, Lamentations, and Esther. Each one was read publicly at one of the annual festivals of the Jews, although it is not known how ancient this custom was.[38]

---

[38] Rowley, *The Growth of the Old Testament*, p. 148.

1. Ecclesiastes.

Because it is more closely related to Job and The Proverbs than other books in the Five Rolls, Ecclesiastes will be discussed first. A major emphasis in the book is the meaninglessness of all things: "vanity of vanities! All is vanity" (1:2; cf. 12:8). The author by personal testing of the way of wisdom and the way of folly (2:12; 7:25) found them equally futile (1:17). Wisdom leads to sorrow (1:18) and pleasures are vain (2:1ff.).

There are some rather significant and relevant observations concerning the futility of wealth: He who "loves money will not be satisfied with money" (5:10); the accumulation of possessions is like striving after the wind (2:4–11); one is never satisfied with wealth—he constantly craves for more (4:8; cf. 6:7); it robs its owner of sleep (5:12) and is not secure since it can be lost through accident (5:13–14) and certainly will be lost at death (5:15), when it will have to be left to someone who has not labored for it (2:18–23; cf. 2:25; 4:7–8).

In spite of the author's pessimism and skepticism the book includes some gems of moral and spiritual instruction. The following are a few of these: "Better is a poor and wise youth than an old and foolish king" (4:13); "Sweet is the sleep of a laborer" (5:12); "A good name is better than precious ointment" (7:1); "The patient in spirit is better than the proud in spirit" (7:8); and "Wisdom is better than might" (9:16) or "weapons of war" (9:18).

Furthermore, the author of Ecclesiastes in spite of his skepticism "never surrenders the conviction that God is sovereign over human affairs."[39] It is God who "has appointed a time for every matter" (3:17). The righteous and the wise, and by implication all others, and their deeds "are in the hand of God" (9:1). The tragic thing from the perspective of Ecclesiastes is that man cannot fathom the purposes of God. The latter "has put eternity into man's mind, yet so that he cannot find out what God has done from the beginning to the end" (3:11).

The book closes with the following summary: "The end of the matter; all has been heard. Fear God, and keep his command-

---

[39] Anderson, p. 480.

ments; for this is the whole duty of man. For God will bring every deed into judgment, with every secret thing, whether good or evil" (12:13–14).

The paradoxical nature of the book is so pronounced that there seems to be a dichotomy in it. Whether this dichotomy was the result of the conscious construction of the author or was derived from the character of the author himself cannot be known.

2. The Song of Solomon or the Song of Songs.[40]

This book is an anthology of love poems expressing the feeling of and sung by the bride, the bridegroom, and their friends. The climax of the book is the bride's or maiden's description of love (8:6ff.), which one author calls "one of the classics in the erotic poetry of mankind."[41]

The fact that the book is included in the canon is of some significance for biblical ethics. This is particularly true if, as Rowley suggests, it is no more than it purports to be, i.e., a collection of love songs. He says that we should not be surprised that such a book would be included in the canon in the light of God's command to the first man and woman to be fruitful and multiply and in the light of the church's teachings concerning the holy nature of matrimony. Rowley concludes that it is "fitting that these poems should be found in the sacred canon, thus symbolically reminding men that their love should be under the control of God and the life of their home be not remote from their faith."[42]

3. Ruth.

This is "one of the most charming short stories in Hebrew literature."[43] It is a love story, strange in some of its customs but

[40] The expression "the Song of Songs" is the Hebrew way of expressing the superlative. Other examples are "vanity of vanities" and "holy of holies." Thus, "the Song of Songs, which is Solomon's" (1:1) means that this was the most beautiful or the best known of the one thousand and five songs that were credited to Solomon (I Kings 4:32).

[41] Pfeiffer, p. 717.

[42] Rowley, *The Faith of Israel*, p. 132. In contrast, Pfeiffer (p. 714) suggests that the allegorical interpretation of the book made possible its canonization.

[43] Pfeiffer, p. 717.

abidingly appealing in its spirit and beauty. The marriage of
Ruth and Boaz is related to levirate marriage, although their
relationship was more distant and some of the procedures varied
from the provisions in the law (cf. Ruth 4:9 and Deut. 25:9). As
a result of Ruth's devotion to Naomi (1:16–17), she became the
mother of Obed, the great grandmother of David (4:18–22), and
hence was in the ancestral line of Jesus.

4. Lamentations.

The book contains five poems, one for each chapter. The first
four are alphabetic acrostics. The main emphasis throughout is
a lament over the destruction of Jerusalem, a destruction that
had come because of "the multitude of her transgressions" (1:5).
She had "sinned grievously" (1:8), and had rebelled against the
word of God (1:18). Even her prophets had been false, deceptive,
or misleading. They had not exposed the iniquity of the people
(2:14). The priests had also sinned (4:13).

In spite of the author's rather gloomy outlook regarding the
judgment of God, portrayed in a particularly graphic way in
Chapter 2, he has a strong faith in God and in His goodness. In a
passage that may be primarily personal but which also may apply
to Jerusalem, he says:

The steadfast love of the Lord never ceases,
    his mercies never come to an end; . . .
      great is thy faithfulness. . . .
It is good that one should wait quietly
    for the salvation of the Lord [3:22–23, 26].

He further says that the Lord "will not cast off for ever" (3:31):

But, though he cause grief, he will have compassion
    according to the abundance of his steadfast love;
for he does not willingly afflict
    or grieve the sons of men [3:32–33].

In common with the prophets the author of Lamentations foresaw the return and restoration of Israel. There would come a
time when the punishment of the daughter of Zion would be

accomplished; God would keep her in exile no longer (4:22). The closing note is triumphant:

But thou, O Lord, dost reign for ever;
  thy throne endures to all generations [5:19].

5. Esther.

This book was written primarily to give the reason for or to justify the Feast of Purim, a feast which was not authorized by the law. Possibly for this and other reasons, such as the failure of the book to mention the name of God, Esther had difficulty getting into the canon. One author claims, however, that its portrayal of anti-Semitism and its strong nationalistic spirit gives to the book a "pressing relevance today."[44]

There are some things in the book that are of ethical importance, such as the striking evidence in the life of Haman that whatever a man sows he will also reap. Also, some insight is given into a social, moral, and religious problem which has continued to perplex the world—the problem of race and race relations. Although the differences between the Jews and those among whom they lived were more religious and national than racial, the book does give some understanding of the reasons for minority problems, including those that are racial. While Esther personally violated the Jewish prohibition against marriage with uncircumcised Gentiles, the Jews in general retained their separateness from the people among whom they lived. They were, as they in the main have continued to be, a nation within a nation. Any people who have not been assimilated, whether they or the ones among whom they live are responsible for this failure, are convenient objects for prejudice. The book of Esther also demonstrates that such prejudice is very easily aroused, and the ease with which it can be aroused is frequently taken advantage of by one who, like Haman, is ambitious for power. There were demagogues then as there have been through the years.

[44] Anderson, "Esther," *The Interpreter's Bible*, III, 828.

Conclusion

This chapter concludes the study of the canonical books of the Old Testament. The Law, the Prophets, and the Writings contain a rather closely unified message with diversified emphases. The unity stems from the centrality of God. The Old Testament, in the main, is a record or history of God's attempt to reveal Himself to His people and to achieve His will and purpose with and through them.

The diversity found in the Old Testament stems, to a large degree, from the fact that God had to work through immature, finite men. They could not fully comprehend what He was seeking to reveal to them. They, in turn, had the difficult task of interpreting what they did comprehend to those to whom they ministered. They had to try to speak a language the people could understand. This largely explains the fact that they adopted and in some cases adapted terms common to the neighbors of the children of Israel. For example, such basic concepts as "covenant" and "holiness" were used by other peoples of that time. However, through the consciousness by the children of Israel of the presence of *Yahweh,* these and other terms were gradually changed in their meaning and depth. The children of Israel tended to place their own peculiar stamp upon the language that was utilized. One common trend was for the words borrowed from others to take on an increasingly ethical connotation. This resulted primarily from the Hebrew conception of *Yahweh* as a moral or ethical being.

It was natural that different authors and books in the Old Testament would give major attention to one or more of the central concepts of the faith of Israel. In some cases the particular emphasis was clearly related to the historical situation. For example, the covenant concept is dominant in the Code of the Covenant (Exodus) which was given to the children of Israel at Mount Sinai when God entered into covenant with them. Similarly, the idea of holiness and the Holiness Code are central in Leviticus which majors on laws for the priest and the children of Levi who were peculiarly holy unto God. Hosea's "Gospel of Love" grew out of his experience with a faithless wife. Isaiah's emphasis on holiness and the transcendence of God may have resulted from his vision of God at the time when he was called to the prophetic office. Jeremiah and Ezekiel, ministering during and after the days of the decline and fall of Jerusalem, naturally stressed the responsibility of the individual, with an attendant emphasis on a new heart and an inner covenant. The central messages of other prophets such as Amos, Micah, Zephaniah, Habakkuk, and Malachi were called forth by the conditions they faced.

At least two of the books in the Writings—the Psalms and the Proverbs—are collections. They do not have a clearly defined background that gave them birth. Both of them do have, however, one or more unifying emphases. The Psalms as a song book concentrates to an unusual degree on God and His nature, giving particular attention to "the steadfast love" of God. The Proverbs, which is wisdom literature of a prudential type, is individualistic and practical. Some contemporary Christians would question the theology or philosophy of some of the Proverbs and also some of the Psalms, yet many of them will agree that a serious study of the Proverbs, as is true of other wisdom literature, would give considerable guidance even in the contemporary world. The greatest of the books of the Writings is Job which deals with one of the most disturbing and continuous moral and spiritual problems for the child of God.

There has been little attempt in the survey of the ethical content of the Old Testament to evaluate the material. There is much in the Law, the Prophets, and the Writings that is abidingly relevant and authoritative. This does not mean, however, that the Old Testament is equally authoritative with the New Testament for the child of God. The former is always to be read and evaluated in light of the full revelation found in the New Testament.

Before we come to the New Testament portion of our study, we will devote a chapter to the Apocrypha, Pseudepigrapha, and the Dead Sea Scrolls. Most of this material was produced in the years between the testaments and throws some light on both Old Testament and New Testament. The Apocrypha and Pseudepigrapha have more significance for Old Testament study and the Dead Sea Scrolls for New Testament study, although the latter potentially are very important from the viewpoint of the text of the Old Testament.

CHAPTER IV

THE APOCRYPHA, PSEUDEPIGRAPHA, AND DEAD SEA SCROLLS

The proper name "The Apocrypha" is a technical term that is used to refer to books that have not been considered canonical, although they have at various times been a part of the printings of the Scriptures,[1] including the King James Version of 1611. The Pseudepigrapha[2] is composed of books or writings which cir-

[1] See L. H. Brockington, *A Critical Introduction to the Apocrypha* (London: Gerald Duckworth, 1961), pp. 136–48, for a brief historical sketch of the relation of the Apocrypha to various translations of the Scriptures. Bruce Metzger, *An Introduction to the Apocrypha* (New York: Oxford University Press, 1957), pp. 239–47, briefly discusses "current English translations of the Apocrypha." The Catholic or Douay Version of the Old Testament includes most of the books of the Apocrypha. J. M. Powis Smith's and Edgar J. Goodspeed's *The Complete Bible: An American Translation* (Chicago: University of Chicago Press, 1939) includes the books of the Apocrypha.

[2] Some scholars such as Charles Torrey, *The Apocryphal Literature* (New Haven: Yale University Press, 1945), use "Apocrypha" to refer to all non-canonical writings, including the Pseudepigrapha. See Weiser (*The Old Testament: Its Formation and Development*) for a brief book-by-book analysis of the Apocrypha (pp. 389–412) and the Pseudepigrapha (pp. 413–47). Brockington, Metzger, and an older book by W. O. E. Oesterley, *An Introduction to the Books of the Apocrypha* (New York: Macmillan, 1935) devote chapters to each of the books of the Apocrypha but not the Pseudepigrapha.

culated under false titles and have never been admitted into the canon of the Scriptures. The Dead Sea Scrolls are relatively recent discoveries of major importance for both Old Testament and New Testament study.

Although space will not permit an adequate discussion, it has been considered necessary to give some attention to this literature in a book on biblical ethics. It helps to bridge the years between the close of the Old Testament and the opening of the New Testament. Furthermore, an acquaintance with the Apocrypha, Pseudepigrapha, and Dead Sea Scrolls will provide a basis for a better understanding of a biblically oriented Christian ethic and of Christian theology and of the Christian life in general.

Apocrypha

The most significant book for our purpose in the Apocrypha is Ecclesiasticus. The teachings of the book will be set forth in more detail than those of the other books of the Apocrypha.

1. Ecclesiasticus.

The book of Ecclesiasticus, or The Wisdom of Jesus, the Son of Sirach, frequently referred to as Ben (son of) Sira, is similar in many ways to the Proverbs. Subjects, however, are discussed more frequently at considerable length, occasionally taking the form of brief essays. Like the Proverbs, the advice "is usually full of good sense and as applicable today as it was two thousand years ago."[3] The author "is a moralist of the first rank."[4]

(1) *Basic concepts.* As one would expect, wisdom is emphasized from the first chapter (1:1)[5] to the last (51:13ff.). Ben Sira says that all wisdom comes from God (1:9), and that the fear of the Lord is the beginning (1:14; 15:1; 19:20; cf. Prov.), the crown (1:18), and the root of wisdom (1:20). It is also said that the Lord

---

[3] Metzger, p. 81.
[4] Torrey, p. 96.
[5] References to the Apocrypha will be to the Revised Standard Version published by Thomas Nelson and Sons, 1957.

loves those who love wisdom (4:14), and that many blessings such as security (4:15; 6:29) and rest (6:28) will come to those who seek wisdom. This means that wisdom should be pursued (14:22). The man who meditates upon her will be blessed (14:20). It is also said that the remembrance of wisdom is "sweeter than honey" (24:20) and that those who eat her will hunger for more and those who drink her will thirst for more (24:21). There are places where wisdom seems to be personified (see 1:9; 24:3–5), although this conception is more clearly evident in the Wisdom of Solomon. For other major passages on wisdom, see 4:11–19; 6:18–31; 51:13–22; and particularly 24:1–34, a beautiful chapter in which wisdom is clearly personified, the pronoun "I" frequently being used to refer to wisdom.

In harmony with Jewish thought in general, God is central in Ecclesiasticus and is revealed as a moral person. He is a God of wrath but also of mercy (16:11–12; 17:29). His compassion is compared to the compassion of man in the following beautiful statement:

> The compassion of man is for his neighbor,
> > but the compassion of the Lord is for all
> > > living beings.
> He rebukes and trains and teaches them,
> > and turns them back, as a shepherd his
> > > flock [18:13].

His eyes are upon those who love Him (34:16). He fills the earth "with his good things" (16:29), and gives to man, who was created in His image, authority or dominion over all that is upon the earth (17:2–4).

(2) *Social ethic.* As is true of Proverbs, a social or applied ethic is quite prominent in Ecclesiasticus. For example, there are contrasting pictures of the wicked and the good wife. Concerning the former, Ben Sira says:

> I would rather dwell with a lion and a dragon
> > than dwell with an evil wife.
> The wickedness of a wife changes her appearance,
> > and darkens her face like that of a bear.

> Her husband takes his meals among the neighbors,
>> and he cannot help sighing bitterly.
> Any iniquity is insignificant compared to a
>> wife's iniquity;
>> may a sinner's lot befall her!
>>> [25:16–19; see also 25:23].

He further says,

> An evil wife is an ox yoke which chafes;
>> taking hold of her is like grasping a
>> scorpion [26:7].

On the other hand, Ben Sira says that the man "who acquires a wife gets his best possession." She will give him strength and stability (36:24–26). Furthermore, a "blameless wife" will do more to build a man's reputation than children or the building of a city (40:19), and a good wife "is a great blessing"; her husband, whether rich or poor, will be happy (26:1–4).

The unfaithfulness of either husband or wife is sharply condemned (see 23:16–27; cf. 25:2; 47:19–20). The main emphasis is on unfaithfulness to the Lord, and the main motivation for faithfulness is the fact that God knows. For example, it says of the unfaithful wife: "First of all, she has disobeyed the law of the Most High" (23:23), and to the man who breaks his marriage vows the word is: "The eyes of the Lord are ten thousand times brighter than the sun" (23:19). In other words, God knows. Men are warned not to "go to meet a loose woman" or "give themselves to harlots." They should not "look intently at a virgin" or "at beauty belonging to another," since "many have been misled by a woman's beauty, and by it passion is kindled like a fire." They should never dine or revel with another man's wife (9:3–9).

There are also instructions concerning parents and children. Children are to honor their father (3:8) and respect their mother (3:11; cf. 7:28). The father is to be helped "in his old age" (3:12): "Whoever forsakes his father is like a blasphemer" (3:16). On the other hand, parents should discipline children, making them "obedient from their youth" (7:23). A passage that summarizes the matter of discipline contains the following:

He who disciplines his son will profit by him,
    and will boast of him among acquaintances. . . .
A horse that is untamed turns out to be stubborn,
    and a son unrestrained turns out to be wilful.
           [30:2, 8; cf. 22:3, 6].

There are special instructions for the parents of a daughter. They should be concerned for her chastity and wise marriage (7:24–25). A father's worry regarding his daughter is summarized as follows:

A daughter keeps her father secretly wakeful,
    and worry over her robs him of sleep;
when she is young, lest she do not marry,
    or if married, lest she be hated;
while a virgin, lest she be defiled
    or become pregnant in her father's house;
or, having a husband, lest she prove unfaithful,
    or, though married, lest she be barren [42:9–10].

There are teachings concerning certain aspects of economic life. For example, in the latter part of Chapter 38 (vv. 24–34), a number of vocations are referred to: the scribe, the plowman, the craftsman, the smith, and the potter. The implication is that each has his work from the Lord. The position of some may be humble,

But they keep stable the fabric of the world,
    and their prayer is in the practice of their
        trade [v. 34].

In a rather lengthy passage contrasting the rich and the poor or humble (13:1–26), the key verse says, "Riches are good if they are free from sin" (v. 24). However, one should not seek wealth or go after gold (31:8; 5:1). Many things such as health (30:15) are of greater value. Also, seeking wealth leads to anxiety and loss of sleep (31:1–2). Furthermore, why should one seek wealth when death is certain, and in Hades "one cannot look for luxury" (14:16).

There are temptations that constantly lurk in the path of those who seek wealth (26:29; 27:1–2). Anyone "who pursues money will be led astray by it" (31:5); "it is a stumbling block to those who are devoted to it" (31:7). Furthermore,

A man who builds his house with other people's
        money
    is like one who gathers stones for his burial
        mound [21:8].

Really, the only essentials for life are water, food, clothing, and "a house to cover one's nakedness" (29:21). Men should be content with little or much (29:23).

While the poor may be responsible, to a considerable degree, for their poverty, there is portrayed a kindly attitude toward them. A hand should be stretched forth to them (7:32). It is also stated that the giving of alms "atones for sin" (3:30), is comparable to a thank offering (35:2), "endures forever" (40:17), and along with prayer should not be neglected (7:10; cf. Acts 10:4). For other passages on the poor and almsgiving, see 4:1–6; 12:3–4, 7; 29:8–13.

Although there is not much material in Ecclesiasticus on political life, there is at least one statement of considerable significance. It is as follows:

A wise magistrate will educate his people,
        and the rule of an understanding man will be
        well ordered.
Like the magistrate of the people, so are his
        officials;
        and like the ruler of the city, so are all its
        inhabitants.
An undisciplined king will ruin his people,
        but a city will grow through the understanding
        of its rulers.
The government of the earth is in the hands of
        the Lord,
        and over it he will raise up the right man for
        the time [10:1–4].

Ben Sira also says,

He [God] appointed a ruler for every nation,
        but Israel is the Lord's own portion [17:17].

Here are combined Jewish particularism and God's universalism. He is the God of all the nations but Israel is considered His in a unique way.

(3) *Miscellaneous teachings.* Ecclesiasticus contains a number of miscellaneous ethical or moral teachings. As one would expect in a wisdom book, there is considerable instruction concerning the tongue and speech. It is said that a word may be and is a good gift (18:16–17), but one should learn before he speaks (18:19). He should be quick to hear and slow to answer (5:11).

> The mind of fools is in their mouth,
> > but the mouth of wise men is in their mind
> > > [21:26].

The following somewhat sums up the matter:

> Have you heard a word? Let it die with you.
> > Be brave! It will not make you burst!
> With such a word a fool will suffer pangs
> > like a woman in labor with a child.
> Like an arrow stuck in the flesh of the thigh,
> > so is a word inside a fool [19:10–12].

In a similar vein, the following comes at the conclusion of a considerable section on slander:

> Make balances and scales for your words
> > and make a door and a bolt for your mouth
> > > [28:25].

There are also admonitions against lying (20:25; 51:2, 5); a section on oaths (23:7–13); and another on speaking in general, with particular advice to young men (32:3–9).

Sins or vices specifically mentioned are: anger (10:6; 27:30; 28:7), arrogance and injustice (10:7), pride (10:12–13), indolence (22:1–2), vengeance (28:1), and bribery and injustice (40:12). There is a warning against "an insatiable appetite for any luxury" and even for food (37:29–31; cf. 31:12–21, which also includes some practical advice concerning proper table manners). There is a general admonition to forsake one's sins and turn away from iniquity (17:25-26) and to "flee from sin as from a snake" (21:2; cf. 12:13-14).

On the other hand, Ben Sira admonishes his readers to mourn with those who mourn (7:34), to visit the sick (7:35), to respect the aged (8:6, 9), to be impartial (4:22), to exercise self-control (18:30-31), to be obedient to the law (19:20, 24), to be self-reliant and industrious (40:18), and not to give surety beyond their means (8:13; cf. 29:14, 18, 20). They should lend to a neighbor in need and should repay their neighbor promptly (29:1-2). In a passage that sounds strikingly similar to Matthew 6:14-15, he says:

> Forgive your neighbor the wrong he has done,
>> and then pray your sins will be pardoned when
>> you pray [28:2].

The following may suggest a belief that there is a connection between sin and sickness:

> He who sins before his Maker,
>> may he fall into the care of a physician
>>> [38:15].

Preceding this verse, there are some rather striking statements concerning the physician, prayer, and healing. It says that the physician should be honored "for the Lord created him" (38:1). He also "created medicines from the earth" (v. 4), and "the pharmacist makes of them a compound" (v. 8). It is recognized that "healing comes from the Most High" (v. 2). Therefore, one should "pray to the Lord" (v. 9), while at the same time he should "give the physician his place" (v. 12); for

> There is a time when success lies in the
>> hands of physicians,
>>> for they too will pray to the Lord
> that he should grant them success in diagnosis
>> and in healing, for the sake of preserving
>> life [vv. 13-14].

Possibly the best way to close this section on Ecclesiasticus is to quote the following, which is one of several summary statements of considerable ethical significance:

> With nine thoughts I have gladdened my heart,
> and a tenth I shall tell with my tongue:
> a man rejoicing in his children;
> a man who lives to see the downfall of his
> foes;
> happy is he who lives with an intelligent wife,
> and he who has not made a slip with his tongue,
> and he who has not served a man inferior to
> himself;
> happy is he who has gained good sense,
> and he who speaks to attentive listeners.
> How great is he who has gained wisdom!
> But there is no one superior to him who fears
> the Lord.
> The fear of the Lord surpasses everything;
> to whom shall be likened the one who holds
> it fast [25:7-11]?[6]

2. Other books of the Apocrypha.

Although there is more ethical material by far in Ecclesiasticus than in any other book of the Apocrypha, there is some material in other books. This section will suggest a few of the major emphases in these books. Some of the apocryphal books do not contain ethical material of enough consequence to be included in this study.[7]

(1) *Marriage and the home.* Some of the marriage customs of the times are evident in Tobit. Tobias, following the advice of his father (Tob. 4:12-13)[8] and under the guidance of an angel of

---

[6] For other summaries see 41:17-23—a list of things to be ashamed of—and 42:1-8—a list of things not to be ashamed of.

[7] Included in this list are: Additions to Esther, the Letter of Jeremiah, one brief chapter, and the Prayer of Azariah and the Song of the Three Young Men. The last two are inserted in the Greek version of Daniel between 3:23 and 24. Other additions to Daniel are Susanna, "one of the best short stories in the world's literature" (Metzger, p. 107), which follows the motif of the triumph of virtue over villainy, and Bel and the Dragon, "one of the oldest detective stories in the world" (Metzger, p. 115).

[8] Abbreviations for books of the Apocrypha to which reference will be made will be as follows: Esd. = Esdras; Tob. = Tobit; Jth. = Judith; Wisd. Sol. = The Wisdom of Solomon; Bar. = Baruch; Macc. = Maccabees.

the Lord, entered into a marriage which was closely akin to if it was not actually a levirate marriage (see Tob. 6:11). Still another custom was the writing of the marriage contract and the sealing of it by the parents of the bride (Tob. 7:14).

In the same imaginary story, for it is evidently fiction with a didactic purpose, there are found some high ideals for marriage and the home. For example, the angel said that Sarah was destined for Tobias "from eternity" (Tob. 6:17). Tobias, when he was alone with the bride, said, "Sister, get up, and let us pray that the Lord may have mercy upon us" (Tob. 8:4). In the prayer he quoted Genesis 2:18 and then said: "And now, O Lord, I am not taking this sister of mine because of lust, but with sincerity. Grant that I may find mercy and may grow old together with her." And she said with him, "Amen!" (Tob. 8:7–8).

The Wisdom of Solomon reveals a rather high level of sexual purity (Wisd. Sol. 3:13; 4:6; 14:26), while one of the main problems dealt with in I Esdras, a book which includes most of canonical Ezra, is intermarriage. It is said that "the holy race" had been "mixed with the alien people of the land." The leaders and nobles shared in the iniquity (I Esd. 8:70; see 9:18–36 for the names of those, including priests and Levites, who had taken foreign wives; cf. Ezra 10:18–44).

(2) *Alms and the poor.* The giving of alms is emphasized in Tobit. He admonished Tobias to give alms "to all who live uprightly" and not begrudge the gift when he made it (Tob. 4:7). He further said, "Give of your bread to the hungry, and of your clothing to the naked." He even told Tobias to give all his surplus to charity (Tob. 4:16). The motive was prudential: "Do not turn your face away from any poor man, and the face of God will not be turned away from you" (Tob. 4:7). He also said that charity was an excellent offering in the presence of the Most High" (Tob. 4:11; cf. vv. 7, 9, 10, 14). Furthermore, it is said that prayer is good when accompanied by almsgiving and righteousness. Almsgiving delivers one from death, cleanses from sin, and gives fulness of life (Tob. 12:7–10; cf. 14:11). No wonder it is said, "It is better to give alms than to treasure up gold" (Tob. 12:8).

(3) *Wisdom and truth.* As one would expect, wisdom is central in the book entitled "The Wisdom of Solomon." It is said that

wisdom, which is personified, is "radiant and unfading," "easily discerned by those who love her," and "is found by those who seek her" (Wisd. Sol. 6:12). She is more important than wealth (7:8), and is to be loved "more than health and beauty" (7:10). All good things come "along with her" (7:11).

In the same book wisdom is very closely related to God (9:4; 10:1, 10, 15). One great passage on wisdom (7:25–29) says that "she is a breath of the power of God," "a pure emanation of the glory of the Almighty," "a reflection of eternal light," "a spotless mirror of the working of God, and an image of his goodness." It further says that "she can do all things," "renews all things," and "passes into holy souls and makes them friends of God, and prophets." The conclusion is that "God loves nothing so much as a man who lives with wisdom." The writer closes this rather remarkable passage on wisdom with the statement:

> For she is more beautiful than the sun,
> and excels every constellation of the stars,
> Compared with the light she is found to be
> superior [7:29].

Truth is another ideal that is exalted, particularly in I Esdras. It is stronger than wine, the king, or women (I Esd. 4:15–37). In contrast to these, it endures forever (4:38). "With her there is no partiality or preference, but she does what is righteous instead of anything that is unrighteous or wicked" (4:39). The shout of the people: "Great is truth, and strongest of all!" has been called "an immortal proverb."[9]

(4) *The nature of God.* The books of the Apocrypha, as one would expect in any Jewish literature, are rooted and grounded in the nature of God. He is portrayed as one who is merciful, gracious, patient, compassionate, forgiving, holy (II Esd. 7:62–69; Wisd. Sol. 3:9; 4:15; 9:3; 15:1). Righteousness is His breastplate, impartial justice His helmet, and holiness His invincible shield (Wisd. Sol. 5:18–19). Being impartial in His judgment, He takes "thought for all alike" (Wisd. Sol. 6:7). God expects His people to have these same qualities. A particular emphasis is given to the righteous man, especially in The Wisdom of Solo-

[9] Metzger, p. 19.

mon (3:1; 5:1, 15). If one loves righteousness he will have produced in his life such virtues as self-control, prudence, justice, and courage; all of which are typical Greek virtues. The conclusion is that "nothing in life is more profitable for man than these" (8:7).

(5) *God and history*. In addition to the subjects previously discussed, there are three closely related subjects that receive considerable attention in the Apocrypha. These subjects are: the relation of God to history, the judgment of God, and the suffering of Israel, His chosen people.

The fact that God is a God of history is not stated and defended as much as it is assumed. This philosophy or theology of history should be expected in the Apocrypha since the idea or concept represents the biblical and Jewish perspective in general. It is seen even through the rather gory details of a book like Judith. The author of the book considered the secret of the strength of Israel to be in the God she worshipped. Obedience to Him brought victory; sin brought defeat (see Jth. 5:17–21; 8:15–17). Both I and II Maccabees, the latter of which lacks in general the historical accuracy of the former,[10] portray God as active in the affairs of His people—fighting with them in their battles (see I Macc. 3:19; 3:50–53; 4:24; 9:46; II Macc. 8:18, 23; 10:38; 11:10; 13:15; 15:26–27).

The idea that God is a God of history is particularly prevalent in the writings of the apocalyptists, "who judge history and the end of history in terms of a holy and righteous God."[11] There is more apocalyptic literature in the Pseudepigrapha than in the Apocrypha, although there is some in the latter. In common with Jewish thought in general, the apocalyptists believed that God had a purpose in history, took the initiative in history, was in control of and would be triumphant in or over history. They looked for a "unique divine initiative at the end of history."[12]

---

[10] Robert C. Dentan, in *The Apocrypha, Bridge of the Testaments* (Greenwich, Conn.: Seabury Press, 1954), p. 62, says of I Maccabees: "If accuracy is the chief test for judging a book of history, I Maccabees would rate very high."

[11] D. S. Russell, *The Method and Message of Jewish Apocalyptic* (Philadelphia: Westminster Press, 1964), p. 101.

[12] H. H. Rowley, *The Relevance of Apocalyptic*, 2nd ed. (London: Lutterworth Press, 1947), pp. 154–55.

The apocalyptists were closely related to and yet rather sharply different from the prophets of the Old Testament. Both had a strong faith in the ultimate achievement of God's purposes in history. They were both preachers of righteousness and social justice, although the ethical was considerably more central in the prophets. The predictive element was more prevalent in the apocalyptists. The prophets saw with keen insight the evils of their day and pronounced the judgment of God. They foretold the future that should arise out of the present. In contrast, the apocalyptists "foretold the future that should break into the present."[13]

(6) *The judgment of God.* Judgment is under the control of the God of history. The emphasis on the judgment is particularly prevalent in the books most closely related to the prophets such as II Esdras and Baruch.[14] The authors of these books used prophetic concepts and at times used language strikingly similar to the prophets. The judgment of God was coming upon Israel because she had deserted Him and had sinned against His ordinances (Bar. 1:18, 21; 2:12). In terms that sound as though they were lifted directly from Isaiah, the Lord is represented as saying, "When you call upon me, I will not listen to you; for you have defiled your hands with blood, and your feet are swift to commit murder" (II Esd. 1:26; cf. Isa. 1:15). Again God says, "When you offer oblations to me, I will turn my face from you; for I have rejected your feast days, and new moons, and circumcisions of the flesh" (II Esd. 1:31; cf. Isa. 1:13–14; Amos 5:21f.). Similar to Jeremiah and Ezekiel, it is said that in the day of judgment "every one shall bear his own righteousness or unrighteousness" (II Esd. 7:[105]).

Again in terms common to the prophets, the people are admonished to "guard the rights of the widow, secure justice for the fatherless, give to the needy, defend the orphan, clothe the naked, care for the injured and the weak . . . protect the maimed, and let the blind man have a vision" of God's splendor. They were

---

13 *Ibid.*, p. 35.
14 Metzger (p. 89) suggests that Baruch is the only book of the Apocrypha that is formed on the model of the Old Testament prophets and says that "though it is lacking in originality, one can still detect, even at second-hand, something of the ancient prophetic fire."

also not to ridicule a lame man and were to protect the old and the young (II Esd. 2:20–22).[15]

In Baruch, as in the Prophets, there is considerable emphasis on the restoration of Israel. The restoration would be the work of God's grace. God was kind and compassionate. He foresaw that in the land of exile they would come to themselves (Bar. 2:30). God would give them "a heart that obeys and ears that hear" (Bar. 2:31), would bring them again to the land He had promised to their fathers (2:34), and would make an everlasting covenant with them (2:35).

(7) *The suffering of Israel.* There is still another matter dealt with particularly in II Esdras, which represents a recurring problem in Jewish thought: the suffering of God's people, particularly at the hands of those who were less righteous than they (cf. Habakkuk). The author of II Esdras struggles with this problem through at least four chapters (3–6). He claims that Israel was the chosen of God, his "one vine," "one region," "one lily," "one river," "one dove," "one sheep," and "one people" (5:23–27). He then asks why God had delivered the one to the many. Why had those who opposed the promises of God been allowed to tread under foot those who had believed the covenants of the Lord? His final cry was, "If thou dost really hate thy people, they should be punished at thy own hands" (5:28–30). He also pointedly asks: "If the world has indeed been created for us, why do we not possess our world as an inheritance? How long will this be so?" (6:59). There is no entirely adequate answer in II Esdras to this recurring moral and spiritual problem in Jewish thought.

In II Maccabees it is suggested that the purpose of God's punishment of His own people was not to destroy but to discipline them (II Macc. 6:12; cf. 6:16). To punish His own immediately was "a sign of great kindness" (6:13). In dealing with other nations, God waits patiently "until they have reached the full measure of their sins" (6:14).

---

[15] The similarity of II Esdras to the Prophets was not accidental. The author was familiar with the work of the prophets, listing the names of the twelve minor prophets (1:39–40).

Pseudepigrapha[16]

1. The Testaments of the Twelve Patriarchs.

The most significant book by far in the Pseudepigrapha from the perspective of ethics is The Testaments of the Twelve Patriarchs. The book is rather remarkable in its construction. The author puts his words into the mouths of the twelve sons of Jacob. The patriarchs are represented as approaching death. They recount something of their lives and ask their sons, and in some cases others, to emulate their virtues and shun their vices.

(1) *Vices to be shunned.* There is a recurring warning against fornication, particularly in Reuben. It is suggested that fornication is "a pit unto the soul" (Reub. 4:6),[17] and has destroyed many (4:7). The author even lists as one of the seven spirits of deceit "the power of procreation, and sexual intercourse, with which through love of pleasure sin enters in" (2:8). To avoid fornication one must be pure in mind and guard his senses "from every woman" (6:1). There is a somewhat similar warning to women (6:2). (For other references to fornication in Reuben, see 1:6, 10; 3:10; 5:1). Elsewhere, fornication is portrayed as the "mother of all evils" (Sim. 5:3). Even a king can be stripped "of his kingship by becoming the slave of fornication" (Jud. 15:2).

From a more positive perspective it is said that the Lord "loveth him who in a den of wickedness combines fasting with chastity, rather than the man who in kings' chambers combines luxury with licence" (Jos. 9:2; cf. 10:2). There is even a proper season "for a man to embrace his wife" and also "a season to abstain therefrom for his prayers" (Naph. 8:8; cf. I Cor. 7:5).

There are warnings in The Testaments against deceit, envy (Sim. 3:1-7; 4:7), and jealousy (Sim. 4:5; Gad 7:1). The poor

[16] References to the Pseudepigrapha will be to R. H. Charles, *The Apocrypha and Pseudepigrapha* (II). Charles places II Esdras in the Pseudepigrapha and III Maccabees in the Apocrypha. This plan will not be followed in this study.

[17] Abbreviations for various sections of the Twelve Patriarchs will be as follows: Reub. = Reuben; Sim. = Simeon; Jud. = Judah; Iss. = Issachar; Zeb. = Zebulun; Naph. = Naphtali; Ash. = Asher; Jos. = Joseph; Benj. = Benjamin. Levi, Dan, and Gad will not be abbreviated.

man, if he is free from envy, "is blessed beyond all men" (Gad 7:6). A good man does not envy; he is not jealous (Benj. 4:4). There are also warnings against hatred (Gad 3:1; 4:2, 6; 5:1–2) and anger. The latter troubles the soul, gets the mastery over it, and blinds it to what is right (Dan 3:1–3). Anger encompasses a man "with a net of deceit," blinds his eyes, darkens his mind, and gives him "its own peculiar vision" (Dan 2:4). Other vices that are condemned are lying (Dan 5:1; 6:8), covetousness (Naph. 3:1), the love of money (Jud. 17:1; 18:2; 19:1), and the use of wine. The last turns "the mind away from the truth, and inspires the passion of lust, and leadeth the eyes into error" (Jud. 14:1). The right limits of wine should be observed (Jud. 16:1), it should be used modestly (Jud. 16:2), but if one would live soberly he should not touch it at all (Jud. 16:3).

(2) *Virtues to be cultivated.* Righteousness is one virtue to be cultivated, although it is not as prominent in The Testaments as in some other books of the Apocrypha and Pseudepigrapha. A part of Levi's raiment was to be "the crown of righteousness" and "the garment of truth" (Levi 8:2). He instructed his children to work righteousness on the earth (13:5). The closing admonition in Dan is to "cleave unto the righteousness of God" (Dan 6:10). The central emphasis of Asher is on the two ways; the way of righteousness and the way of unrighteousness (Ash. 5:1–3; cf. 1:3–4).

There are some teachings of a high order concerning love, compassion, mercy, and forgiveness. Gad admonished his children to "love one another in deed, and in word, and in the inclination of the soul" (Gad 6:1; cf. 6:3). Love is coupled with generosity (Jos. 17:2). Good is to be returned for evil (Jos. 18:2); in this way one can overcome evil (Benj. 4:3; cf. Rom. 12:21). It is said that a good man loves "the righteous as his own soul" (Benj. 4:3) and shows "mercy to all men, even though they be sinners" (Benj. 4:2).

Love for God and man are united in a way strikingly similar to the New Testament. One such statement is the following:

Love the Lord through all your life,
> And one another with a true heart [Dan 5:3; cf. Iss. 5:2;
> 7:6; and Matt. 22:34–40].

There is an admonition to "show compassion and mercy without hesitation to all men" and to "have compassion . . . in bowels of mercy" even if one is unable to help (Zeb. 7:2–3). One should have compassion "because even as a man doeth to his neighbor, even so also will the Lord do to him" (Zeb. 5:3). There is a negative form of the Golden Rule in The Testaments: "None should do to his neighbor what he doth not like for himself" (Naph. 1:6, late Hebrew text; cf. Tob. 4:15, in the Apocrypha, which reads as follows: "And what you hate, do not do to any one.")

A high level of forgiveness is found in The Testaments, particularly in Gad 6:3–7. Charles suggests that the parallels in thought and diction between these verses and Luke 17:3 and Matthew 18:15, 35 are so close "that we cannot but assume our Lord's acquaintance with them." He further suggests: "The meaning of forgiveness in both cases is the highest and noblest known to us, namely, the restoring the offender to communion with us, which he had forfeited through his offence," which is likewise the essence of divine forgiveness.[18]

Another recurring note in The Testaments which approaches the spirit of the New Testament is an appeal for singleness of heart or mind. Issachar admonishes his children to walk in singleness of heart (Iss. 4:1), and says:

> The single-minded man coveteth not gold,
> > He overreacheth not his neighbour,
> > He longeth not after manifold dainties,
> > He delighteth not in varied apparel [Iss. 4:2].

The main appeal in Asher is also for singleness of mind and life. The appeal is to follow the truth "with singleness of face" (Ash. 6:1; cf. Sim. 4:5, Benj. 6:5–6).

The power of the clean or pure mind is particularly prevalent in Benjamin. It is said that just as "the sun is not defiled by shining on dung and mire, but rather drieth up both and driveth away the evil smell; so also the pure mind, though encompassed by the defilements of earth, rather cleanseth (them) and is not itself defiled" (Benj. 8:3).

[18] R. H. Charles, *Religious Development between the Old and the New Testaments* (New York: Henry Holt, 1919), p. 154.

(3) *Climax of the Testaments*. Nowhere do The Testaments attain a higher ethical level or approach more closely the spirit of the New Testament than in some statements attributed to Issachar. In tones somewhat similar to Job 31, Issachar says that he was not conscious of having committed any sin. He claimed for himself that he was not a busybody, not envious of his neighbor (Iss. 3:3), had never slandered anybody (3:4), and except for his wife he had "not known any woman." He had never committed fornication even "by the uplifting" of his eyes (7:2). He further adds:

> I drank not wine, to be led astray thereby;
>> I coveted not any desirable thing that was my neighbour's.
>> Guile arose not in my heart;
>> A lie passed not through my lips.
>> If any man were in distress, I joined my sighs with his,
>> And I shared my bread with the poor.
>> I wrought godliness, all my days I kept truth [7:3–5].

He then sums up the matter as follows:

>> I loved the Lord;
>> Likewise also every man with all my heart [7:6].

2. Other books of the Pseudepigrapha.

While no other book of the Pseudepigrapha is as important from the perspective of biblical ethics as The Testaments of the Twelve Patriarchs, there are teachings of considerable significance scattered through most of the other books.

(1) *The nature of God*. The logical subject with which to begin this brief survey is God. In Aristeas[19] most of the replies of the seventy-two men to the questions of the Egyptian king included

---

[19] This letter, supposedly written by Aristeas, an officer at the court of Ptolemy Philadelphus (285–247 B.C.) to his brother Philocrates, purportedly gives an account of the circumstances which led to the Septuagint translation of the Jewish scriptures. The heart of the letter (187–294) is composed of a series of questions by the king and answers by the seventy-two who had been sent by Eleazer, the high priest, in response to the king's request, to make the translation. The king asked one question of each of the seventy-two.

some reference to God. The king himself said after the first ten had replied to his questions that they "made God the starting-point of their words" (Ar. 200).[20] The same could be said of most of the writers of the other books of the Pseudepigrapha. They begin with God. Their view of God is the basis for whatever ethical content their books contain.

God is presented as holy (Bk. Jub. 21:4)—"all holy among the holy ones" (III Macc. 2:21), faithful (Bk. Jub. 21:4), true (III Macc. 2:11), merciful (I En. 24:4; III Macc. 5:8; 6:9), with a mercy that endures forever (Ps. Sol. 10:8; 16:3), longsuffering toward both sinners and the righteous (II Bar. 24:2), good and gentle (Ps. Sol. 5:14), and just and kind (Ps. Sol. 10:6). God is particularly kind in His treatment of the poor, being a refuge for them (Ps. Sol. 5:2) and responding to their prayers (Ps. Sol. 18:3).

An emphasis on the righteousness of God is found in the Book of Jubilees (21:4), but particularly in I Enoch. It could properly be considered the theme of the latter book. Enoch is called the "scribe of righteousness" (I En. 12:4; 15:1), and the Garden of Eden is referred to as the Garden of Righteousness (32:3). God is portrayed predominantly as righteous. His righteousness is revealed in His judgments (50:4) and is beyond man's comprehension (63:3). One of several titles for the Messiah in I Enoch is "Righteous One" (38:2; 53:6; cf. Acts 3:14; 7:52). The "Son of man" is "born unto righteousness" (71:14); "righteousness dwells with him" (46:3). God's righteousness expresses itself through His impartiality or His lack of respect of persons, which is a recurring theme in the literature (I En. 63:8; cf. II Bar. 44:4; Ps. Sol. 2:19).

God is also presented, as is true in other Jewish literature, as the highly exalted One, the creative sovereign God of the nations, who will judge the peoples of the world. This is the major emphasis in the Sibylline Oracles and is very prominent elsewhere

---

20 Books of the Pseudepigrapha will be abbreviated as follows: Bk. Jub. = The Book of Jubilees; Ar. = The Letter of Aristeas; En. = Enoch; Sib. Or. = The Sibylline Oracles; Assump. M. = Assumption of Moses; Bar. = Baruch; Ps. Sol. = The Psalms of Solomon; Macc. = Maccabees; Ah. = The Story of Ahikar; Eth. F. = Ethics of the Fathers or Pirke Avoth.

There are some books, such as the Books of Adam and Eve and The Martyrdom of Isaiah, that do not contain enough material to justify their inclusion in this study.

(see Assump. M. 12:4–5; II Bar. 24:2; Ps. Sol. 2:36; 8:27; III Macc. 2:2–3; 7:9). The Jews were His people in a unique way. He chastened His own but "as a beloved son" or as the firstborn (Ps. Sol. 13:8; *cf.* 18:4). The purpose of whatever chastening He meted out to them was that they might return unto Him (Ps. Sol. 16:11).

(2) *The Law.* An emphasis on the Law is prominent in the Book of Jubilees,[21] which was written primarily to defend Judaism against the prevalent Hellenistic spirit. As a part of this defense the Law was glorified. The author considered it the final and complete expression of divine truth. While the major emphasis is on the external observance of the Law, there is some attention given to its inner and deeper meaning (Bk. Jub. 1:23). The Law is magnified in other books of the Pseudepigrapha, particularly in II Baruch (see 32:1; 48:22–24; 51:3, 7; 77:3, 13–16), whose author considered sin the conscious and deliberate violation of the Law (15:5–6; 19:1–3). In Pirke Avoth, or Ethics of the Fathers,[22] the Law or Torah is equated with the will of God. It is also said that "where there is no Torah, there is no proper conduct; where there is no proper conduct, there is no Torah" (Eth. F. 3:21). The Torah is represented as "rich in rules of conduct" (4:29). Aristeas suggests that all rules were for "the object of teaching us a moral lesson" (Ar. 150). This was even true of ritualistic laws, such as those regarding unclean animals. These laws "were made for the sake of righteousness to aid the quest for virtue and the perfecting of character" (144: cf. 168–69). The good life consists in keeping the Law (127).

An extreme emphasis on the Law that tended to make it a burden to the people is found in a few places. An example is the discussion of the Sabbath in the last chapter of the Book of

---

21 It is claimed that the Book of Jubilees was received by Moses as a secret revelation (1:26–29). The history of the world from creation to Mount Sinai is divided into jubilee periods of forty-nine years each. The history is re-edited from the Pharisaic viewpoint and includes many rather interesting additions and embellishments.

22 This is the title used by Philip Birnbaum, whose translation will be used (New York: Hebrew Publishing Co., 1949). Birnbaum gives both the Hebrew and English on opposite pages. *Ethics of the Fathers* contains utterances by Jewish teachers from the third century B.C. to the third centutry A.D. It is one of the sixty-three treatises in the Mishnah and is rich in religious and ethical content.

Jubilees. It is stated that a man who lies with his wife, sets out on a journey, buys or sells, draws water, takes up a burden to carry it out of his tent or house, lights a fire, rides a beast, travels by a ship, strikes or kills anything, catches an animal, a bird, or a fish, fasts, or makes war on the Sabbath shall be put to death (Bk. Jub. 50:8, 12–13).

(3) *Righteousness*. As one might expect, there is considerable material on righteousness in the books of the Pseudepigrapha. The author of II Maccabees, for example, accepts the classic Greek virtues—temperance, courage, wisdom, and justice—but adds to these righteousness, which is the keynote of the book. While righteousness in this book and elsewhere is closely related to the observance of the ritualistic requirements of the Law, yet it expresses itself in practical and ethical ways. For example, the righteous men from Ur of the Chaldees, as described in the Sibylline Oracles, were men of sound minds and fair deeds (Sib. Or. III, 219–20), who practiced justice and virtue (III, 234). They did not remove a neighbor's landmark but rather assisted their neighbor. They helped the widow, and the wealthy among them shared their harvest with those who had nothing (III, 240–47).[23]

Typical of the Jewish perspective in general, the righteous will be blessed. God will give them peace; will protect, preserve, and prosper them, and will extend His mercy to them (I En. 1:8; cf. 5:9; 45:6; 48:7; 58:4; 71:17). His blessings to the righteous will not be restricted to this life. At the time of the judgment there will be a separation of the righteous and the wicked. The "Elect One" will choose the righteous (I En. 51:1–2); their days will be unending (I En. 58:3). This means that the righteous should not fear when they "see the sinners growing strong and prospering in their ways" (I En. 104:6).

(4) *Social ethic*. In contrast to a personal or basic ethic, a social or applied ethic is not as prominent in the Pseudepigrapha as it is in the canonical writings, or even in the Apocrypha. There are a few hints of a domestic ethic, one or two of which are quite interesting. In the Sibylline Oracles it is suggested that there would be "a holy race of God-fearing men," who would honor their

---

[23] For additional references to righteousness, see the Book of Jubilees 7:20; 20: 2, 9; 22:14; 36:8.

parents, would be "mindful of the purity of marriage," and would not have "unholy intercourse with boys" as was true of those of surrounding nations (Sib. Or. III, 594–600), which is evidently a reference to homosexuality or possibly some other unnatural sex expression (cf. III, 764–66; V, 166, 387–91, 430). In the Psalms of Solomon there are warnings against gross sensual sins (Ps. Sol. 2:13; 8:9–11, 24), including unnatural intercourse, which in this place may refer to incest (2:15). Ahikar instructs his sister's son Nadan not to "look upon a woman that is bedizened and painted" nor to lust after her (Ah. 2:5).[24] He should not commit adultery with the wife of his neighbor (2:6), nor be "inquisitive into beauty" that does not belong to him, "because many have perished through the beauty of woman, and her love has been as a fire that burneth" (2:72).

There is a rather strong implication in the Book of Jubilees that the sin involved in the temptation and fall was sexual. God covered the shame of Adam and Eve with coats of skin and clothes (Bk. Jb. 3:26–27; cf. 3:31). They did not sin, so it says, until after the first Jubilee which was spent in Eden, and "after this" Adam "knew" Eve. This suggests that sex relations caused their expulsion from the Garden of Eden.

There are also admonitions in Jubilees against the marriage of Jews to Gentiles, which was considered as serious an offense as fornication. A man who gave his daughter or sister to a Gentile should be stoned to death, and the woman should be burned (Bk. Jb. 30:7). Such a marriage was "abominable before the Lord" (Bk. Jub. 30:11).

There is found in Ahikar some advice on the discipline of a son (Ah. 2:22–23), also advice against living in the house of a father-in-law (2:46), and against being a matchmaker: if it does not work out well, one will be cursed for it; if it works out well, one will be ignored (2:68).

There is material on a political ethic, particularly in the Letter of Aristeas. The political philosophy and teachings of the letter are of considerable interest. The ideal monarch is portrayed as a benevolent despot and a philosopher-king. Many specific

---

[24] Reference to The Story of Ahikar will be to the Syriac Version A, found in Charles.

qualifications for the king, moral and otherwise, are set forth (see particularly Ar. 187–292). The greatest achievement in ruling an empire was that the subjects of the king would "dwell in peace," and that justice would "be speedily administered in cases of dispute" (291).

(5) *Vices and virtues.* In addition to the teachings previously set forth, there are warnings against other vices and an exaltation of certain virtues. In I Enoch there is a whole series of warnings or woes against "sinners." A few of the vices or sins specifically condemned are deceit (I En. 94:6), lying (95:6), godlessness (99:1), and the use of deceitful and false measures (99:12). Woes are pronounced, in particular, upon those "who build their houses with sin" (94:7; cf. 99:13), acquire silver and gold in unrighteousness (97:8), trust in their riches and forget God (94:8), and are proud of their wealth (97:9). In the Sibylline Oracles the love of money is called "the shepherd of evils to many" (Sib. Or. III, 642).

In III Baruch there is a special condemnation of the drinking of wine. It is said that evils "such as murders, adulteries, fornications, perjuries, and thefts, and such like" come from drinking wine, and "nothing good is established by it" (III Bar. 4:16–17). In Ethics of the Fathers there are admonitions against envy, lust, and vainglory (Eth. F. 4:28). In I Enoch there appears to be an exhortation against the signing of contracts or agreements: one's word should be sufficient (I En. 69:8–10). There is also an evident reference to and condemnation of abortion: "the smitings of the embryo in the womb" (69:12).

In the Story of Ahikar there are some relevant warnings concerning the tongue. The author says, "It is better for a man to stumble in his heart than to stumble with his tongue" (Ah. 2:53). One's mouth should be guarded "for the tail of a dog gives him bread, and his mouth gets him blows" (2:38). Nadan, the adopted son of Ahikar, is counselled to put any evil matter he has heard "seven fathoms deep under ground" (2:54). Similarly, in Ethics of the Fathers it is suggested that one should be careful with his words (Eth. F. 1:11), remembering that "a fence to wisdom is silence" (3:17).

Quite a long list of virtues or moral ideals could be compiled, particularly from the replies of the seventy-two to the questions of the king in the Letter of Aristeas and from II Enoch. In the former the following virtues or ideals are mentioned and commended: fairness (Ar. 191), courage (199), righteousness (209, 267), justice (212), kindness (225), liberality and generosity (227), gratitude (228), purity (234), temperance (237), and humility (263). There is also included a negative form of the Golden Rule (207). Among the personal virtues recommended in II Enoch are the following: meekness (1:2-3; 66:6), patience (51:3), longsuffering (66:6), sincerity (52:14), honesty (66:6), peace and love (52:11), justice (61:1; 66:1, 7), humility (52:13). Some admonitions in II Enoch somewhat more social are: generosity in general but particularly toward the poor (51:1), the naked and the hungry (63:1), and the fallen (52:7). In Ethics of the Fathers, in addition to many negative exhortations, there are admonitions to be generous to the poor (Eth. F. 1:5), to love work (1:10), and peace (1:12). It is also suggested that every man should be judged favorably ("with a leaning to his merit," Charles) (1:6). Generosity, unselfishness (2:13), teachableness and contentment (4:1), humility (4:4, 12), and friendliness (4:20) should characterize one's life.

(6) *Some distinctive emphases.* There are a few other emphases, more or less peculiar to certain books. In I Enoch, in a highly figurative portrayal of the preservation of Noah and his family, there seems to be a crude attempt to explain the different races. Evidently the white bull that became a man and later "departed from them" (I En. 89:9) was Noah. There were three bulls with him in the ark: one white, one red, and one black.

The main positive ethical emphasis in the Assumption of Moses is its doctrine of merit or good works, while the freedom of man is emphasized in II Baruch and in the Psalms of Solomon. In II Baruch the consequences of Adam's fall were largely limited to Adam (II Bar. 54:15). Really, each individual is the Adam of his own soul (54:19). In the Psalms of Solomon freedom of choice is summarized as follows:

Our works are subject to our own choice and power
    To do right and wrong is the works of our hands
    [Ps. Sol. 9:7].

The Fourth Book of Maccabees is a moral discourse which concentrates on "Inspired Reason," reason guided by the law (IV Macc. 2:21–23) or "religion-guided Reason" (16:4). This "Inspired Reason" is master of the passions (13:1; 16:1) and of pain both from within and from without (18:1–2). It can control the sexual passions and all kinds of coveting (2:1–6). There is nothing in this book of the Stoic conception that the passions are the result of wrong thinking. Rather, the passions are natural but they are to be brought under rigid control and can be by "Inspired Reason" or a religiously oriented Reason.

Dead Sea Scrolls

Biblical scholars and theologians in general have been tremendously challenged by the Dead Sea Scrolls since the discovery of the first ones in 1947. Since that time scholars have continued to translate, interpret, and evaluate the Scrolls[25] that have been discovered, while they search for additional ones. It has been suggested that there are enough available now to keep the scholars busy for fifty years, with thousands of fragments awaiting publication.

1. Significance of the Scrolls.

One author, referring to the impact of the discovery of the Scrolls, in a rather extreme statement says that "all the problems

[25] The following is a representative group of books on the Scrolls: F. F. Bruce, *Second Thoughts on the Dead Sea Scrolls*, 2nd ed. (Grand Rapids: Eerdmans, 1961); Millar Burrows, *The Dead Sea Scrolls* (New York: Viking Press, 1955), and *More Light on the Dead Sea Scrolls* (New York: Viking Press, 1958); A. Dupont-Sommer, *The Essene Writing from Qumran*, trans. G. Vermes (Oxford: Basil Blackwell, 1961); A. R. C. Leany, ed., *A Guide to the Scrolls* (London: SCM Press, 1958); and Helmer Ringgren, *The Faith of Qumran*, trans. Emile T. Sander (Philadelphia: Fortress Press, 1963). Leany would serve as a helpful, brief introduction to the Scrolls. Burrows' books are standard works. Dupont-Sommer, in the main, introduces and translates the non-biblical or sectarian documents of the Scrolls. Ringgren, a paperback, is more of a systematic study of the content of the Scrolls than any of the other books. For a translation of certain Scrolls see Theodore H. Gaster, *The Dead Sea Scriptures*, rev. ed. (Garden City, N. Y.: Doubleday, 1964).

relative to primitive Christianity henceforth find themselves placed in a new light which forces us to reconsider them completely."[26] It is quite clear that there are some teachings in the Scrolls that are strikingly similar to teachings in the New Testament.[27] Included are the condemnation of impurity, a rather general hostility to wealth, which is particularly evident in Luke and James, and the ideal of brotherly love. These and other similarities are evident in the Sermon on the Mount, and especially in Matthew 5, which means, among other things, that "many of the contacts between Jesus' sayings and the Dead Sea Scrolls are in the area of moral teachings."[28]

It should be remembered, however, as Burrows and others suggest, that there are marked contrasts between certain of the teachings of Jesus and the Scrolls. For example, the Qumran community emphasized asceticism, legalism, strict Sabbath observance, ritualism, and exclusiveness, all of which were foreign to the spirit and teachings of Jesus. Furthermore, there is nothing in the Scrolls comparable to the teachings of Jesus on the Fatherhood of God and the Kingdom of God. His teachings regarding moral perfection transcend anything found in the Scrolls.

While some have pointed out similarities between Paul's epistles and the Epistle of James and the Scrolls, "the closest and

---

26 A. Dupont-Sommer, *Dead Sea Scrolls: A Preliminary Survey* (Oxford: Basil Blackwell, 1952), p. 100.

27 In addition to sections and, in some cases, chapters in the books previously mentioned, the following will be found helpful for those who want to study more thoroughly the relation of the Dead Sea Scrolls not only to the New Testament but to the Bible in general: Matthew Black, *The Scrolls and Christian Origins* (New York: Scribner's, 1961)—the subtitle is "Studies in the Jewish Background of the New Testament"; William Hugh Brownlee, *The Meaning of the Qumran Scrolls for the Bible* (New York: Oxford University Press, 1964)—about half of the book is Part II on "The Significance of the Complete Isaiah Scroll"; F. F. Bruce, *Biblical Exegesis in the Qumran Texts* (Grand Rapids: Eerdmans, 1959); and Krister Stendahl, ed., *The Scrolls and the New Testament* (New York: Harper, 1957). See also Chapter XI, "The Rise of Christianity and the Qumran Texts," in Kurt Schubert's *The Dead Sea Community* (London: Adam and Charles Black, 1959).

28 Burrows, *More Light on the Dead Sea Scrolls*, p. 95. Burrows (pp. 95–100) also mentions a number of additional teachings or emphases that are found in both the Sermon and the Scrolls. Kurt Schubert has a chapter on "The Sermon on the Mount and the Qumran Texts" in Stendahl's book.

most impressive parallels with the Qumran texts" are found in the Johannine writings.[29]

Based on the foregoing suggestions of the possible points of contact between the community that produced the Scrolls and the early Christian movement, it can correctly be concluded that the Scrolls have considerable significance for the study of the early days of Christianity. This does not mean that Jesus or the early leaders of the Christian movement were dependent on or consciously and directly borrowed from the Qumran sect. As Bruce suggests, however, even if the Scrolls "provide us simply with a new background against which we can study the New Testament and the beginnings of Christianity with greater understanding, that is a great contribution."[30] When an object is viewed against a new background, it takes on a fresh appearance. At least the Scrolls show, as Albright has suggested, that the writers of the New Testament "drew from a common reservoir of terminology and ideas which were well known to the Essenes and presumably familiar also to other Jewish sects of the period."[31]

The Scrolls have some particular significance for a study of biblical ethics. If it is correct, as generally agreed, that the Scrolls were produced by the Essenes[32] or a sect closely akin to them, then the following statement about the Essenes, based on a description of them by Philo, has significance for our study: "They were chiefly preoccupied with ethics, and taught piety, holiness, justice, love of God and man."[33] It is evident from the Scrolls themselves that the people of Qumran were primarily concerned with daily living. Charles, in writing concerning the Fragments

[29] *Ibid.*, p. 123. Burrows gives approximately ten pages to an examination of these "parallels," including some in the Revelation. Raymond E. Brown has a chapter on "The Qumran Scrolls and the Johannine Gospel and Epistles" in Stendahl's book.

[30] Bruce, *Second Thoughts on the Dead Sea Scrolls*, p. 150.

[31] Burrows, *More Light on the Dead Sea Scrolls*, p. 132.

[32] A. Powell Davies in *The Meaning of the Dead Sea Scrolls* (London: Frederick Muller, 1957) has a considerable section on the Essenes (pp. 79–105) as is also true of Bruce (*Second Thoughts on the Dead Sea Scrolls*, pp. 125–35). A. Dupont-Sommer (*The Essene Writings from Qumran*) gives particular attention to the Essenes with introductory chapters on "The Essenes in Ancient Literature" and "The Essene Origin of the Qumran Writings." The closing chapter of his book is "Essenism and Christianity."

[33] Birnbaum, *A Treasury of Judaism*, p. 247.

of a Zadokite Work, says: "The movement that gave them birth was of an intensely ethical and religious character."[34] In the light of the preceding it is surprising that so little attention has been given to the ethical content of the Scrolls.[35]

The ethical emphasis is particularly prevalent in the Rule of the Community or the Manual of Discipline. There is also considerable ethical material in the Book of Hymns, the Damascus Document,[36] and the War of the Sons of Light and the Sons of Darkness.

2. The Manual of Discipline.

The Manual or Rule reveals the customs of the community, which in turn reveal a major emphasis on the ethical or moral. One who wished to join the community was required, among other things, to enter into covenant or pledge to "do what is good and upright" in God's sight, keep away from evil and "cling to all good works." He must also "act truthfully and righteously and justly on earth."[37] When one entered the covenant and wished formally to be joined to the community there were two main areas of his life that were investigated: "his temper in

34 Charles, *The Apocrypha and Pseudepigrapha*, II, 785. This statement by Charles was made several years before the discovery of the Dead Sea Scrolls. The Fragments are now generally called "The Damascus Document" (see footnote 36).

35 In contrast to most writers, Ringgren gives some specific attention to the ethical content of the Scrolls. In his chapter on "Man" he has a section (pp. 132–44) on "Ethical Ideas," with another section (pp. 144–51) on "Reward and Punishment."

36 This document was discovered in 1896–1897, translated in 1910, and since the discovery of the Dead Sea Scrolls it has been definitely linked with the Qumran community. For a discussion of the document see H. H. Rowley, *The Zadokite Fragments and the Dead Sea Scrolls* (Oxford: Basil Blackwell, 1952).

37 Gaster, p. 46. Quotations from the Scrolls will be from the revised edition (1964) of Gaster's translation. Page references to his book will be given in parentheses in the body of the material. It is believed that this will be more convenient for the average reader than references to the Scrolls themselves. For other translations see G. Vermes, *The Dead Sea Scrolls in English* (A Penguin Book, 1962), Burrows, *The Dead Sea Scrolls*, pp. 349–415, *More Light on the Dead Sea Scrolls*, pp. 387–404, and Dupont-Sommer where translations are found in various chapters. Burrows (*More Light on the Dead Sea Scrolls*, p. 382) says that truth, righteousness, and justice as used in the Manual are practically synonyms for the law.

human relations and his understanding and performance of doctrine" (p. 56). Typical of the perspective of the community, which considered itself "The Elite of a Chosen People,"[38] the covenanter had to pledge himself "to love all the children of light . . . and to hate all the children of darkness" (p. 46), the latter in sharp contrast to the spirit of the New Testament.

The community required that its members separate themselves from others. They were to keep apart from all who "walk in the path of wickedness" (p. 55), they were not to associate "in work or in goods" with men who transgress the word of God. They were to keep away from such men "in every respect" (p. 55). There is even the instruction "to bear unremitting hatred towards all men of ill repute, and to be minded to keep in seclusion from them" (p. 68).

One thing of interest to students of the New Testament is the provision for a community of goods in the Qumran community. Those who became members of the community had to be willing to "bring all of their mind, all of their strength, and all of their wealth unto the community of God" (p. 46). They were "to belong to the community in both a doctrinal and an economic sense" (p. 54). They were "to dine together, worship together, and take counsel together" (p. 57).

Full participation in the life of the community, however, was not immediate. One's performance was to be reviewed after a full year "in the midst of the community." Previous to this review he had "no stake in the common funds." If at the end of a year he was approved by the priests and by "a majority of their co-covenanters," then he was to bring all his property "and the tools of his profession," which were to be committed to "the community's 'minister of works.'" This officer was to keep a special account of what was brought, but it was not to be disbursed "for the general benefit." It was only after the candidate had been subject to another review and approved at the completion of a second year in the community that he was "to be admitted to the common board" (p. 59).

There was a rather interesting mixture in the community of adherence to rank and order and the practice of considerable

[38] Davies, p. 53.

democracy. For example, as indicated above, approval for admission to the community was by the priests and a majority of the covenanters. There was to be an annual review of priests, levites, and laity, to see that all were functioning properly in their particular rank and in relation to one another (p. 49). Each person in the community was "to obey his superior in rank in all matters of work and money" (p. 57). The priests were the highest rank, and determined the rank of the other members of the community. In one place it says that they alone had "authority in all judicial and economic matters" (p. 66), while in another place it suggests that decisions in those areas, along with doctrinal matters, were shared with a majority of the community who were faithful to the covenant (p. 54).

Democracy in the community was not only evident in the admission of members but also in the operation of the community. One who was admitted "to the formal organization of the community" entered into covenant to be faithful to the commandments of the Law of Moses, as that Law was "revealed to the sons of Zadok . . . and to a majority of their co-covenanters who have volunteered together to adhere to the truth of God and to walk according to His pleasure" (p. 55). In sessions of the common council of the community everyone was to have an opportunity to give his opinion, although no one was "to speak in advance of his prescribed rank" (p. 58).

Also, some democracy was practiced in the establishment of standards of conduct for members of the community. At least laymen were members of the group that set the standards. This is set forth in the following passage, which is very rich in ethical content:

> In the deliberative council of the community there shall be twelve laymen and three priests schooled to perfection in all that has been revealed of the entire Law. Their duty shall be to set the standards for the practice of truth, righteousness and justice, and for the exercise of charity and humility in human relations; and to show how, by control of impulse and contrition of spirit, faithfulness may be maintained on earth; how, by active performance of justice and passive submission to the trials of chastisement, iniquity may be

cleared, and how one can walk with all men with the quality of truth and in conduct appropriate to every occasion [p. 63].

There is present in the Manual, as in the Scrolls in general, considerable evidence of a dualism. This is not a metaphysical dualism of matter and spirit; as Burrows says, it is "primarily ethical but with a cosmic dimension."[39] God created man "and appointed for him two spirits": the good spirit and the evil spirit. The good spirit is associated with light, truth, and righteousness. The evil spirit is associated with darkness, error, and perversity. God, who created both spirits, has set the limits of their activity. They are to exist "in equal measure until the final age" (p. 53), when truth will be triumphant.

Through communion with the spirit of truth there comes to men "a zeal for righteous government, of a hallowed mind in a controlled nature, of abounding love for all who follow the truth, of a self-respecting purity which abhors all the taint of filth, of a modesty of behavior coupled with a general prudence" (p. 52). In contrast, the following belong to or are the product of the spirit of perversity: greed, falsehood, pride, deception, cruelty, insolence, "shortness of temper," folly, "arrogant passion," lewdness, unchastity, blasphemy, and "blindness of eyes, dullness of ears, stiffness of neck and hardness of heart" (p. 52).

3. The Book of Hymns.

As is true of the canonical Psalms, most of the ethical material in the hymns is related to the character of God. Before we come to the Book of Hymns proper there is the Hymn of the Initiants, which contains some rather rich ethical material. God is revealed as sovereign; all things exist by His will (p. 133). He is the "cause of all good," the

Fountain of all knowledge,
    Spring of holiness,
    Zenith of all glory,
    Might omnipotent [p. 128].

[39] Burrows, *More Light on the Dead Sea Scrolls*, p. 281. Ringgren (pp. 68–80) has a chapter entitled "Dualism."

Possibly as a result of his relation to God, the writer promises that he will "pursue all men with good," "will not be envious of the profit of wickedness," "will harbor no angry grudge against those that indeed repent," "will cherish no baseness" in his heart, will not use his mouth for coarse speech nor his lips for deceit and lies. In contrast, he says, "The fruit of holiness shall be on my tongue" (p. 129). He further says that he will temper justice with mercy, "will show kindness to men downtrodden" will "reply to the proud with meekness" and "with humility answer the base" (p. 130).

Some of the qualities attributed to God in the Book of Hymns[40] or Psalms of Thanksgiving are mentioned over and over again. For example, his mercies are "beyond number" (p. 134), are multitudinous or abundant (pp. 152, 165, 166, 181), and "are shed upon all who do" God's will (p. 178; cf. p. 194). The writer was overwhelmed by the mercies of God (p. 174). Also, God's loving-kindness is plenteous (p. 152) and is frequently coupled with or closely related to His mercy (pp. 165, 171, 179).

God is also "longsuffering in judgment" (p. 134). He always deals justly (p. 153) and His "justice holdeth firm for ever" (p. 166). He is truth and His "works are righteousness" (p. 152). He is a God of forgiveness and "abundant goodness" (p. 166; cf. p. 175). His compassion is also abundant (p. 175; cf. p. 181). As one would expect, God is revealed as a covenant-keeping God: "and ne'er shall Thy word be revoked" (p. 187). He is the "essence of right" (p. 189). His truth cannot be equaled with any amount of wealth and His holiness has no match (p. 192).

The love of God is freely bestowed upon the righteous, but He is portrayed as hating the perverse (p. 190). His care of His people is compared in a beautiful way to the care of a father, a mother, and a nurse:

> Yet Thou art a father to all that [know] Thy truth,
>   and Thou wilt rejoice over them

40 Gaster (p. 124) considers the Book of Hymns as "the most original literary creation in the Dead Sea Scriptures." Some scholars consider the Teacher of Righteousness the author of the hymns. See Burrows, *More Light on the Dead Sea Scrolls*, pp. 324–30, for a review of the literature on this subject.

> like a mother that pitieth her babe,
> and Thou wilt feed all Thy works
> as a nurse feeds her charge at the bosom [p. 174; cf. p. 166].

Typical of the Jewish perspective in general and of the Old Testament in particular, God is revealed as having a special concern for the underprivileged. He helps the needy and weak and snatches him from the grasp of one who is stronger than he (p. 142). He never abandons the orphan or despises the poor (p. 155).

While the sovereignty of God may not be frequently stated in a specific way in the Psalms of Thanksgiving, it is assumed throughout (see pp. 174–75). The sovereign God has assigned to men their tasks or roles (p. 183) and prescribed their works (p. 135). He is the source of all might, "the wellspring of all power" (p. 134), the secret of truth (p. 136), and the source of stoutness of heart and "fortitude in the face of affliction" (p. 138).

God has taught the writer not to rely on riches and even to abhor "all worldly wealth and gain" (p. 176). It is only through the goodness and mercy of God that man "can ever do right" (p. 187). Likewise, it is God who gives the power to discern between the good and the wicked and the power to love what God loves and abhor that which He hates (p. 188). It is God who creates the righteous, preparing him to walk in the ways of God (p. 191). Really, no man can be righteous without God's help (p. 194):

> . . . righteousness lies not with man,
>   nor perfection of conduct with mortals.
>   Only with God On High
>   are all works of righteousness [p. 151].

A man may be more righteous than another man, but no man can prove his righteousness in the presence of God (p. 172): "No man is righteous with Thee" (p. 183). God's righteousness is at the center of His nature, and particular attention is focused in the Scrolls on His "absolute righteousness in contradistinction to man's total depravity."[41]

41 Ringgren, p. 65.

The following prayer will be an appropriate conclusion to this section on the Book of Hymns or Psalms of Thanksgiving:

> Strengthen, then, the stand of this Thy servant
> > against all spirits of perverseness,
> > that he walk in all the ways which Thou lovest,
> > reject all that Thou hatest,
> > and do what is good in Thy sight [p. 197].

4. Other documents.

There are additional Dead Sea Scrolls that contain considerable ethical material. For example, the introductory part of the Damascus Document or the Zadokite Fragment "is a brief philosophy of history or, more correctly, theology of history."[42] It also spells out rather specifically the things that are required of one who enters into the covenant. Some of the requirements are ritualistic but most of them are moral. One who has entered the covenant is "to keep away from men of ill repute" and to remain "aloof from ill-gotten gain." He is not to rob the poor or make widows his prey. He is not to nurse grudges and is to abstain from whoredom. From the more positive perspective, the one who enters the covenant is "to grasp the hand of the poor, the needy and the stranger," to seek "the welfare of his fellow," and "to love each man his neighbor like himself" (pp. 78–79).

There are some instructions concerning the family. The men of the community were not to take two wives at the same time, which some interpret to mean no divorce, although it seems more logical that it refers to bigamy. The covenanters were not to marry within the degrees forbidden by the Law (p. 76). Since there are no instructions in the Manual of Discipline regarding family relations, some assume that the covenanters of Qumran were celibate. The evidence, however, is not clear.

There is another provision, different from the community of property required in the Manual of Discipline. The Damascus Document says that the wages of two days per month were to be handed over to the overseer. The judges took what was thus collected and used it for the benefit of orphans and to support "the

42 *Ibid.*, p. 59.

poor and needy," the aged, "persons captured by foreign peoples, unprotected girls, unmarriageable virgins, general communal officials" (p. 94).

This document contains some of the extreme requirements for Sabbath observance that had made the day a burden to the people in the days of Jesus. A few of the many requirements were the following: one was not to eat food on the Sabbath that had not been prepared in advance, he was not to raise his hand to strike his fist, he was not to take anything out of his house or bring anything in, he was not to pick up a rock or dust in a dwelling place. Nurses were not to carry babies around on the Sabbath. A provision that sounds cruel was the following: "No one is to foal a beast on the Sabbath day. Even if it drop its young into a cistern or a pit, he is not to lift it out on the Sabbath" (pp. 88–89).

The War of the Sons of Light and the Sons of Darkness has been described as "a kind of G.H.Q. manual for the guidance of the Brotherhood at 'Armageddon.' "[43] The main thing of interest from our perspective is the prominent place that is given to God as a factor in the wars of His people. In language strikingly similar to the Maccabees, the people are told that victory belongs to God. Logically, then, the name of God was to be on all the trumpets (pp. 303–4) and on the standards or banners that were carried into battle (p. 305). For example, as they went out to battle they were to write upon their several standards: *Truth of God, Righteousness of God, Glory of God, Justice of God*, and thereafter the specific name of each division" (p. 306). The priests were to encourage the troops as they went into battle. They sounded the trumpets which directed the battle (pp. 309–10). The exhortation to the troops included such expressions as: "Your God is marching with you to do battle for you against your foeman to the end that He may save you" (p. 313). In addressing God it is said that the issues of war belong to Him:

> Thine is the battle; from Thee comes the power; and it is not ours. It is not our strength nor the might of our hands that achieveth this valor, but it cometh through Thy strength and through Thy great valorous might [p. 314].

[43] Gaster, p. 294.

He is the Lord of battles, waging battle from heaven against the enemies of His people (p. 315). The congregation of His holy beings were in their midst "as a perpetual help" (p. 316). The war was God's war (p. 323). There was a special prayer for the battle line (p. 321) and a prayer of thanksgiving for victory (p. 325).

CHAPTER V

THE SYNOPTIC GOSPELS

The centrality of God and His expectations that His children should be like Him are as evident in the life and teachings of Jesus as they are in the Old Testament. There are some differences, however, in the terms that are used and in the emphases that are made. For example, Jesus spoke of God as His Father and our Father, an idea that is present to a limited degree in the Old Testament. Jesus also revealed that our Father is meticulous in His care of His children. In turn, they are to trust Him, are to pray for His will to be done on earth as in heaven, are to seek first the Kingdom of God, and are to attempt to be like Him. The latter means that they are expected to be perfect as their Father in heaven is perfect.

The present chapter will be a brief discussion of certain aspects of the ethical teachings of Jesus as revealed in the Synoptic Gospels.[1] Whatever else Jesus was, He was a great ethical teacher.

---

[1] The following books will be helpful for those who want to study the "Synoptic Problem" along with other critical problems of the New Testament: Vincent Taylor, *The Formation of the Gospel Tradition*, 2nd ed. (London: Macmillan, 1935); a more recent book by the same author entitled *The*

Jesus and the Law

The fact that God was the point of reference in the life and teachings of Jesus can be seen clearly in His relation to the Law and His attitude toward the scribal use and interpretation of the Law.

1. Attitude toward the Law.

Jesus knew and respected the Law. He "recognized the nucleus of the Torah as the revealed will of God."[2] This nucleus, in the main, contained the apodictic in contrast to the casuistic laws. On the other hand, Jesus rejected most of the scribal interpretations of the Law, which had made it a burden to the people. Also, His emphasis was on the moral law rather than on the ceremonial law. The former, from His perspective, was nullified at times by the traditions of the Scribes and Pharisees. On one occasion He spelled this out pointedly. He said, "You have a fine way of rejecting the commandment of God, in order to keep your tradition." They had left or rejected the commandment to honor father and mother by having a tradition that a man could say, "It is Corban" (given to God), and thus avoid using what he had to help his needy parents (Mark 7:1–13; cf. Matt. 15:1–9).

Jesus revealed His general attitude toward and relation to the Law in His introductory statement to the comparisons He made between the Law and His teachings. His statement was: "Think

Text of the New Testament (New York: St. Martin's Press, 1961); F. F. Bruce, *Are the New Testament Documents Reliable?*, 3rd ed. (London: Inter-Varsity Fellowship, 1950), a brief book which gives an affirmative answer to the author's question; Reginald H. Fuller, *The New Testament in Current Study* (New York: Scribner's, 1962), related in the main to the writings of Bultmann, his followers, and his critics; and Bruce M. Metzger, *The Text of the New Testament* (New York: Oxford University Press, 1964), a scholarly book on "The Science and the Art of Textual Criticism." Of the many introductions to the New Testament, two that are somewhat representative of different theological perspectives are: Robert M. Grant, *Historical Introduction to the New Testament* (New York: Harper and Row, 1963), and Everett F. Harrison, *Introduction to the New Testament* (Grand Rapids: Eerdmans, 1964). Grant has four chapters on the Synoptic Gospels in which he discusses the major critical problems. Harrison has a brief section on the Synoptic Problem as well as sections on other critical problems in the New Testament.

2 Hans Windisch, *The Meaning of the Sermon on the Mount*, trans. S. MacLean Gilmour (Philadelphia: Westminster Press, 1951), p. 101.

not that I have come to abolish the law and the prophets; I have come not to abolish them but to fulfil them ["to complete," NEB; "to fill them up to the brim," Williams]" (Matt. 5:17; cf. Luke 16:17). He fulfilled the Law by going beyond it, by bringing its essential teaching to its full development, by giving "a penetrating insight into the true moral principles underlying the enactments of the Mosaic Code" (ICC), and by going behind the Law and expressing the original purpose of the Lawgiver. As Manson says, "The ethical demands of the Law and the Prophets are not cancelled; they have become flesh and dwelt among us in the person and work of our Lord Jesus Christ."[3]

To underscore what He had just said, Jesus stated that "the law will not lose a single dot or comma until its purpose is complete" (Phillips), completed by His life and death, but, in the immediate context, primarily by what He taught. With this statement as a background, Jesus said to His disciples, "Unless your righteousness exceeds that of the scribes and Pharisees, you will never enter the kingdom of heaven" (Matt. 5:20). He then proceeded to compare His teachings with the Law, teachings that filled the Law full to the brim, and went beyond the righteousness of the Pharisees.

2. Comparison of His teachings with the Law.

The six comparisons (Matt. 5:21–48) are all in the horizontal or ethical area, man-to-man or this worldly relations. With the exception of the one regarding divorce, which is sometimes not considered a separate comparison, they follow the same formula: "You have heard . . . But I say to you."

They had heard it said:	Jesus said:
No murder	No anger
No adultery	No adulterous thought
Divorce for "some indecency"	No divorce[4]
No false oaths	No oaths
An eye for an eye	No retaliation
Love neighbor	Love enemy

[3] T. W. Manson, *Ethics and the Gospel* (New York: Scribner's, 1960), p. 65.

[4] Matthew, in two places (5:32; 19:9), includes the exception clause—"except for unchastity"—which is not found in Mark or Luke.

In the first two of these comparisons, Jesus fulfilled the Law and went beyond the righteousness of the Scribes and Pharisees by making sin internal as well as external. In the next three He went beyond the requirements of the Law; in the matter of divorce, He went behind the Law and expressed the purpose of the One who was the giver of the Law (cf. Mark 10:2–12; Matt. 19:3–12). In the last comparison He evidently went beyond the common interpretation of the Law.[5] This one, with its stress on love of enemy, is the climax of the comparisons. In it Jesus swept away "all casuistical distinctions between neighbours and enemies, Jews and Gentiles. The neighbour of the Old Testament is to include the enemy" (ICC).

Furthermore, Jesus placed no limits on any of His basic teachings. They were demands for perfection. This is what Hunter calls "Christ's doctrine of the extra." The same author says, "To return evil for good is the devil's way: to return good for good is man's: to return good for evil is God's."[6] And Jesus challenges His disciples to be like God. "He does not wish them to be moral mediocrities, men of average morality, but to be morally superior, uncommon" (Ex. G).

In what was evidently the conclusion to the section on the comparison of the Law and His teachings, Jesus said, "You, therefore, must be perfect, as your heavenly Father is perfect." From that day until now many of His followers have tried to take away the sharpness of this challenge. Some have argued that the word translated "perfect" (*teleios*) could properly be translated "full-grown," "complete," or "mature." Such a change in translation, however, would not make any real difference; the words that give meaning and depth to the statement are: "as your heavenly Father." These words call for absolute "maturity" or "completeness" and, hence, for perfection.

---

5 The injunction in the Dead Sea Scrolls to hate the enemies of God may reveal an attitude rather common in the days of Jesus, which could provide the background for the statement by Jesus, "You have heard that it was said, 'You shall love your neighbor and hate your enemy'" (Matt. 5:43).

6 Archibald M. Hunter, *A Pattern for Life* (Philadelphia: Westminster Press, 1953), p. 58.

3. Fulfillment of the Law.

When Jesus was asked, "Which is the great commandment in the law?" or "What sort of command is greatest in the law?" (Matt. 22:36; Williams), He replied, "You shall love the Lord your God with all your heart, and with all your soul, and with all your mind" (Matt. 22:37; cf. Deut. 6:5). He then added: "And a second is like it, You shall love your neighbor as yourself" (Matt. 22:39; cf. Lev. 19:18): "like it" because it was also a commandment of love, but possibly, too, like it in importance. There follows the statement: "On these two commandments depend ["hangs," NEB; "is summed up," Weymouth] all the law and the prophets." The truthfulness of the latter statement can be clearly seen in relation to the Ten Commandments. The commandments summarize the basic moral law of the Old Testament. If a man loved God supremely, he would keep the first of the commandments; if he loved his neighbor as himself, he would keep the last ones: he would not kill, commit adultery, steal, bear false witness, or covet. After citing for the rich young ruler the commandments concerning one's relation to his fellowman (Matt. 19:16–19; Mark 10:17–19; Luke 18:18–21), Jesus, according to Matthew's account (Matt. 19:19), quoted to him Leviticus 19:18, implying that love of neighbor belonged with and would fulfill the so-called Second Table of the Law (cf. Rom. 13:8–10; Gal. 5:14; James 2:8). It may be quite significant that Jesus omitted the tenth commandment: "You shall not covet."

Evidently, when Jesus was asked about the chief or great commandment, He was only expected to give one commandment, but He gave two. Why did He give the second? There may have been more than one reason, but no doubt one reason was that either commandment was incomplete without the other. Kline suggests that "the two commandments of Jesus do not distinguish two separate areas of human life but two complementary aspects of human responsibility." He further says, "Our Lord's perspective is one with the duplicate tables of the covenant which comprehend the whole duty of man within the unity of his consecration to his covenant Lord."[7] Furthermore, no one can love God supremely

7 Kline, *Treaty of the Great King*, p. 26.

and not love those God loves. On the other hand, one cannot love
his neighbor with a love that partakes of the divine quality without loving God supremely.

The following should also be noted about the statement of Jesus
concerning the commandments of love: (1) Love for God comes
first—it is basic. Love of neighbor is a derivative, but so closely
related that it is an inevitable derivative. (2) In these two commandments and elsewhere Jesus "demands love with such exclusiveness that all other commandments are included in it."[8] (3)
The commandments, typical of the ethical emphasis of Jesus,
touched the inner life. They were commandments that could not
be enforced. They must be responded to freely and voluntarily.
(4) Religion and ethics are united. Love for God and man, as implied earlier, must support and pervade one another. (5) We know
by what Jesus said elsewhere that "love" and "neighbor" were for
Him as broad as human need. He set no limits for love (*agape*).[9]
When asked, "Who is my neighbor?" Jesus told a story (Luke
10:25–37) that answered a much more important question: "How
can I be a good neighbor?" (6) Jesus demonstrated in His own
life supreme love for God and equal love for His neighbor.

The emphasis of Jesus on love of neighbor was epitomized in
the "Golden Rule" (Matt. 7:12; Luke 6:31), to which is added in
Matthew: "for this is the law and the prophets." The statement
of the Rule by Jesus was positive rather than negative, as it is expressed elsewhere.[10] A. B. Bruce suggests that "the negative con-
fines it to the region of *justice;* the positive takes us into the
region of *generosity* or *grace,* and so embraces both law *and*

---

[8] Ethelbert Stauffer, "Love," *Kittel's Bible Key Words,* I, 45.

[9] The standard work, under some criticism in recent years, on two
of the Greek words translated "love" is Anders Nygren's *Agape and Eros,*
trans. Philip S. Watson, rev. ed. (London: S.P.C.K., 1953). C. S. Lewis' *The
Four Loves* (London: Geoffrey Bles, 1960) deals with the same topic but in a
nontechnical way.

[10] For example, Tobit 4:15 is as follows: "And what you hate do
not do to anyone." The negative form is also found in *The Testament of the
Twelve Patriarchs* (Naph. 1:6, Hebrew text). It reads as follows: "None should
do to his neighbour what he does not like for himself." *Also see* the Letter
of Aristeas (207).

prophets" (Ex. G). Barclay claims that "this saying is the topmost peak of social ethics, and the Everest of all ethical teaching."[11]

4. Conflict with the Pharisees regarding the Law.

In addition to the matter of "Corban," mentioned previously, there were other areas of conflict between Jesus and the Pharisees regarding the Law. The sharpest and most continuous one was regarding the Sabbath (Matt. 12:1–14; Mark 2:23–3:6; Luke 6:1–11; 13:10–17; 14:1–6). The Pharisees were especially critical of His healing on the Sabbath, which was contrary to their interpretation of the Law; the Mishnah somewhat arbitrarily lists thirty-nine main classes of work forbidden on the Sabbath.[12] In His controversy with the Pharisees, Jesus stated at least three principles: (1) "The Son of Man is lord even of the sabbath." (2) It is lawful to do good on the Sabbath. (3) Most important from our perspective: "The sabbath was made for man, not man for the sabbath"; every basic requirement of God is for man's good.

Then there are the woes that Jesus pronounced upon the Scribes and Pharisees (Matt. 23). These woes are related more or less directly to the Law. They are introduced with a warning to the crowds and to His disciples. They were to listen to what the Pharisees said, but not to follow their example. He said that the Pharisees preached, but did not practice, and then spelled this out in three specific ways: (1) They bind heavy burdens on the backs of people but will not so much as use a little finger to move them. (2) They do their deeds to be seen of men. (3) They love the place of honor at feasts.

He then pronounced six woes upon the Scribes and Pharisees, at least three of which are definitely in the ethical area. For example, He said that they tithed the smallest of herbs and then added that they, at the same time, "overlooked the weightier

11 William Barclay, *The Gospel of Matthew,* 2nd ed. (Philadelphia: Westminster Press, 1958), I, 277.
12 See W. O. E. Oesterley's *Tractate Shabbath* (London: Society for Promoting Christian Knowledge, 1927), which introduces and translates this tractate from the Mishnah.

demands ["more vital matters," Williams] of the Law, justice, mercy, and good faith ["trueheartedness," Ex. G]" (NEB). He then added: "These you ought to have done, without neglecting the others." The "weightier demands" or "more vital matters" of the Law had to do primarily with their treatment of their fellowman. Their religion was largely formal, and formalism is "the deadliest poison which can contaminate theological ethics."[13] Faithfulness to formalities is no substitute for the realities of daily living. The Scribes and Pharisees were primarily concerned with conformity to the Law, with its 613 specific precepts. They were externalists. Jesus was concerned with the inner attitude toward the Law. They were interested primarily in conduct; He in character.

The Kingdom of God[14]

We cannot possibly discuss in detail the Kingdom of God; we can only touch on a few things more or less closely related to the ethical teachings of Jesus.

1. Its centrality.

The Kingdom, Realm, Reign, or Rule of God was the central theme of the preaching (Matt. 4:23; Luke 4:43) and ministry of Jesus. The subject of His earliest preaching was, "The kingdom of God is at hand; repent, and believe in the gospel" (Mark 1:15;

[13] Lindsay Dewar, *An Outline of New Testament Ethics* (London: Hodder and Stoughton, 1949), p. 22.

[14] Three of the better recent books on the Kingdom, which represent different approaches and emphases are: George Eldon Ladd, *Jesus and the Kingdom: The Eschatology of Biblical Realism* (New York: Harper, 1964), a more comprehensive study than his earlier *The Gospel of the Kingdom* (Grand Rapids: Eerdmans, 1959); Norman Perrin, *The Kingdom of God in the Teaching of Jesus* (Philadelphia: Westminster Press, 1963), a critical analysis of the position on the Kingdom of many prominent scholars beginning with Schleiermacher; and Rudolf Schnackenburg, *God's Rule and Kingdom* (New York: Herder and Herder, 1963), a study of the Kingdom in the Old Testament and later Judaism, in "The Preaching of Jesus," and in "Early Christian Teaching," including Paul, John, and others. William Barclay, *The Mind of Jesus* (New York: Harper, 1960, 1961) has an excellent chapter on the Kingdom of God, which is largely a study of the sayings of Jesus concerning the Kingdom.

cf. Matt. 4:17). Following His Resurrection, He spoke to His disciples concerning the Kingdom of God (Acts 1:3). It was His continuing theme. He sent His disciples out "to preach the kingdom of God" (Luke 9:2). Marshall sums up the place of the Kingdom as follows: *"All the ethical teaching of Jesus is simply an exposition of the ethics of the Kingdom of God, of the way in which men inevitably behave when they actually come under the rule of God."*[15] In other words, the ethic of Jesus was primarily an eschatological ethic.

If there is such a thing as a *summum bonum*, supreme value, or highest good, in the Christian ethic, it is the Kingdom of God. At least, Jesus said that it was to be sought by His disciples before material wealth or even the necessities of life. Their Heavenly Father knew that they had need of the latter. They were to trust Him and "seek first his kingdom and his righteousness" (Matt. 6:33), and if they did, the necessary things would be added. Two of the Kingdom parables (and most of His parables related to the Kingdom), the treasure hid in a field and the pearl of great value (Matt. 13:44–46), emphasized the centrality and supremacy of the Kingdom for the child of God. The Model Prayer implies that before one prays for his daily bread, he should pray:

Thy kingdom come,
Thy will be done,
On earth as it is in heaven [Matt. 6:10].

2. Its nature.

It is Marshall who says that Jesus "thought and spoke of the Kingdom of God in so many different ways that to harmonise them and present them systematically is out of the question."[16] In spite of this evident difficulty many have sought to systematize the teachings of Jesus regarding the Kingdom. Bultmann, and others, consider the Kingdom *"supernatural, super-historical"*[17]

---

15 L. H. Marshall, *The Challenge of New Testament Ethics* (London: Macmillan, 1946), p. 31.

16 *Ibid.*, p. 25.

17 Rudolf Bultmann, *Jesus and the Word,* trans. Louise Smith and Erminie Lantero (New York: Scribner's, 1958), p. 35.

and *"entirely future,"* although Bultmann does say that it *"wholly determines the present* . . . because it now compels man to decision."[18] There are others, such as Dodd[19] with his concept of *realized eschatology,* who think of the Kingdom as largely, if not exclusively, a present reality.[20]

Still others such as Kümmel and Fuller[21] suggest that the Kingdom is both a present reality and a future hope, a position "firmly established by the modern discussion" of the Kingdom.[22] While there is tension between the "already" and "not yet" concepts of the Kingdom, still, as Alan Richardson suggests, the apparent dilemma between the present and futuristic concepts of the Kingdom is unreal. He suggests that we shall see this "if we recall that the Kingdom of God means essentially God's reign, or, even less abstractedly, God's reigning."[23] It will also help if we remember that it is *God's* Kingdom: He gives it (Luke 12:32), although men must accept and even seek and work for that which is given. There is a sense in which the Kingdom or the Realm of God has been present all the time. There is also a deep sense in which it came in a unique and dramatic way in the life, death, and resurrection of Christ; and there is also a sense in which it will be consummated in the future.

Whatever one's viewpoint concerning the basic nature of the Kingdom, in some way the will and righteousness of God are related to it. In the Model Prayer, "Thy kingdom come" is closely

18 *Ibid.,* p. 44.

19 C. H. Dodd, *The Parables of the Kingdom,* rev. ed. (New York: Scribner's, 1961).

20 For a compact examination of various theories concerning the Kingdom, beginning with Schweitzer's view, see Amos N. Wilder, *Eschatology and Ethics in the Teaching of Jesus,* rev. ed. (New York: Harper, 1950), pp. 37–52.

21 Werner Georg Kümmel, *Promise and Fulfilment: The Eschatological Message of Jesus,* trans. Dorothea M. Barton, rev. ed. (Chicago: Alec R. Allenson, 1957) and Reginald Horace Fuller, *The Mission and Achievement of Jesus,* 2nd ed. (Chicago: Alec R. Allenson, 1956). The first chapter of Kümmel is "The Imminent Future of the Kingdom of God," while the third chapter is entitled "The Presence of the Kingdom of God." Fuller, in chapters II and III, gives a careful critique of Dodd and Bultmann.

22 Perrin, p. 185.

23 Alan Richardson, "Kingdom of God," *A Theological Word Book of the Bible,* ed. Alan Richardson, p. 121.

related to, if not equated with, "Thy will be done, On earth as it is in heaven." His Kingdom comes, His Realm, Reign, or Rule is extended as His will is done, and since He is the sovereign God of the universe, His will is as broad as life. Similarly, righteousness is related to the Kingdom in that wonderful challenge in Matthew 6:33: "Seek first his kingdom and his righteousness, and all these things shall be given you as well." As God's righteous rule is increasingly accepted in our hearts and lives and in our world, His Kingdom is coming.

The preceding means that there is significant ethical content in the teachings of Jesus concerning the Kingdom. Craig says that one of the new elements in the teachings of Jesus concerning the Kingdom was the fact that "he took the kingdom hope of his people with a new seriousness in his ethical appeal to his contemporaries."[24] Marshall concludes that the moral teaching of Jesus "sets forth the way of the Kingdom, the way in which God's Will may be done on earth as it is done in heaven."[25] While this statement may make the Kingdom excessively "this worldly," there can be no doubt that the ethical teachings of Jesus, to a large degree, revolve around and stem from His conception of the Kingdom. His ethic is the absolute ethic of the Kingdom. It represents the perfect or radical will of God, which will be done when the Kingdom comes in its fulness, but which also represents His will for men of the Kingdom in the present world order.

3. Entrance into the Kingdom.

It has been suggested that the Kingdom of God is a gift. However, God's gifts have to be accepted and sometimes fought for. Seldom, if ever, are they unconditional. They really represent a covenant. God promises the gift or the blessing, but man must meet God's conditions. The gift of the Promised Land to the children of Israel is a good example. It was God's gift to them, but they still had to conquer the area. So it has been with God's gifts to His children through the centuries. At least, God will not and cannot give His good gifts to unwilling minds and hearts. There

[24] Clarence Tucker Craig, "The Teaching of Jesus," *The Interpreter's Bible*, VII, 148.
[25] Marshall, p. 14.

must be a response to His offer. This is just as true of His King-dom as it is of any of His other gifts.

It should also be remembered that the Kingdom of God is basically spiritual rather than physical. This means that the conditions for entrance into it are spiritual; they relate primarily to the individual's relation to God. These conditions, however, contain a considerable ethical overtone and deep ethical significance.

There are several conditions for entrance into the Kingdom that Jesus plainly stated. (1) Repentance (Mark 1:15; Matt. 4:17): "Repentance implies decisive change, the reorientation of man and the reversal of his values, the surrender by him of his own royalty and his own righteousness."[26] (2) Childlikeness: "Whoever does not receive the kingdom of God like a child shall not enter it" (Mark 10:15; Luke 18:17; cf. Matt. 18:3). What did Jesus mean when He said "like a child"? Possibly He simply meant that one must accept the Kingdom as a child receives a gift. He has little to give in exchange except his love and devotion. One of the Beatitudes expresses something of this idea:

How blest are those who know that they are poor;
    the kingdom of heaven is theirs [Matt. 5:3, NEB].

(3) Obedience: "Not every one who says to me, 'Lord, Lord,' shall enter the kingdom of heaven, but he who does the will of my Father who is in heaven" (Matt. 7:21). (4) Righteousness: "Unless your righteousness exceeds that of the scribes and Pharisees, you will never enter the kingdom of heaven" (Matt. 5:20).

(5) There is at least one other major condition for entrance into the Kingdom of God. It is single-minded devotion to the Kingdom and the things of God. This was the point where the rich young ruler failed. On the basis of the young man's failure Jesus made a statement that was quite perplexing to His disciples. "How hard it is for those who have riches to enter the kingdom of God!" (Luke 18:24; Matt. 19:23; Mark 10:23). One must be willing to give up anything that stands between himself and supreme devotion to the Kingdom of God. This emphasis on

[26] H. Roux, "Kingdom," *A Companion to the Bible,* ed. J.-J. Von Allmen, p. 219.

single-minded devotion is the background for the hyperbolic statement by Jesus to cut off, if necessary, a hand or a foot, or to pluck out an eye. He said, "It is better for you to enter the kingdom of God with one eye than with two eyes to be thrown into hell" (Mark 9:47; Matt. 18:9). The Kingdom is worth any sacrifice; it is life's supreme value.

4. Greatness in the Kingdom.

The subject of greatness and the question as to which of them was greatest were evidently frequent topics of conversation and even dispute among the disciples. On one occasion after they had argued "which of them was the greatest" (Luke 9:46) they asked Jesus the question, "Who is the greatest in the kingdom of heaven?" (Matt. 18:1). He called a child and putting him in the midst told them that unless they turned and became like children they would never (a double negative) even enter the Kingdom of Heaven. He then said to them, "Whoever humbles himself like this child, he is the greatest in the kingdom of heaven" (Matt. 18:4). Greatness involves humility. The truly great are unassuming. However, as A. B. Bruce says, the humbling of oneself is "the most difficult thing in the world for saint as for sinner." Bruce further says, "The really humble man is as great in the moral world as he is 'rare'" (Ex. G).

On one occasion John and James (Mark 10:35), evidently with their mother (Matt. 20:20), requested the chief seats in Christ's Kingdom. The other ten Apostles were indignant. Jesus called them all to Him and reminded them that in the world those who were great or were rulers lorded it over the people. But in His Kingdom it was to be different. He said, "It shall not be so among you; but whoever would be great among you must be your servant; and whoever would be first among you must be slave of all" (Mark 10:43–44; Matt. 20:26–27). He then gave Himself as an example: "For the Son of man also came not to be served but to serve, and to give his life as a ransom for many" (Mark 10:45; Matt. 20:28).

The Way of the Disciple

Some qualities that should characterize the follower of Christ, such as love and righteousness, have been discussed to some degree previously. In this section, we shall suggest a few additional qualities that should characterize all disciples and not just an elite few. We shall see that all that Jesus expected His disciples to be He had been before them. In other words, here again there is present the kinship motive or appeal.

1. The way of humility.

This quality or character trait, mentioned in the last section, should be spelled out more fully. While Marshall goes too far when he says that "humility might fairly be regarded as the motif of all the teaching of Jesus,"[27] it is an important item in His teachings. On at least three distinct occasions Jesus enunciated the paradoxical principle that "whoever exalts himself will be humbled, and whoever humbles himself will be exalted" (Matt. 23:12; Luke 14:11; 18:14).

The background varies for each of the three statements of the basic principle. The background in Matthew is provided by the Pharisees who did "all their deeds to be seen by men," and who loved "the place of honor at feasts and the best seats in the synagogues, and salutations in the market places, and being called rabbi by men." It is interesting that there is inserted in Matthew just before the statement of the principle in verse 12 the following: "He who is greatest among you shall be your servant." There is a close connection between humility and the spirit of service. The first statement of the principle in Luke (14:11) comes at the conclusion of a parable about seats of honor at a marriage feast. The familiar story or parable of the Pharisee and the publican or tax-collector at prayer in the temple provides the background for the other statement of the principle that exaltation comes through humility (Luke 18:14).

It may be necessary or wise to say that one does not really humble himself if he is conscious of doing so and goes about it delib-

[27] Marshall, p. 92.

erately. Notice also that Jesus does not say, "Humble yourself *that* you may be exalted." There must be real humility, which involves forgetfulness of self, for there to be a resultant exaltation. The source of true humility is a consciousness of the presence and majesty of God. Such a consciousness will cause one, like the tax-collector, to "beat his breast" and say, "God, be merciful to me a sinner!" It will also inspire one to give himself in unselfish devotion to the needs of his fellowman.

2. *The way of forgiveness.*

One of the petitions in the Model Prayer is

And forgive us our debts,
   as we also have forgiven our debtors [Matt. 6:12].

Augustine called this "the terrible petition," terrible because of the condition attached—"as we." This is the only petition in the prayer that is commented on. It is plainly said that God's forgiveness is conditioned by our forgiveness of others (Matt. 6:14–15). Whether the comment was by Jesus, by Matthew, or by someone else does not affect its validity. As T. H. Robinson says, "God forgives only the forgiving." He further concludes that "this is not an arbitrary sanction, but a fundamental law which springs from the very nature of personal relations" (MC).

The "as" in the petition, which is missing in Luke's record of the prayer (Luke 11:4), does not carry the idea of a business deal or bargain. God has to forgive much more than we shall ever have to forgive. Our situation would be tragic if He was not unusually generous in His forgiveness of us. The petition, with the comment, simply teaches that no man can be right with God and wrong with his fellowman.

Jesus taught this same truth on another occasion. He said, "Whenever you stand praying, forgive, if you have anything against any one; so that your Father also who is in heaven may forgive you your trespasses" (Mark 11:25). He also taught that forgiveness of others was to be unlimited: until "seventy times seven" (Matt. 18:22; cf. Luke 17:3–4).

The statement concerning unlimited forgiveness is followed in

Matthew with a parable or story of two servants: one was for-given a huge debt of possibly a million dollars by his king and in turn refused to forgive a small debt of approximately twenty dol-lars by a fellow servant. "And in anger his lord delivered him to the jailers, till he should pay all his debt" (Matt. 18:34). Jesus then drew the following lesson: "So also my heavenly Father will do to every one of you, if you do not forgive your brother from your heart" (Matt. 18:35). Are we, in relation to our heavenly Father, the big debtor; and is our fellowman, in relation to us, the little debtor? The answer seems obvious, and we should not forget that our forgiveness must be real; it must be "from the heart."

It is sometimes argued that one cannot be forgiven unless he repents. It is true that the act of forgiveness is incomplete with-out repentance followed by forgiveness and restoration. But, as already suggested, one can have the willingness to forgive or the spirit of forgiveness regardless of the attitude of others. After all, forgiveness is more an attitude than an act; at least the attitude precedes the act. It may be, as Dewar suggests, that two words are needed: forgiveness, spelled "forgivenness," and "forgivingness." At least a clear distinction needs to "be drawn between the will-ingness to forgive and the *fait accompli* which cannot come to pass without repentance on the part of the offender."[28]

3. The way of service.

Jesus sets forth the place of service most pointedly in the par-able of the last judgment, which closes the major eschatological discourse in Matthew (25:31–46). Buttrick suggests that "there is no finer writing in the Gospel, and no finer truth" (IB). The truth in the parable or story has major ethical significance.

Notice the following about the parable: (1) The basis for the separation and the subsequent blessing or curse was not what they believed, their faithfulness to religious formalities, or their stand-ing in the community—but their service to their fellowman. (2) Both those on the right and the left were unconscious of the service they had rendered or failed to render. "They had just done the thing natural to them . . . their acts had value . . . because

28 Dewar, p. 65.

they were illustrations of character" (MC). A self-consciousness in goodness is a sign of immaturity. (3) The service rendered was in the area of the everyday needs of the common people: feeding the hungry, giving drink to the thirsty, taking in the stranger, clothing the naked, and visiting those in prison. It was self-forgetful rather than spectacular service. (4) Christ identified Himself with those in need: "in as much as" (vv. 40, 45, KJV). Buttrick says, " 'Inasmuch' is almost the burning heart of the parable" (IB). Notice that Jesus identified Himself with "one of the least of these."

The service approved by Him is illustrated in the cup of water given to a disciple (Mark 9:41), including one of the little ones who was a disciple (Matt. 10:42). Such unselfish service is an evidence of love for Christ and of likeness to Him.

4. The way of fruit-bearing.

An emphasis on the fruitful life is particularly prominent in the Gospel of John and especially in the great chapter on the vine and the branches. There is some material, however, in the Synoptics. For example, Jesus said in the Sermon on the Mount that false prophets could be known by their fruit (Matt. 7:16, 20). He also asked a question with an obvious answer: "Are grapes gathered from thorns, or figs from thistles?" (Matt. 7:16; cf. Luke 6:44 for some variation). A grapevine bears grapes and a fig bush or tree bears figs. It is just as natural and inevitable that a "sound tree" will bear "good fruit" and a "bad tree" will bear "evil fruit." Windisch suggests that "the true disciple of Jesus is a good tree that brings forth good fruit." He also says, "By good fruit is meant good works, proofs of genuine humaneness and brotherliness, and unalloyed devotion to God."[29]

It is the good man out of the good treasure of his heart who produces good, "and the evil man out of his evil treasure produces evil" (Luke 6:45). The good treasure within is the product of the indwelling Christ. The direction or the flow of the Christian life is from within outward. The child of God is to bear fruit, but if his fruit-bearing is to be approved by God it must not be deliberate and self-conscious; it must be the spontaneous

[29] Windisch, p. 71.

response of an inner relationship. Let us never forget, however, that the test of the tree or the man is the quality of fruit.

5. The way of the cross.

The cross, with all that it symbolizes, permeates and gives meaning and unity to all the ethical teachings of Jesus. One writer suggests that love and self-denial are the two great characteristics of the Christian life as taught by Jesus.[30] These, as well as other basic teachings of His, speak the language of the cross. For example, *agape*, the distinctive New Testament word for love, gives itself unselfishly to the object loved (John 3:16; 15:13; Eph. 5:25).

At Caesarea Philippi, which has been called the watershed of the gospels, Jesus definitely ties together self-denial and the cross. After Peter's great confession for himself and the others, Jesus began to reveal more fully to them that he "must go to Jerusalem and suffer many things from the elders and chief priests and scribes,[31] and be killed, and on the third day be raised" (Matt. 16:21; Mark 8:31; Luke 9:22). It was then that Jesus said, "If any man would come after me, let him deny himself and take up his cross and follow me ["keep on following me," Williams]" (Matt. 16:24; Mark 8:34; Luke 9:23). Here the denial of self and the taking up of a cross are not two separate things. They are two ways of expressing the same idea. They represent, as Wilder suggests, "the supreme expression" of the appeal of Jesus to His generation.[32]

Bonhoeffer says, "When Christ calls a man, He bids him come and die. . . . In fact every command of Jesus is a call to die."[33] He further correctly suggests that the cross is laid on every Christian. We follow Christ only as we take up a cross.

But what does it mean to "take up a cross"? The relating of the cross to self-denial by Jesus helps us to understand. It means that the self, with selfish motives and purposes, will no longer be the

---

30 William Lillie, *Studies in New Testament Ethics* (Edinburgh and London: Oliver and Boyd, 1961), p. 161.

31 The three groups represented in the Sanhedrin.

32 Wilder, p. 169.

33 Dietrich Bonhoeffer, *The Cost of Discipleship*, trans. R. H. Fuller, rev. ed. (New York: Macmillan, 1959), p. 79.

center around which one builds his life. To use Phillips' translation of Matthew 16:24, "One must give up all right to himself." The will and purposes of God must become dominant in his life. This will mean a radical reorientation of life. Love will be directed to God and neighbor rather than to one's self. We can understand more clearly the meaning of the cross if we will remember that it is something on which a person is crucified. Paul expressed this idea of crucifixion in several ways and places (Rom. 6:6, 8; Gal. 5:24; 6:14), but possibly best of all when he said, "I have been crucified with Christ; it is no longer I who live, but Christ who lives in me" (Gal. 2:20). This, basically, is what it means to deny self and take up a cross: it means to let Christ live in us and express Himself through us.

A marvelous and abiding truth is that crucifixion and resurrection are linked together. Jesus in the same breath that He mentioned His death mentioned also His resurrection. There is no truth more fundamental in His teachings than the statement that follows His invitation for the disciples to take up their cross and follow Him. The statement is, "For whoever would save his life will lose it; and whoever loses his life for my sake and the gospel's will save it" (Mark 8:35; Matt. 16:25; Luke 9:24; cf. Matt. 10:39 and John 12:25), which has been termed a "great ethical principle" (Ex.G). This is not an appeal to a selfish motive; it is a simple statement of fact. There must be a real crucifixion for there to be a real resurrection. In turn, there is no real crucifixion unless it is voluntary and redemptive in purpose.

6. The way of the Lord.

The disciple of the Lord should walk in the way of the Lord. Just as Jesus came into the world to reveal the Father, His disciple is sent into the world to reveal Him. He was God Incarnate; the disciple is to be Christ incarnate.

The initial invitation of Jesus to Simon and Andrew was, "Follow me" (Mark 1:17; Matt. 4:19), which was specifically repeated to Levi or Matthew (Mark 2:14; Matt. 9:9). This was also His continuing invitation. To the rich young ruler He said, "Sell what you have, and give to the poor . . . and come, follow me" (Mark 10:21; Matt. 19:21). This is also the initial and continuing invitation of Jesus to His disciples in the contemporary period.

What did and does it mean to follow Jesus? For the chosen few that Jesus gathered around Him, it meant the abandonment of everything. Peter, on one occasion, said to Him: "Lo, we have left everything and followed you" (Mark 10:28; Matt. 19:27; Luke 18:28). That may not have been literally true, but they had left their businesses and, evidently for most of the time, their families. At least a disciple must be willing to give up anything that might interfere with his following his Lord. This includes not only what he has (Luke 14:33), but also his loved ones and even his own life (Luke 14:26). Plummer asks the pointed question: "Would any merely human teacher venture to make such claims" (ICC)? Bultmann is correct when he says that Jesus "conceived radically the idea of obedience."[34] He is also correct when he suggests that "radical obedience exists only when a man inwardly assents to what is required of him."[35]

As we seek to follow Jesus, His life and teachings give us the sense of direction we need. Let us never forget that the object of His teaching "is to give direction rather than directions, to point to the goal of all good living rather than to legislate for particular cases."[36] His teachings and His life provide a compass, not a road map.

As we follow Him, as we walk in His way, we can be assured that the way is not an uncharted course. He has traveled that way before us. It may sound paradoxical, but He has not only traveled that way; He walks with His disciples on the way now. His word is: "Go . . . and lo, I am with you always" (Matt. 28:19-20). He not only provides a pattern of life for us to follow, He gives us the desire, the dynamism, and the strength to walk in that way, although our walk is admittedly imperfect. Manson has expressed the relation of Christ to the disciple in the following statement: "The living Christ still has two hands, one to point the way, and the other held out to help us along."[37]

---

34 Bultmann, p. 58.
35 *Ibid.*, p. 61.
36 Manson, *The Sayings of Jesus*, p. 37.
37 Manson, *Ethics and the Gospel*, p. 68.

General Characteristics

How can the ethical teachings of Jesus, as revealed in the synoptics, be summarized? What are some of the general characteristics? We shall discuss briefly a few of those characteristics, some of which have been referred to formerly.

1. A disciples' ethic.

Hunter suggests that the ethic of Jesus "is essentially a disciples' ethic."[38] Marshall similarly says: "The ethical ideal of Jesus is an ideal only for the man who is in touch with . . . God."[39] Wilder suggests that there is a close relation between "the general ethical principles of Jesus, as represented for instance in the Sermon on the Mount" and what he calls "the drastic summons to personal discipleship."[40] Discipleship, in turn, "means decision, Jesus' decision as regards certain individuals, but then it means no less their own decision to follow him."[41] Jesus called for radical commitment or obedience. Men like Tolstoy who have seen in the ethical teachings of Jesus a blueprint for society have overlooked the fact that His ethic is basically a disciples' ethic.

Those who are committed to follow Jesus, however, are not to withdraw from the world and live in isolation. There is a sense in which they are liberated from the world, but, in turn, they are sent back into the world to pervade, to preserve, to reveal, to heal (Matt. 5:13–16). This means, among other things, that the teachings of Jesus which are directed primarily to His disciples are to be carried by them into the world, and to be applied by them to the structures of society.

It possibly should be repeated that His teachings were and are for *all* who claim to be disciples. They are not meant for any restricted group. The ethical precepts of Jesus apply to everyone who has responded to His invitation, "Follow me." Since those precepts represent the original purpose of God, the Creator, and

38 Hunter, p. 109.
39 Marshall, p. 200.
40 Wilder, p. 167.
41 Günther Bornkamm, *Jesus of Nazareth*, trans. Irene and Fraser McLuskey with James M. Robinson (New York: Harper, 1960), p. 146.

the ultimate ideal of God, the Sovereign Ruler of the universe, they also are the norms or standards for all men and for the world in every age.

2. Religious.

Religion and ethics are inseparable in both the Old Testament and the New Testament. Jesus, for example, fused religion and ethics "into one indissoluble whole—the religion is inconceivable without the ethics, and the ethics is unintelligible and impracticable without the religion."[42] Marshall expresses the same general idea in a slightly different way, as follows: "For Him, ethics is part and parcel of religion, and completely inseparable from it, and morality springs out of a new relation to God."[43] This new relation is the most significant and distinctive element in the ethic of Jesus. He does not say, "Be good that you may please God." Rather, He says, "Get into right relation with God and He will help you to be good." And to be good was to be like God. Through his fellowship with God, the disciple also has a new sense of direction, accompanied with an inner urge and dynamic to move in that direction. The movement is to God and then from God, but in fellowship with Him, into the world to make Him and His will a living reality among men.

The close relation of "religion," using the term in its restricted sense, and ethics is seen in the order, in general, of *kerygma* and *didache* in the New Testament. Logically, *kerygma*, the proclamation of what God has done for man, comes first, followed by *didache*, the teaching of what God expects of man. This is the order that one would expect in a religiously oriented ethic. The order, however, is not always followed. At times the two are interspersed or mixed. The Christian ethic has been called a "kerygmatic" ethic.[44]

42 Marshall, p. 15.
43 *Ibid.*, p. 13.
44 See A. N. Wilder, "Kerygma, Eschatology, and Social Ethics," *The Background of the New Testament and Its Eschatology*, eds. W. D. Davies and D. Daube (Cambridge: University Press, 1954). See particularly pp. 517–22 where Wilder analyses and evaluates "a kerygmatic social ethic." For a compact discriminating analysis of C. H. Dodd's distinction between and use of *kerygma* and *didache*, see Floyd V. Filson, *Three Crucial Decades: Studies in the Book of Acts* (Richmond: John Knox Press, 1963), pp. 30–35.

3. Internal.

For Jesus, the good life, as well as the evil life, flowed outward from within. This was one of the chief points of His controversy with the Pharisees. They criticized His disciples for eating "with hands defiled" or unwashed. It was from this kind of a background that Jesus called the people to Him and said, "There is nothing outside of a man which by going into him can defile him; but the things which come out of a man are what defile him" (Mark 7:15). In answer to a question by Peter, He further said: "Do you not see that whatever goes into the mouth passes into the stomach, and so passes on? But what comes out of the mouth proceeds from the heart, and this defiles a man" (Matt. 15:17–18).[45] Again Jesus said: "For out of the heart come evil thoughts, murder, adultery, fornication, theft, false witness, slander. These are what defile a man; but to eat with unwashed hands does not defile a man" (Matt. 15:19–20).

Dewar goes too far when he says that Jesus here was "concerned with *thoughts* rather than deeds."[46] He was primarily concerned "with *thoughts,*" but He had some concern with outer deeds, else why would He have mentioned murder, adultery, and the others? He was simply saying that evil deeds stem from an evil heart. In other words, sin may have many expressions as branches, but only one root, an evil or corrupt heart, and "heart" for the Jew included the entire inner life—"intelligence" as well as "emotions." What we generally consider the motive was, for Jesus, essentially the act itself; one could commit murder or adultery within the heart. The insight of Jesus into the nature of sin is the reason why He was more concerned about the cleansing of the inside than the outside of the cup (Matt. 23:25–26). Likewise, His concern about the inner explains the fact that He condemned more sharply sins of the spirit such as covetousness and self-righteous-

---

[45] There is a parenthetical sentence in Mark (7:18–20) between the above question by Jesus and his statement that followed. It is "(Thus he declared all foods clean.)" It is interesting to conjecture that this statement may have been inserted as a result of Peter's experience on the housetop (Acts 10).

[46] Dewar, p. 73.

ness than the sins of the flesh. The latter may be more disgusting but the former are more dangerous and hurtful.

Similarly, the good life flowed from within. For Jesus, it stems from a new relation with God, a relation that touches the deepest recesses of the human spirit. It gets deep enough to affect ambitions, motives, and purposes. It provides within a well of living water or a spring that never fails. Ours is an "internalized morality." Jesus demands of us "a morality in the blood and bone," a morality that "calls for truth in the inward parts."[47] Scott similarly says, "Even the best conduct is worthless when it is . . . not the revelation of a man's inner self."[48]

4. Emphasis on principles.

Most writers on the ethics of Jesus stress that His emphasis was on principles rather than laws or rules. Principles are more general and inclusive than laws and are more concerned with inner spirit or attitude. This distinction between principles and laws or rules may be more apparent than real. This is particularly true if we include under the term "law" not only legal requirements, but also the natural law as the basic law of God. Life's basic laws represent the purposes of God. The principles of Jesus are in harmony with and really an expression of those basic laws. When this is understood, one can see that it makes little difference whether the teachings of Jesus are considered principles or laws.

The basic laws, which are an expression of God as Creator and Sovereign, are to be obeyed. The penalty for their violation is not external to the laws but inherent in them. This means, among other things, that the penalty, sooner or later, is inevitable. It is written into the nature of things.[49] This means that it is good common sense to seek to discover what those laws are and then to conform to them. In the deepest and truest sense God's laws are best for us; they are for our good. And let us not forget that the

[47] Hunter, p. 44.

[48] Ernest F. Scott, *The Ethical Teaching of Jesus* (New York: Macmillan, 1924), p. 19.

[49] This does not mean that God's punishment is always restricted to the operation of basic laws. There may be times when God's wrath is expressed in ways that are not restricted to the evil consequences that result from the violation of some law.

principles of Jesus are an expression of the laws of God. This means that they are to be taken seriously; they are to be obeyed. They are not merely "beautiful generalities" that are to be admired, they are also to be applied to life, and once applied we shall find that they likewise are for our good and God's glory.

Christians are frequently confused and sometimes thoroughly frustrated when they seek to apply some of the principles of Jesus. One reason for the frustration is the tendency, on the part of many, to identify the illustrations of Jesus with the principles and to believe that the illustrations are to be applied literally. A good example of the problem or problems is the interpretation of what Jesus said concerning non-retaliation, non-vindictiveness, or non-resentment (Matt. 5:38–42). Following the statement of the general principle, Jesus gave four illustrations or applications of the principle: the other cheek, the "cloak as well," the extra mile, and the non-refusal of the borrower. One can be helped in properly interpreting this and similar teachings by understanding a distinction that is sometimes made between *mandata* and *exempla*. The former "are moral imperatives stating deep broad principles"; the latter "are illustrations of these principles in action."[50] The latter should never be confused with the former and should not be taken literally. After all, Jesus did not turn the other cheek but He did demonstrate to the fullest the non-vindictive or non-resentful spirit.

5. Perfectionistic.

A. D. Lindsay's book,[51] which is primarily a study of Matthew 5:43–48, has a chapter entitled "The Gospel of Perfection." The perfectionistic emphasis in the teachings of Jesus, however, is not limited to this one passage. It pervades everything He taught. For example, Jesus makes love limitless in its application. So it is with forgiveness and every other basic teaching of His. Knox concludes that He asks for "an absolute perfection," that He

---

[50] Hunter, p. 20; cf. Marshall, p. 102, and C. A. Anderson Scott, *New Testament Ethics* (New York: Macmillan, 1930), p. 11f.

[51] A. D. Lindsay, *The Moral Teaching of Jesus* (London: Hodder and Stoughton, 1937).

seems "to lay on us an impossible obligation."[52] Knox further says, "Jesus never dilutes the righteous demands of God or adjusts them to our moral capacities. On the contrary, he presses every moral requirement to its extreme limit."[53]

The ethic of Jesus has been labelled an "impossible ethic," or to use a frequently quoted term of Reinhold Niebuhr, the ideals of Jesus are "impossible possibilities."[54] They are constantly held out before us as possibilities, but we can never fully attain to them. Even the Apostle Paul said, "I have not yet reached perfection, but I press on, hoping to take hold of that for which Christ once took hold of me" (Phil. 3:12, NEB).

The impossibility of living up to the high demands of Christ creates some real problems for the conscientious child of God. John Knox in a particular way struggles with these problems. One problem which he considers "a perplexing logical problem" is stated as follows: "How can we be really obligated to do what we cannot do?" The other, a "poignant personal existential problem," is: "How can I actually live in so impossible a position?"[55] Paul's "I press on" is one man's response, if not a logical answer to the first of these questions. It is only those who are continually challenged by the high calling of God who can be salt and light in the world. And after all, there is no movement toward the ideals of perfection unless one feels an obligation to measure up to them.

Knox himself gives what might be considered the ultimate answer to the "existential problem." He says that peace comes to us as children of God "not in the awareness of being worthy, but in the assurance of being accepted in spite of our unworthiness, not in the consciousness of being good enough to be loved, but in the knowledge that another is good enough to love us."[56] In other words, we can get release from the tension created by Christ's demands for perfection through the love and forgiveness of God.

[52] John Knox, *The Ethic of Jesus in the Teaching of the Church* (New York and Nashville: Abingdon Press, 1961), p. 18.

[53] *Ibid.*, p. 22.

[54] Reinhold Niebuhr, *An Interpretation of Christian Ethics* (New York: Harper, 1935), p. 113.

[55] Knox, p. 28.

[56] *Ibid.*, p. 54.

Our release, as is true of our salvation, is by grace and not by works.

There seems at times to be an almost endless round of tension and release from tension for the conscientious Christian. When he attempts to live up to the perfectionistic demands of his faith, he becomes deeply conscious that he falls far short. He asks God to forgive him. God graciously forgives and restores to fellowship. In the forgiveness and restoration there comes to the Christian new insights into the nature, character, and will of God. The child of God, in turn, seeks to live up to the new insights. As he falls short he asks God to forgive. God does forgive and in the process the Christian again sees more clearly the purposes of God in his life and in the life of the world. The process then starts all over. This has been the experience of many mature Christians.

The preceding may be, in one sense, an endless round, but it is not for the sincerely seeking Christian a meaningless round. It represents for the latter a movement toward God's ideal for him and his world. And it is possible that God judges His child more by the direction of his life than by his present attainment. We also should remember that there is no progress toward the purposes of God for us without some tension. On the other hand, there is a wonderful paradox in the Christian life: in the midst of the tension between the real and the ideal, the "is" and the "ought," the imperfect part and the perfect whole, the child of God can have as a backdrop for his life the peace "which passes all understanding"—a peace that comes from a deep sense of the presence of the sovereign God, who is the Father of our Lord Jesus Christ and our Heavenly Father.

6. Relevant.

Is such a perfectionistic ethic relevant for us today? Did Jesus then expect those to whom He spoke, and does He now expect His contemporary followers, to practice what He preached and taught? Or, were His teachings, as Schweitzer and others have claimed, only for the brief period between the Resurrection and the Parousia? Or, were they for the Kingdom Age, which would come after a brief interim? In other words, was the ethic of Jesus an interim ethic?[57] The closing words of the Sermon on the Mount (Matt. 7:24–27) plainly reveal that Jesus expected His teachings to be applied to life. The one who not only hears but does what He had taught was likened to the wise man who had built his house on the rock. In contrast, the foolish man was one who had heard His teachings but did not do them. His house was built upon the sand and would not be able to withstand the storms of life. The ethic of Jesus is not restricted to any particular "interim" of life unless it be from the time He walked among men until the Kingdom is consummated when He comes again.

When we suggest that His teachings are relevant for His followers we do not mean that all of His teachings, particularly His illustrations, as suggested earlier, are to be taken literally. Neither do we mean that His followers can live in complete harmony with those teachings: "Their rigorous radicalism is beyond most men's reach."[58] The only kind of ideals that will be abidingly relevant, however, will be ideals of perfection. If we could attain fully any ideal of Jesus within a day, a week, a month, a year, or even years, it no longer would be challenging or relevant for us. Certainly our inability to measure up creates tension within us, but there is no hope for progress without such tension. This tension is inherent in our faith and is the secret to any creative, constructive contribution we make to the cause of Christ. Walther Eichrodt says that "the whole life of the believer is lived under constant tension: the tension between the Now and the Hereafter, between the part and the perfect whole, between defeat and triumph."[59]

There is another sense in which the teachings of Jesus are abidingly relevant. As implied earlier, they stand in judgment over 'our imperfect approximation of them. Dewar suggests that "the Christian ethic is for every age, because it stands above every age,"[60] and it could not be for every age if it did not stand above and beyond every age. Hunter somewhat similarly says that Jesus'

---

57 See Marshall (pp. 191–96) for a good brief analysis of "The 'Interimsethik' Idea."

58 Windisch, p. 97.

59 Alan Richardson and W. Schweitzer, eds., *Biblical Authority for Today* (London: SCM Press, 1951), p. 273.

60 Dewar, p. 60.

"design for Life is the only one which will last,"[61] and one reason it will last is because it will never be fully attained. Marshall strikingly says, "There is nothing that is purely local or transient in the ethical teaching of Jesus. It transcends all the limits of space and time. It is adaptable to all nations, to all races, to all types of civilization, to all conditions. It can never be out of date until man himself is out of date."[62] At least as we seek to face up to the teachings of Jesus our faces will be set in the right direction of additional light and insight. As we do our best to follow Him we can have the assurance of His presence and of the strength and guidance of the Holy Spirit.

7. *Exemplified.*

"The most distinctive element in the Christian ethic is Jesus himself";[63] and "it is from him that it derives its content, its form, and its authority."[64]

If one had the space or time to review all of the teachings of Jesus, he would not find a basic truth that He did not exemplify in His life. He taught his disciples to seek first the Kingdom, the Realm, the Reign, the Will of God; His prayer in the Garden was, "not my will but thine be done" and His frequent statement was, "I have come down from heaven, not to do my own will, but the will of him who sent me" (John 6:38). His disciples were to walk in the way of humility; "he humbled himself and became obedient unto death" (Phil. 2:8). They were to have the forgiving spirit; He prayed for those who crucified Him, "Father forgive them; for they know not what they do" (Luke 23:34). They were to walk in the way of service; He was among them as one who served (Luke 22:27). They were not to be vindictive in their spirit: "When he was reviled, he did not revile in return" (I Peter 2:23). They were to deny self and take up a cross; He walked that way before them. They were challenged to be perfect; He was

61 Hunter, p. 92.
62 Marshall, p. 191.
63 Georgia Harkness, *The Sources of Western Morality* (New York: Scribner's, 1954), p. 228. This is the last of eight distinctive elements in the teachings of Jesus suggested by the author. For a similar list see E. F. Scott, *The Ethical Teaching of Jesus*, pp. 17–21.
64 Manson, *Ethics and the Gospel*, p. 102.

perfect. How glorious it is to have a teacher, yes, more than a teacher—a Saviour and Lord, who demonstrated fully in His own life the way He would have us to go!

He also exemplified in His life the attitude of His Father toward suffering, sinning humanity: *"He did not avoid sinners, but sought them out. . . . He opened a new chapter in men's attitude towards sin and sinners."*[65] He loved people simply because they were people, all kinds of people: little children, the crippled, the demented, the sorrowing, the suffering, the social and moral outcasts. For example, the majority of His recorded miracles were healing miracles. Why? His miracles were signs or proofs that He was the Messiah. But He could have used His miraculous power in other ways, in ways that might have been even more spectacular and convincing. Could it be that He used His miraculous power primarily to relieve human need simply because He wanted to? When He came into contact with a person whose body was broken or twisted or whose mind was demented, there was something within Him that naturally yearned to relieve men of such affliction. Also, in this way He revealed the attitude of His Father toward suffering mankind.

Two chapters in Matthew (8 and 9) record the following healing miracles: a leper, the servant of a centurion, Peter's mother-in-law, two demoniacs, a paralytic, the daughter of a ruler, a woman with a hemorrhage, two blind men, and "a dumb demoniac." In addition, it says that He healed "many who were possessed with demons," "rebuked the wind and the sea; and there was a great calm," and healed "every disease and every infirmity." The secret to all that He did was His compassion. He had compassion on the multitudes (Matt. 9:36) but also on individuals. His compassion was not only generalized; it was also particularized. He wept over Jerusalem (Luke 19:41); He also wept with Mary (John 11:35). He had compassion on the hungry multitude and fed them (Mark 8:1–10; Matt. 15:32–39); but He also had compassion for a leper and healed him (Mark 1:40–42), the widow of Nain and raised her only son back to life (Luke 7:13–14), and two blind men and opened their eyes (Matt. 20:34). The ultimate expression of His

[65] C. G. Montefiore, *The Synoptic Gospels,* 2nd ed. (London: Macmillan, 1927), I, 55.

love and compassion was His death on the cross. It is John who says, "It is by this that we know what love is: that Christ laid down his life for us" (I John 3:16).

Two of His greatest parables, found only in Luke, were parables of compassion. They were the Good Samaritan who had compassion on the man who fell among robbers (Luke 10:33–34) and the Forgiving Father (or Prodigal Son) who saw his son coming "and had compassion, and ran and embraced him and kissed him" (Luke 15:20).

CHAPTER VI

THE PAULINE EPISTLES

Paul wrote primarily as a missionary statesman, as one who had a consuming passion to bring men into union with Christ and to lead them to maturity in Christ. The latter meant that inevitably there was an important place in his epistles for the ethical. As James Stewart says, there was no place in his thought for a religion that did not "issue in a morally strenuous and elevated life."[1] This life for Paul included the totality of life; every relationship of life was to be brought under the lordship of Christ. To adopt one of Paul's own expressions, anything less than this would be as "a noisy gong or a clanging cymbal" (I Cor. 13:1).

There is an abundance of ethical material in Paul's epistles. We shall attempt to compress as much as possible into the following major divisions: a comparison of the ethical teachings of Jesus and Paul, the relation of theology and ethics in the Pauline epistles, formative factors in Paul's ethics, and a brief summary of the place of vices and virtues in his epistles.[2]

[1] James S. Stewart, *A Man in Christ* (New York: Harper, 1935), p. 28.

[2] The epistles credited to Paul in the ordinary English translations—Romans through Philemon—are included, to some degree, in this study. It is recognized that many New Testament scholars question the Pauline au-

Jesus and Paul

In this section we are not concerned with the relation of Jesus and Paul in general, but with the relation between their ethical teachings.

1. Paul's use of the teachings of Jesus.

It is safe to assume that Paul had considerable knowledge of the life and teachings of Jesus. Occasionally he cited a saying of Jesus as "a word of the Lord." This could be a reference to special revelation, but it seems more logically to refer to a written record or an oral tradition concerning the "word of the Lord." Regarding divorce, Paul says, "To the married I give charge, not I but the Lord, that the wife should not separate from her husband" (I Cor. 7:10). In contrast he regrets that he has "no command of the Lord" regarding virgins (I Cor. 7:25). In the same epistle he cites the Lord regarding the support of those who "proclaim the gospel" (I Cor. 9:14), and the initiation of the Lord's Supper (I Cor. 11:23–26). In other places he cites "the word of the Lord" concerning the Second Coming (I Thess. 4:15); and in his farewell address to the Ephesian elders he reminded them of "the words of the Lord Jesus, how he said, 'It is more blessed to give than to receive' " (Acts 20:35). Any "word of the Lord" was considered authoritative by Paul.

In addition to the direct quotations of "the words of the Lord," there is considerable evidence of Paul's indebtedness to the teach-

thorship of the pastorals (I and II Timothy and Titus), and some his authorship of other epistles, particularly Ephesians. Most of these same scholars agree, however, that all of these epistles are Pauline in perspective and that some of them contain material originally from Paul. For example, speaking concerning Ephesians, Richard Longenecker (*Paul, Apostle of Liberty* [New York: Harper & Row, 1964]) says that "even those who most staunchly oppose its Pauline authorship insist upon its faithfulness to the Pauline teaching" (p. 15).

There are some critical problems, other than authorship, regarding other Pauline epistles such as Galatians—to whom was it written? and the Corinthian correspondence—the number of letters and whether or not one or more of "the lost letters" are incorporated, in part or in whole, into the existing letters. These critical problems do not change the ethical content of the epistles, and this is our major interest.

ings of his Master. That indebtedness is quite clear in two hortatory sections of the epistles. One, Romans 12–14, includes "too many echoes and adaptations of the teachings of Jesus . . . to put it all down to the 'nicest coincidence of sentiment' between Paul and his master." The other, I Thessalonians 4 and 5, is "permeated with the ethical teachings of Jesus."[3] Paul exhorted the Thessalonians "in the Lord Jesus" (I Thess. 4:1) and instructed them "through the Lord Jesus" (I Thess. 4:2). Other possible echoes of the teachings of Jesus that are not particularly ethical in emphasis are found in Romans 16:19 (cf. Matt. 10:16), I Corinthians 13:2 (cf. Mark 11:23), Philippians 4:6 (cf. Matt. 6:25), and I Thessalonians 5:2 (cf. Luke 12:39).

Although Paul's direct references to the teachings of the historical Jesus are comparatively few, there is "an essential harmony of thought and expression."[4] Paul may "supplement but he never contradicts his Master."[5] He did not come with a new gospel or a new ethic. He was used by the Lord to introduce "the leaven of the ethical teaching of Jesus into European society,"[6] and that leaven was a major factor in creating Western civilization and continues to be a creative force in our way of life.

2. Paul more specific.

It has already been implied that the major, if not the only, difference in the ethic of Jesus and Paul was a matter of emphasis. Furthermore, their distinctive emphases stemmed largely from the difference in the situations they faced. Jesus ministered primarily to Jews who were grounded in the Law. In contrast, Paul wrote largely to Gentile Christians who were recent converts and had little, if any, knowledge of the Old Testament Law. Also, since Paul's converts lived in centers of wickedness such as Corinth and Ephesus, they faced some unusual problems and temptations. Under these conditions, Paul would not have met the needs of those to whom he ministered if he had simply set forth his theol-

[3] A. M. Hunter, *Paul and His Predecessors*, new rev. ed. (Philadelphia: Westminster, 1961), p. 49.
[4] Morton Scott Enslin, *The Ethics of Paul* (New York: Harper, 1930), p. 115.
[5] C. A. Anderson Scott, *New Testament Ethics*, p. 75.
[6] Marshall, *The Challenge of New Testament Ethics*, p. 216.

ogy and his basic ethic without applying what he said to the immediate needs of the people.

Paul's primary concern was the new life in Christ, but he was a realist and he knew that many who had been brought into union with Christ were still babes in Christ. They needed someone who was more mature to point out the application of the basic principles of the Christian way to the daily problems and decisions of their lives. As immature Christians they needed some signposts or highway markers along the way. Paul provided many of those signposts or markers. Sydney Cave may be correct when he says that "the great Apostle of Christian liberty" was compelled against his wish "to give not only warning and exhortation but definite instruction on particular issues."[7] Whether or not he felt "compelled" to do so, such instructions are quite prominent in his epistles. He sought "to make explicit *all* that is implicit in the Christian ideal."[8]

Some of these instructions, such as those concerning women (I Cor. 11:3–16; 14:34–36; I Tim. 2:9–15) and the eating of certain meats (Rom. 14:15–23; I Cor. 8:1–13; and elsewhere), are largely, if not entirely, irrelevant for us today. However, if we examine carefully enough we shall discover even in what seems to be the most irrelevant portions of his epistles deep-seated principles that governed the life of Paul and principles that are abidingly relevant for the child of God. For example, an examination of Paul's teachings concerning the eating of meat offered to idols will reveal the following principles that will serve as guides to the contemporary Christian in many of his moral decisions: (1) one who is in Christ is not only to consider what he thinks is right; he is also to give serious consideration to what others think is right for him to do; (2) a thing that may be all right within itself for one to do becomes a sin against Christ if it is a cause of stumbling to one who is weaker (I Cor. 8:13); (3) the Christian is not to seek his own good but the good of others (I Cor. 10:24); (4) he is to do all things to the glory of God (I Cor. 10:31).

---

7 Sydney Cave, *The Christian Way* (London: Nisbet, 1949), p. 80.
8 Marshall, p. 219.

3. Paul more negative.

Since Paul dealt so largely with immature Christians, he emphasized the negative in his ministry. The former life of his Gentile converts provided a type of negative standard for their lives. They were to flee the old life with its habits and practices. They were to make a sharp break with the past. This is expressed in various ways. For example, in that wonderful passage on the resurrected life, he says, "If then ["since" or "assuming that"] you have been raised with Christ" (Col. 3:1), and then proceeds to describe the resurrected life. Among other things, he says, "Put to death therefore what is earthly in you" (v. 5) and spells out what he means. Again he says, "Put them all away: anger, wrath, . . ." (v. 8). After saying "put off the old nature with its practices" (v. 9) he is ready for the positive emphasis. Since you have been raised with Christ, he says, "Put on the new nature [v. 10]. . . . Put on then, as God's chosen ones . . . compassion, kindness [v. 12] . . . and above all these put on love" (v. 14). See Ephesians (4:17–32) for a strikingly similar passage, where the positive aspects of the statement are summarized as follows: "Put on the new nature, created after the likeness of God in true righteousness and holiness" (Eph. 4:24).

The balancing of the negative and positive, with the former stated first, is also seen in that striking passage concerning the works of the flesh and the fruit of the spirit. The opening statement of the passage is: "If you are guided by the Spirit you will not fulfil the desires of your lower nature" (Gal. 5:16, NEB). Williams, bringing out the verb tense and the double negative of the Greek, translates the verse as follows: "Practice living by the Spirit and then by no means will you gratify the cravings of your lower nature." This might be called a negative fruit of the Spirit. Just as we get darkness out of a room by turning on the lights, so we get the works of the flesh—the darkness of sin—out of our lives by walking or living in or under the guiding impulse of the Holy Spirit.

4. Paul more community-centered.

Since Paul's epistles were written largely to Churches, it is natural that they should contain a major emphasis on a Church or community ethic. This emphasis was not entirely lacking in the teachings of Jesus. It is true that His teachings were primarily for the disciples as individuals, but they did not live in isolation. Insofar as Jesus had a community ethic, His tended to be for the broader world community. The Church as an organization was not in existence, except in a very embryonic form.

In contrast, the community loomed so large in Paul's thought that Beach and Niebuhr suggest that "the Christian ethics of Paul is the ethics of life in the community."[9] That community was the body of Christ, and those who had been brought into union with Him were members of that body. Those "who are many are one body" (I Cor. 10:17). Each member of the body had his own peculiar function to perform for and in the body. Also, they were so closely knit together that if one member suffered, they all suffered. What was right for a member was to be determined largely by the effect of one's action on the body and the members of the body. Paul's admonition was: "Let all things be done for edification" (I Cor. 14:26). There is to be unity in the body (I Cor. 1:10, 13; Eph. 4:3) and a sharing with those in need within the Christian community (Rom. 12:13; 15:25; II Cor. 8:1–9, 15).

The community-centeredness of Paul's ethic is particularly evident in his use of love (*agape*). One author suggests that for Paul "*agape* . . . belongs essentially within the Christian community and has meaning there which it cannot have outside."[10] Christians, in a peculiar sense, were to love those within the Christian fellowship. A favorite word for this fellowship, which involved sharing with one another, was *koinonia* and related words. There is a *koinonia* in the faith, in the Spirit, and with Christ. "The Christian *koinonia* is that bond which binds Christians to each other, to Christ and to God."[11] That it involves the idea of sharing is seen in the fact that Paul uses the word three times in connection with the collection he took for the saints at

9 Waldo Beach and H. Richard Niebuhr, *Christian Ethics* (New York: Ronald Press, 1955), p. 44.

10 Knox, *The Ethic of Jesus in the Teaching of the Church*, p. 92.

11 William Barclay, *A New Testament Wordbook* (London: SCM Press, 1955), p. 72.

Jerusalem (Rom. 15:26; II Cor. 8:4; 9:13).[12] One might almost say that the "sense of *koinonia* produced his ethics, or at least gave to it its distinctive form."[13] His ethic could be properly called a *koinonia* ethic. The *koinonia* or community nature of Paul's ethics is revealed in his statement to the Galatians: "Let us do good to all men, and especially to those who are of the household of faith" (Gal. 6:10). This statement reflects a universal element but a peculiar emphasis on "the household of faith."

Can one justify on the basis of Paul's teachings the sectarian strategy—a withdrawal from the world? Does Paul expect the Church or the Christian community to be primarily "a saved remnant" or "a saving remnant?" It is true that he said:

Therefore come out from them,
and be separate from them, says the Lord
[II Cor. 6:17; cf. Isa. 52:11].

But in his earlier letter to the same Christian group he said: "I wrote to you in my letter[14] not to associate with immoral men; not at all meaning the immoral of this world, . . . since then you would need to go out of the world" (I Cor. 5:9–10). He explains to them that he had intended that they not associate "with any one who bears the name of brother if he is guilty of immorality . . . not even to eat with such a one" (v. 11). In other words, the separation was to take place within rather than outside the Christian community. The application of the Christian ethic was to begin in the Christian community, but its expression was not and could not be limited to the community. After all, the members of the fellowship lived in the world. They should be just as Christian in the home, in the community, and in the shop or store as they were in the *koinonia*. They were to express, as best they could, the Christian spirit and principles in every relationship of their lives.

12 *Ibid.*
13 Enslin, p. 78.
14 A reference to a lost letter. Some scholars believe that II Corinthians 6:14—7:1 is a fragment of that letter.

Theology and Ethics

When we speak of the theology of Paul we are using the term "theology" in a general sense. He was not a speculative or even a systematic theologian. As James Stewart says: "No system in the world could satisfy that untrammelled spirit, that mind of surpassing boldness, that heart of flame."[15] His heart had been set aflame by his encounter with Christ. His main concern was to share with others his experience, with all its breadth and depth. His primary interest was not theology but religion. His religion, however, which was fused with his ethics, was undergirded by great theological concepts, which in turn were derived from or closely related to his experience with Christ.

1. Structure of his epistles.

While some of Paul's epistles are largely practical (I Corinthians and the pastorals), most of his major epistles first lay down a theological or doctrinal base followed by moral exhortations. As Dodd suggests, "The twofold character of Christianity as ethical religion is reflected in the very structure of these documents."[16] Usually, the more practical portion of the epistle is introduced with a "therefore," a favorite word of Paul's.

The structure of Romans, the most formal of his letters, will serve as an illustration. The applied or hortatory section of the epistle begins with the twelfth chapter. He says, "I appeal to ["beseech," KJV; "implore," NEB] you therefore, brethren, by the mercies of God, to present your bodies as a living sacrifice, holy and acceptable to God, which is your spiritual worship" (Rom. 12:1). There follows in the next four chapters one exhortation after another. But what was the background of the "therefore"? It seems quite clear that the "therefore" refers to the preceding eleven chapters. What are "the mercies of God" that are found in those chapters?

The chapters which provide the doctrinal base or background

15 Stewart, pp. 24–25.
16 C. H. Dodd, *Gospel and Law: The Relation of Faith and Ethics in Early Christianity* (New York: Columbia University Press, 1951), p. 5.

reveal (1) that all are under condemnation for sin—both Jew and Gentile; (2) that salvation, which comes through faith, is available to all; (3) that this salvation brings freedom from the enslavement of sin; (4) freedom from the condemnation of the Law; (5) freedom from death and its destruction; and (6) brings us into the family of God. In addition, (7) the failure of the Jews to accept the proffered salvation works to the gain of the Gentiles.

It was from this kind of background that Paul says, "I appeal to you therefore." What follows the "therefore"? What kind of life does he appeal to them to live in the light of the blessedness of the salvation that they have? He appealed to them (1) for self-dedication (12:1); (2) for a transformed life (12:2); (3) for humility (12:3–5); (4) for faithfulness in their distinctive ministry (12:6–8); (5) for mutual love (12:9–21); (6) for obedience to "the governing authorities" (13:1–7); (7) for love as a fulfillment of the law (13:8–10); (8) for honest and decent conduct (13:11–14); (9) for liberality in judging (14:1–12); and (10) for an exemplary life —not putting a stumbling block in the way of others (14:13– 15:13). It will give added meaning to each exhortation if we think of each as being preceded with "I appeal to you therefore, brethren, by the mercies of God" and remember what was the background for the appeal.

Although the preceding division of Romans is legitimate, it should be remembered that when Paul comes to 12:1 he is not abruptly turning his attention from the theoretical to the practical. "On the contrary, the theory . . . is the theory of the practice of religion . . . the ethical problem has nowhere been left out of account."[17]

2. Paul's basic ethic.

The place to look for Paul's basic ethic, in contrast to his applied or social ethic, is in the first portions of his more theological epistles. For example, the first chapters of Romans are possibly the one best source for the underlying and unifying ethical concepts of his thought. Space will not permit a detailed analysis of the ethical content of these chapters. We shall restrict

[17] Karl Barth, *The Epistle to the Romans*, trans. from 6th ed. by Edwyn C. Hoskyns (London: Oxford University Press, 1933), p. 427.

ourselves to a listing of the moral qualities of God that are revealed in those chapters. He is revealed as righteous (1:17; 3:21, 22, 25), kind, forbearing, and patient (2:4), impartial (2:11), faithful (3:3), truthful (3:7), loving (5:5, 8; 8:39), generous (5:15), and merciful (9:15–16; 12:1). Paul could have properly said, "I plead with you on the basis of the kind of God we serve to present your bodies . . . to be transformed, etc." Beach and Niebuhr claim that "next to the Sermon on the Mount no other Biblical document has had greater influence on the ethical reflection of the Christian Church than the letter to the Romans."[18]

The Ephesian letter[19] will serve as a good illustration of the balancing of the theological and the applied in Paul, and also of the fact that his basic ethic is found primarily in the more theological portions of his epistles. The transition from the more theoretical to the more practical is found in words strikingly similar to Romans 12:1: "I therefore . . . beg you to lead a life worthy of the calling to which you have been called" (Eph. 4:1). Here, as elsewhere, "therefore" is used to bridge or tie together the doctrinal and applied portions of the epistle. This does not mean, however, that these two—doctrine and application or theology and ethics—are divorced. They belong together.

This is seen in what Paul had to say concerning faith and works, particularly in Ephesians 2:8–10, which, incidentally, is in the so-called theological portion of the epistle. Paul is quite clear here and elsewhere that salvation[20] is by grace through faith apart from works. The Christian is God's workmanship created in or through his union with Christ. But there is a purpose in

18 Beach and Niebuhr, p. 36.

19 In the present study, the Ephesian letter is accepted as genuinely Pauline. There are some reputable contemporary scholars who support this position. For example, Robert M. Grant (*Historical Introduction to the New Testament*) lists the arguments against the authenticity of Ephesians and then says that the "arguments do not seem conclusive" (p. 201). His personal conclusion is as follows: "Since the authenticity of the letter cannot be disproved it should be regarded as genuine" (p. 202).

20 For an excellent analysis of Paul's idea of salvation see Marshall (pp. 250–66), where he discusses the component parts of salvation: justification, redemption, reconciliation, sonship or adoption, sanctification, life, and a new creation. He suggests that "all these elements—some, more; others, less—raise ethical issues of vital import" (p. 251).

that experience that goes behind and also beyond the experience itself. We are created in Christ Jesus "for,"—for the purpose of, with a view to—good works, or "to devote ourselves to the good deeds for which God has designed us" (v. 10, NEB). This purpose of God in our salvation is so central that it becomes the proof of the experience. One commentator has summed up Paul's position as follows: "No one more wholeheartedly than Paul repudiated good works as a *ground* of salvation" and yet "no one more wholeheartedly insisted on good works as the *fruit* of salvation."[21] It was Martin Luther who said: "Our faith in Christ does not free us from works, but from false opinions concerning works."[22]

The verses immediately following Ephesians 2:8–10 reveal that union with Christ is the real hope for unity among men. In Christ those who were "far off" (Gentiles) "have been brought near" (v. 13). Paul says it is Christ who "is our peace," who has made Jew and Gentile one, "and has broken down the dividing wall of hostility" (v. 14), which was evidently a reference to the wall in the Temple area that set apart the court of the Gentiles. Christ created "in himself one new man in place of the two" (v. 15), and reconciled both Jew and Gentile, as He will every other human division, "to God in one body through the cross" (v. 16). It is through Him that "both have access in one Spirit to the Father" (v. 18). This passage suggests, among other things, that reconciliation of man to God and man to man belong together. Men can be reconciled to one another only as they are reconciled to God, but on the other hand "men cannot be reconciled to God without being also reconciled to one another."[23] It is evident that "God proposes to relate to Himself in one great family people whom historical hates, cultural differences, and social status, have held apart."[24] This He proposes to do through

21 F. F. Bruce, *The Epistle to the Ephesians: A Verse by Verse Exposition* (Westwood, N.J.: Revell, 1961), p. 52.

22 Martin Luther, "A Treatise on Christian Liberty," trans. W. A. Lambert, *Works of Martin Luther* (Philadelphia: Holman, 1915), II, 344.

23 William Owen Carver, *The Glory of God in the Christian Calling: A Study of the Ephesian Epistle* (Nashville: Broadman Press, 1949), pp. 120–21.

24 John A. Mackay, *God's Order: The Ephesian Letter and This Present Time* (New York: Macmillan, 1953), p. 61.

the oneness of men in Christ, a oneness that is made possible through the cross.

All of the preceding from Ephesians is from the so-called theological portion of the epistle. A study of other epistles would reveal similar significant material relevant to basic ethics in the first part of the epistles. This is true because "theology" and "ethics" for Paul are simply two sides of the same coin, and the two sides represent "the total Christian approach to life."[25]

3. Paul's applied ethic.

Romans has been used as an illustration of an epistle with a clear-cut twofold division, with the applied or hortatory section in the latter part of the epistle. The first or more theological division, which also contained his basic ethical principles or concepts, provided a background for his applied ethic. A reading of his epistles will reveal, however, that the applied or hortatory portions of his epistles are thoroughly saturated with theological or religious ideas and concepts. In other words, Paul's ethic, basic or applied, was thoroughly religious.

Whether we are considering the more strictly personal or the broader social aspects of Paul's applied ethic, his point of reference or the motivation appealed to is religious with at least some theological overtones. For example, he appealed to the Thessalonians "to lead a life worthy of God" (I Thess. 2:12). He prayed that God might make them to "increase and abound in love to one another and to all men" (3:12), that they might be "taught by God to love one another" (4:9), and that their hearts might be established "unblamable in holiness before our God and Father" (3:13). He said it was the will of God that they be sanctified, which meant that they should abstain from immorality (4:3). After all, God had not called them for uncleanness "but in holiness" (4:7). Later he suggests that since the day of the Lord will come as a thief in the night, the Thessalonians should "keep awake and be sober" (5:6), putting on "the breastplate of faith and love" (5:8). It was "the will of God in Christ Jesus" (5:18) for them to "be at peace" among themselves, to exhort but also

25 Ray Summers, *Ephesians: Pattern for Christian Living* (Nashville: Broadman Press, 1960), p. vi.

to be patient with the idle, the fainthearted, and the weak, not to repay evil for evil but to "seek to do good to one another and to all," to "rejoice always, pray constantly," and "give thanks in all circumstances" (5:13–18).

When we turn to Paul's broader social ethic, the same theological or religious orientation is evident. In the letter to the Ephesians, after stating the general principle that they should "be subject to one another out of reverence for Christ" (5:21), he applies the principle in a particular way to wives, who should be subject to their husbands "as to the Lord" ("as is fitting in the Lord," Col. 3:18). Throughout this passage (Eph. 5:22–33), Paul compares in a beautiful way the relation of Christian husbands and wives to the relation of Christ and His Church, which is His body. Husbands should love their wives as Christ loved the Church and gave Himself for her. He further suggests that children should obey their parents "in the Lord" ("for this pleases the Lord," Col. 3:20) and that fathers should bring their children up "in the discipline and instruction of the Lord" (Eph. 6:1–4).

The instructions concerning masters and slaves are likewise grounded in their relation to the Lord. Slaves were to be obedient to their "earthly masters . . . as to Christ." "As servants of Christ" they were to do "the will of God from the heart, rendering service . . . as to the Lord and not to men," knowing that the Lord would reward them (Eph. 6:5–8; cf. Col. 3:22–25). On the other hand, masters should remember that they and their slaves have the same Master in heaven and "there is no partiality with him" (Eph. 6:9; cf. Col. 4:1). In Philemon, where Paul comes as close to saying "free Onesimus" as he could without actually saying it, the point of reference throughout is Christ or the Lord: "in Christ" is found three times and "in the Lord" two times in the one chapter. He was sending Onesimus back "as a beloved brother . . . both in the flesh and in the Lord" (v. 16). What did Paul mean when he said, "I want some benefit from you in the Lord. Refresh my heart in Christ"?

The religious element is likewise prominent in what Paul said concerning the State. The fullest statement on the State in the entire New Testament is in the letter to the Romans (13:1–7). The word "God" appears seven times in the seven verses. Why should a Christian be "subject to the governing authorities"? Because those authorities are "instituted by God," and when one resists the authorities he "resists what God has appointed." The ruler is "God's servant," for the good of the people and to execute God's "wrath on the wrongdoer." Taxes are to be paid because "the authorities are ministers of God." In I Timothy there is the admonition "that supplications, prayers, intercessions, and thanksgivings be made for all men, for kings and all who are in high positions, that we may lead a quiet and peaceable life, godly and respectful in every way" (I Tim. 2:1–2). This is followed with the statement: "This is good, and it is acceptable in the sight of God our Savior" (v. 3).

Formative Factors

We shall not discuss in this section such matters as the Hebrew and Greek influence on Paul's thought.[26] To make a fine but valid distinction, our concern in this section is not the formative factors *of* Paul's ethic but the formative factors *in* his ethic. These factors or basic concepts give direction and unity to his ethic. We shall concentrate on four or five factors, recognizing that there are others of major significance, some of which have been mentioned previously, such as unity in Christ and faith and works.

[26] For a discussion of the Greek influence in general on the Christain movement see the classic work, which has been republished in a paperback: Edwin Hatch, *The Influence of Greek Ideas on Christianity* (New York: Harper, 1957). A. M. Hunter's *Paul and His Predecessors* discusses in general the background for Paul's thought, while both A. B. D. Alexander in *The Ethics of St. Paul* (Glasgow: James Maclehose and Sons, 1910) and Morton Scott Enslin in *The Ethics of Paul*, which has been made available in a paperback (Abingdon, 1957), give considerable attention to the influence of Jewish and Stoic thought on Paul. Two books by Jewish scholars, which will provide background for a better understanding of Paul and his thought, including his ethics, are: Samuel Sandmel, *The Genius of Paul* (New York: Farrar, Strauss and Cudahy, 1958), an analysis of Paul as a person for the general reader, and H. J. Schoeps, *Paul: The Theology of the Apostle in the Light of Jewish Religious History*, trans. Harold Knight (Philadelphia: Westminster Press, 1961), a scholarly book majoring on the theology of Paul. Still another of many important books on the background of Paul is W. D. Davies, *Paul and Rabbinic Judaism* (London: S.P.C.K., 1948).

1. The law.

A glance at a good concordance will indicate that the term "the law" is quite prevalent in Paul's epistles, particularly in Romans and Galatians. He uses the term to refer to the ceremonial law and the moral law, and in at least one place (Rom. 2:14–15) he evidently refers to the natural law, a law written on the hearts or in the consciences of Gentiles. In at least one place he speaks specifically of "the law of Christ" (Gal. 6:2; cf. Rom. 8:2; I Cor. 9:21), a term which for Paul may have meant not only the teachings of Christ "but also the example of the person of Christ."[27]

Paul considered the law holy, just, and good (Rom. 7:12). It was spiritual, but Paul himself was carnal—"sold under sin" (Rom. 7:14). The problem basically was man and not the law. He said that he delighted in the law of God in his "inmost self" but he was captive to the law of sin (Rom. 7:22–23). From this background he expressed the heart cry of every man face to face with his sinful condition: "wretched man that I am! Who will deliver me from this body of death?" Paul did not stop with the question. He had discovered the answer:

> Thanks be to God through Jesus Christ our Lord! . . . There is . . . no condemnation for those who are in Christ Jesus. For the law of the Spirit of life in Christ Jesus has set me free from the law of sin and death. For God has done what the law, weakened by the flesh, could not do: sending his own Son in the likeness of sinful flesh and for sin, he condemned sin in the flesh, in order that the just requirement of the law might be fulfilled in us [Rom. 7:24–8:4].[28]

The deliverance that Paul knew from the enslavement of sin and the condemnation of the law was a major factor in his religion and hence in his ethic.

There were two ways for justification before God: the way of the law and the way of faith. The former was hopeless; man could not keep the law, and it was the doers of the law and not

---

[27] Longenecker, p. 191.
[28] Longenecker has three chapters (IV, V, VI) on Paul and the Law. The first two of these chapters are discussions related, in the main, to an interpretation of Romans 7.

the hearers who were righteous before God (Rom. 2:13). Paul's conclusion was that none was righteous (Rom. 3:10), that all, both Jew and Gentile, had sinned and had fallen "short of the glory of God" (Rom. 3:23). In Galatians he plainly says that "a man is not justified by works of the law but through faith in Jesus Christ" (Gal. 2:16). He concludes that "if justification were through the law, then Christ died to no purpose" (Gal. 2:21). Does this mean that "we are using faith to undermine law"? Paul's reply is, "By no means: we are placing law itself on a firmer footing" (Rom. 3:31, NEB). However, any who "rely on works of the law are under a curse," since they are under obligation to keep all of the law, which they are unable to do (Gal. 3:10). It is Christ who redeems us from the curse of the law (Gal. 3:13). Justification comes by faith apart from the works of the law (Rom. 3:28), Abraham being an illustration of this fact (Rom. 4:1–14).

Paul's position might be summed up by two statements in the Roman epistle. They are: "No human being will be justified . . . by works of the law" (Rom. 3:20); and "Christ is the end of the law, that every one who has faith may be justified" (Rom. 10:4). In another place, he says, "The written code kills, but the Spirit gives life" (II Cor. 3:6). For the Christian, right conduct does not result "from the strained attempt to obey detailed commands, but from the response of faith to God's supreme gift to men in Jesus Christ. Paul's ethical teaching can be understood only as it is related to his faith and experience."[29]

One of the reasons for Paul's repudiation of the law as a way of salvation was "his insight that the highest righteousness possible for men was not the achievement of moral effort but was the free gift of God."[30] As Knox also says, "True goodness, wherever we meet with it . . . is God's creation, not man's construction."[31]

Does the preceding mean that the law did not serve any good purpose? It at least served as "our custodian until Christ came" (Gal. 3:24) or as "a kind of 'tutor' in charge of us until Christ should come" (NEB). Since Christ has come we no longer need

[29] Cave, *The Christian Way*, pp. 72–73.
[30] Knox, p. 104.
[31] *Ibid.*, p. 106.

the custodian or tutor. The law also serves a good purpose by convicting us of sin. "Where there is no law there is no transgression" (Rom. 4:15); "sin is not counted where there is no law" (Rom. 5:13); "law came in, to increase the trespass" (Rom. 5:20). Paul further says that our sinful passions are "aroused by the law" (Rom. 7:5) and that he himself would not have known the sin of covetousness if it had not been for the commandment: "You shall not covet." Sin working in or through the commandment wrought in him "all kinds of covetousness" (Rom. 7:7–8). There are two senses in which the law tends to produce sin. First, by defining it: there is no transgression without the law, and second, by provoking men to sin: it is characteristic of human nature to desire the thing that is forbidden. The law can define sin, can stimulate to sin, and can even convict of sin, but it cannot free one from sin.

Paul's position regarding the law created some problems for some of his converts and an opportunity for criticism by some of his opponents. The latter evidently charged him with antinomianism, "which is the devil's misinterpretation of God's grace."[32] Paul faced up to this charge or problem. For example, he asks the question: "Are we to sin because we are not under the law but under grace?" (Rom. 6:15). He does not answer directly this question which is the major problem of the entire chapter. Paul simply makes a statement of fact: he suggests that everyone is someone's slave. We are either slaves of sin, or we are slaves of righteousness and of God. If we continue in sin we continue to be the slaves of sin and do not belong to God and the righteousness which comes from God.

One or two other statements should be made concerning the law. We have been freed from it like a wife is freed whose husband has died (Rom. 7:1–4). Paul further suggests that love is the fulfillment of the law (Rom. 13:8–10; Gal. 5:14). This love that fulfills the law is the fruit of the Spirit (Gal. 5:22) and the Spirit comes "by hearing with faith" and not "by works of the law" (Gal. 3:2–5). Love, along with other fruit, "cannot be achieved by our efforts or earned by our merit. What we need is the living Spirit whom we cannot summon, the living Fire which we can-

---

[32] Lillie, *Studies in New Testament Ethics*, p. 72.

not kindle but can only pray for as Elijah prayed for the fires at Carmel. The goodness of love is always and entirely God's gracious giving of Himself to us."[33]

2. Union with Christ.

This is another formative factor or basic concept in the thought of Paul. It is expressed in various ways but most frequently and pointedly in the two words "in Christ." These words have been variously interpreted, but they are frequently if not usually used by Paul in a mystical sense.[34] Paul himself had been brought into a vital life-changing union with the resurrected Christ. The encounter he had with Christ on the Damascus road had completely changed the direction of his life. He went down that road "breathing threats and murder against the disciples of the Lord," against those who belonged "to the Way"(Acts 9:1–2); he came back that road a disciple, one who walked in the Way. This initial experience with the resurrected Christ became more meaningful as he walked and worked in fellowship with Christ. He says, "I have been crucified with Christ; it is no longer I who live, but Christ who lives in me" (Gal. 2:20). Again he says, "For me to live is Christ" (Phil. 1:21).

[33] Knox, p. 108.

[34] The emphasis on the mystical has been particularly prevalent since the work of Adolf Deissmann as found in two of his books: *St. Paul: A Study in Social and Religious History,* trans. Lionel R. M. Strachan (London: Hodder & Stoughton, 1912) and his later and simpler book, which incorporated considerable material from the earlier volume: *The Religion of Jesus and the Faith of Paul,* trans. William E. Wilson, 2nd ed. (London: Hodder & Stoughton, 1926). Two books that accept, define, and defend the mystical viewpoint are William Barclay's *The Mind of St. Paul* (New York: Harper, 1958), and Stewart's *A Man in Christ.* Among writers who interpret "in Christ" in ways different from Deissmann are: F. C. Porter (*The Mind of Christ in Paul* [New York: Scribners, 1932]), who interprets "in Christ" in terms of friendship and love; Eric Wahlstrom (*The New Life in Christ* [Philadelphia: Muhlenberg Press, 1950]), who in the main would make "in Christ" mean "in dependence upon Christ" or "belonging to Christ"; and C. H. Dodd (*Gospel and Law*), who equates "in Christ" and "in the church," which is the body of Christ (pp. 31f.). Two additional books that deal in a general way with Pauline mysticism are Albert Schweitzer, *The Mysticism of Paul the Apostle,* trans. William Montgomery (New York: Macmillan, 1931)—a standard work with a chapter on "Mysticism and Ethics," and Alfred Wikenhauser, *Pauline Mysticism,* trans. Joseph Cunningham (New York: Herder and Herder, 1960)—an objective examination of the biblical material by a Roman Catholic.

No wonder the idea of union with Christ permeated all his writings and that the term "in Christ," "in the Lord," or "in the Lord Jesus Christ" is found, according to Deissmann,[35] 164 times in his epistles. For Paul "the Christian life is begun, continued and ended in Christ."[36] Our main concern is with its continuance, which operates in the area of ethics or morality.

Union with Christ was not only "the mainstay of Paul's religion," but also "the sheet-anchor of his ethics."[37] When Paul said, "If any one is in Christ, he is a new creation" (II Cor. 5:17), he meant a new creation in every area of his life. When he said, "The old has passed away, behold, the new has come" he not only referred to a new way of thinking about and evaluating Christ but a new way in daily life. "There is, of course, no such thing as a union with Christ which does not have the most far-reaching effects in the moral sphere."[38] Alexander rather strikingly concludes that the expression "in Christ" "determines the content and scope" of the ethic of Paul, "giving to it its distinctiveness, its absoluteness, and its universality."[39]

Baptism for Paul was a symbol of the Christian's relation to Christ. To the Galatians he wrote, "For as many of you as were baptized into Christ have put on Christ" ("put on Christ as a garment," NEB; Gal. 3:27). Again he says, "We were buried therefore with him by baptism into death, so that as Christ was raised from the dead by the glory of the Father, we too might walk in newness of life" (Rom. 6:4; cf. Col. 2:12). The newness of life, referred to in Romans, involves a break with sin and a dedication to God and righteousness.

To the Colossians Paul wrote, "If then [since or assuming that] you have been raised with Christ" (Col. 3:1), and then proceeds to describe the kind of life one should live who has been raised through union with Christ. This union should and inevitably will make a difference in the quality of life one lives for Christ. Earlier in the same letter Paul had pleaded with the Colossians

---

[35] Deissmann, *St. Paul: A Study in Social and Religious History*, p. 128.

[36] Barclay, *The Mind of St. Paul*, p. 126.

[37] Stewart, p. 194.

[38] *Ibid.*, p. 164.

[39] Alexander, p. 125.

"to lead a life worthy of the Lord, fully pleasing to him, bearing fruit in every good work and increasing in the knowledge of God" (Col. 1:10). Again he admonishes them: "So, just as you once accepted Christ Jesus as your Lord, you must continue living in vital union with Him, being continuously built up in Him" (Col. 2:6–7, Williams). To the Ephesians he said that we who are "in Christ have been destined and appointed to live for the praise of his glory" (Eph. 1:12). We live for the praise of His glory as we let the resurrected Christ live in us and express Himself more fully through us.

The preceding correctly suggests that there is growth in this relationship. No one is a Christian unless he has been brought into a vital life-changing union with the resurrected Christ. However, he is not born full grown. He is a babe in Christ, but the "in Christ" assures life and vitality. The ultimate goal of this relationship is that we may attain "to a mature manhood and to a perfect measure of Christ's moral stature" (Eph. 4:13, Williams). Again Paul says that "we are to grow up in every way into him who is the head, into Christ" (Eph. 4:15). Here is an ideal that will challenge us to the end of life's journey. To use an expression of Paul's, there is a sense in which we "have put on the new nature" but at the same time this new nature "is being renewed in knowledge after the image of its creator" (Col. 3:10). The new nature is past event, present reality, and even future hope. We have been brought into union with the one who is "the image of the invisible God" (Col. 1:15), the one who "bears the very stamp" of the nature of God (Heb. 1:3). This One who is the image of God lives within us, but we have not let Him stamp that image fully upon us. We "are being changed into his likeness from one degree of glory to another" (II Cor. 3:18). The image will be fully restored when we awake in His likeness.

The high ideal for the Christian's growth or maturity, as found in Ephesians 4, is preceded and followed by some challenging moral exhortations. In the beginning of the practical or hortatory portion of the epistle Paul says, "I therefore . . . beg you to lead a life worthy of the calling to which you have been called" (4:1). This is spelled out more specifically as follows: "Be humble always and gentle, and patient too. Be forbearing with one another and charitable" (4:2, NEB). They were to put off the old nature, which belonged to their former manner of life (v. 22), and were to put on the new nature, "created after the likeness of God in true righteousness and holiness" (v. 24). Among the specific things they were to put off were falsehood, anger, stealing, evil talk, bitterness, slander, and malice. On the other hand, they were to put on truthfulness, generosity, kindness, tenderheartedness, and the forgiving spirit (vv. 25–32). They were admonished to forgive one another as God had forgiven them (v. 32) and to "be imitators of God, as beloved children" (5:1).

There follows a threefold exhortation: "Walk in love" (5:2); "walk as children of light" (5:8); and "look carefully . . . how you walk, not as unwise men but as wise" (5:15). The metaphor "to walk" is a favorite of Paul's, appearing twice as much in his epistles as in all of the rest of the New Testament. Following the first of these admonitions of Paul to "walk in love" there are a number of specific negative exhortations: things that love would demand that they leave out of their lives. Following the second admonition to "walk as children of light," there is an excellent parenthetical statement with a positive emphasis: "(For the fruit of light is found in all that is good and right and true)" (5:9). All of the preceding is clearly related to one's union with Christ. He is the example for the disciple. The latter is to "walk in love, as Christ loved us and gave himself for us" (Eph. 5:2). Here is both motive and example. Then there is the statement in the Philippian letter: "Have this mind among yourselves, which you have in Christ Jesus" (Phil. 2:5)—either which is revealed in Christ or "which you have in your relation to Christ." Regardless of the correct interpretation, this is in the midst of a Christological passage of major importance, but it "occurs in a strictly ethical context where Paul is concerned to create in his readers an attitude of humility, unity, and benevolence."[40] Here and elsewhere Paul finds in Christ "an objective standard of ethical conduct."[41]

Christ is an example but He is more than an example. If He was not, then to seek to follow Him would be extremely dis-

---

[40] Wahlstrom, p. 168.
[41] Dodd, *Gospel and Law*, p. 39.

couraging, since none of us can follow His example perfectly. However, He is not merely an external or objective standard. We have been brought into union with Him: He is in us and we are in Him. Christ within is our hope of glory (Col. 1:27). There is not much we can do consciously to become like Him. We become like Him as we let Him live in us and have His way through us. As we are conscious of our union with Him, the high or "upward call of God in Christ Jesus" (Phil. 3:14) is no longer a source of discouragement to us. It becomes a constantly thrilling challenge as we seek to walk in fellowship with Him in response to the upward call of God.

3. The work of the Holy Spirit.[42]

The Spirit is basic in the thought of Paul. "One might as well try to explain Paul's Christianity without the Spirit as modern civilization without electricity."[43] He set "the whole Christian life within the sphere and control of the Spirit."[44] For him, "the believer's life must ultimately be guided and empowered by the Spirit if it is to be truly Christian."[45] He relates the Spirit so closely to the indwelling Christ that one wonders if he does not at times equate the two. They were "blended in a remarkable degree."[46] Nevertheless, Paul never fully equates the Spirit and the resurrected Christ, although to be "in Christ" is also to be "in the Spirit." James Stewart, quoting Wheeler Robinson, says that through association with Christ the Spirit "was personalized

[42] Barclay (*The Mind of St. Paul*) has an unusually helpful chapter on "Paul's Thinking about the Holy Spirit." A concise chapter on the teachings of the Bible as a whole on the ethic of the Holy Spirit will be found in Henlee Barnette's *Introducing Christian Ethics* (Nashville: Broadman, 1961). Lindsay Dewar in *An Outline of New Testament Ethics* uses the heading "The Ethic of the Holy Spirit" for a discussion of the ethical content of the book of Acts. An unusually helpful unpublished source is Guy H. Greenfield's doctoral dissertation at Southwestern Baptist Theological Seminary (1961) entitled "The Ethical Significance of the Holy Spirit in the Writings of Paul."

[43] Archibald M. Hunter, *Interpreting Paul's Gospel* (London: SCM Press, 1954), p. 108.

[44] Hunter, *Paul and His Predecessors*, p. 97.

[45] Longenecker, p. 195.

[46] Stewart, p. 310.

as never before" and also that "the holiness of the Spirit was ethicized as never before."[47]

In the Pauline epistles there is "an intimate relation between the activity of the Spirit and the moral life."[48] The Spirit is operative within the child of God to produce in him the right kind of life, a life in harmony with the indwelling Christ. The Kingdom of God for him is "righteousness and peace and joy in the Holy Spirit" (Rom. 14:17). It is through the power of the Spirit that the Christian is sanctified or made holy (Rom. 15:16; cf. I Cor. 6:9–11; II Thess. 2:13). All spiritual gifts within the Christian fellowship are from the Spirit and are to be used for the common good (I Cor. 12:4ff.). "The development of the individual Christian and the perfecting of the Church both depend upon the Spirit."[49]

The relation of the Spirit to the maturing of the Christian is illustrated by what Paul says concerning the flesh and the Spirit. This subject is mentioned in several places, but it is discussed most fully in Romans 8. He suggests that we (Christians) "walk not according to the flesh ["lower nature," NEB] but according to the Spirit" (Rom. 8:4). Really, we are not in the flesh but in the Spirit,[50] if the Spirit dwells in us; and Paul adds: "Any one who does not have the Spirit of Christ does not belong to him" (Rom. 8:9). Again he says that those who have been made alive by the indwelling Spirit are "debtors, not to the flesh [lower or carnal nature], to live according to the flesh" (Rom. 8:12), but by implication they are debtors to the Spirit to live according to or under the guiding impulse of the Spirit.

Paul also discusses the relation of the flesh or the lower nature and the Spirit in Galatians, particularly in Galatians 5.[51] He contrasts the works or desires of the flesh or lower nature with the

---

47 *Ibid.*, p. 311; cf. Hunter (*Paul and His Predecessors*) where he makes a similar statement (p. 90), which later in the same volume he evaluates and revises (p. 146).

48 Wahlstrom, p. 112.

49 Barclay, *Mind of St. Paul*, p. 180.

50 Deissmann (*St. Paul: A Study in Social and Religious History*, p. 126) says that the formula "in the Spirit" occurs nineteen times in Paul's Epistles.

51 Barclay's *Flesh and Spirit* (Nashville: Abingdon, 1962) is a helpful study, based on the Greek text, of Galatians 5:16–23.

fruit of the Spirit. To the Galatians he says, "Practice living by the Spirit and then by no means will you gratify the cravings of your lower nature" (Gal. 5:16, Williams).[52] This is a fruit of the Spirit. The only hope for one to get rid of the desires or cravings of his lower nature is to "walk by the Spirit," be "guided by the Spirit" (NEB), or "practice living by the Spirit" (Williams). After spelling out the works of the flesh or lower nature, Paul lists the more positive fruit of the Spirit: love, joy, peace, patience, kindness, goodness, faithfulness ("fidelity," NEB), gentleness, and self-control. Marshall suggests that all of these "lie in the ethical realm and thus provide a striking demonstration of the complete fusion of religion and ethics in Pauline thought."[53] Need we be reminded that fruit is natural and even inevitable? The movement of the Christian ethic is from within to its outer expression.

There are many additional references to the Spirit and His work in Paul's epistles. These are sufficient to suggest that "the great actions and the great qualities of the Christian life are all in the Spirit,"[54] that "all authentic Christian behaviour is a 'walking by the Spirit,' "[55] and that the Spirit's "moral efficacy is a matter of daily experience to the Christian."[56]

4. Freedom and submission.

Paul's concept of freedom or liberty was another formative factor in his ethic. Those who had been made new creations through their union with Christ were free men and women. He pointedly and plainly says, "Where the Spirit of the Lord is, there is freedom" (II Cor. 3:17), and again, "For freedom Christ has set us free" (Gal. 5:1), or "Christ set us free, to be free men" (NEB).

In Romans 8 Paul spells out this freedom in a more specific way. He says that there is "no condemnation for those who are

[52] Notice that Williams here as usual brings out the verb tense, "practice living," and the double negative, "by no means," of the original. The Revised Standard Version stands practically alone in making the last portion of the verse an exhortation: "and do not gratify the desires of the flesh."

[53] Marshall, p. 290; see pp. 291–303 for an excellent analysis based on the Greek text of each of the fruit of the Spirit.

[54] Barclay, *Mind of St. Paul*, p. 181.

[55] Hunter, *Interpreting Paul's Gospel*, p. 109.

[56] C. H. Dodd, *The Meaning of Paul for To-day* (London: The Swarthmore Press, 1920), p. 125.

in Christ Jesus," and then sets forth, as indicated earlier, three areas in which "the Spirit of life in Christ Jesus" has set us free: (1) from sin and its enslavement (cf. Romans 6, where he discusses this aspect of Christian freedom most fully); (2) from the law and its condemnation; and (3) from death and its destruction. This freedom, in all its aspects, comes through union with Christ. It is freedom "in Christ" or "in the Spirit." The more completely the Christian lets the resurrected Christ live in him, and the more constantly and perfectly he walks in or under the guiding impulse of the Spirit the greater will be his freedom from the enslavement of his fleshly nature and the greater his freedom to do as he pleases. The Christian will discover as he matures that the controls for his daily life will be increasingly inner and decreasingly outer.

Another evidence of the Christian's maturity is what he does with the freedom he has in Christ. Nowhere does Paul state his viewpoint more clearly than in the following verse: "You were called to freedom, brethren; only do not use your freedom as an opportunity for the flesh, but through love be servants of one another" (Gal. 5:13). Real Christian freedom will be willing to submit itself to the law of Christian love. Longenecker says the concept of love is "the conditioning factor in the exercise of Christian liberty."[57] In Christ there is freedom from the law, accompanied with an enslavement to the higher law of love. The voluntary surrender of freedom "is the kernel" to Paul's social ethic.

This basic principle is applied in a specific and rather full way to the eating of meat offered to idols (see particularly Romans 14 and I Corinthians 8, with the discussion in the latter carrying over into chapters 9 and 10).[58] Strong or mature Christians might claim that they were free to eat such meat since there was no such thing as an idol. Paul reminded such brethren, however, that if a weaker brother was injured by what they ate, they were "no longer walking in love" (Rom. 14:15). He admonished them to

[57] Longenecker, p. 202.

[58] It could be that Paul's strong insistence on not eating meat offered to idols was related in some way to the instructions of the Jerusalem Church to Gentile converts (Acts 15:20; 21:25).

"pursue what makes for peace and for mutual upbuilding" (Rom. 14:19). He closes the discussion in Romans with the general statement: "We who are strong ought to bear with the failings of the weak, and not to please ourselves" (Rom. 15:1). He uses Christ as an example of one who "did not please himself" (Rom. 15:3).

In discussing the same matter in the first letter to the Corinthians he said, "Take care lest this liberty of yours somehow become a stumbling-block to the weak" (I Cor. 8:9). In the next chapter he gives himself as an example of one who had not made "full use" of his freedom or rights in the gospel. He who was "free from all men" had made himself "a slave to all" that he might "win the more" (see I Cor. 9:1–19).

In the next chapter he concludes the discussion by saying, " 'All things are lawful,'[59] but not all things are helpful. 'All things are lawful,' but not all things build up" (I Cor. 10:23). He then states two general principles that are abidingly relevant: (1) "Let no one seek his own good, but the good of his neighbor" (10:24); and (2) "Whether you eat or drink, or whatever you do, do all to the glory of God" (10:11). These principles, if applied consistently and sincerely, would solve most of the Christian's problems in the area of daily conduct.

Paul also applied the principle of the voluntary surrender of freedom to other areas of human relations. For example, women were theoretically equal with men (Gal. 3:28),[60] but they were to be submissive to their husbands in the home (Eph. 5:22–24) and were to keep quiet in the churches (I Cor. 14:34–35). In Christ there was neither bond nor free, but slaves were to be obedient to their masters (Eph. 6:5–8; Col. 3:22, and elsewhere). Christians were free in Christ, but they were to be obedient to the powers that be or "the governing authorities" (Rom. 13:1). The great apostle of freedom was also the apostle of order and even subordination (Eph. 5:21). The latter is the voluntary subordination of an equal to an equal.

The glorious paradox is that the voluntary surrender of free-

[59] Which may have been a quotation taken from their letter to him (cf. I Cor. 6:12).

[60] In contrast, in I Corinthians (11:3) Paul recognizes a hierarchical structure—God, Christ, man, woman.

dom for the sake of others, for the good of the Christian community and for the glory of God, in the final analysis, will increase rather than decrease the Christian's freedom in Christ. The most meaningful freedom is freedom to do what our better self wants to do. Freedom for Paul does not "mean freedom from restraint to follow our desires, but freedom from the tyranny of futile desires to follow what is really good."[61] What is "really good" for the child of God will be in harmony with and an expression of the will and purpose of the indwelling Christ. To the degree that we let Him live in us and express Himself through us, to that degree we shall be really free. If He makes us free, we shall be free indeed.

5. Motives for moral living.

There is a sense in which almost everything that Paul wrote was used as an encouragement to or a motive for Christian living. His epistles were written to Christians. Most of his great statements of truth or doctrine were written "to secure the performance of ordinary Christian duties."[62] The structure of many of his epistles, as discussed previously, is an evidence of this fact. The theological doctrine or base is followed by moral exhortations, frequently introduced with a "therefore." The former provided the motive for the latter. This is true whether it represents the broad sweep of an entire epistle such as Romans or a more restricted appeal such as I Corinthians 6:20: "You were bought with a price. So ["therefore," KJV] glorify God in your body."

The basic appeal is to "the mercies" or the grace of God. This is the supreme motive in Paul, with practically every other motive evolving from the response of the child of God to what God, through His grace, had done for him. In the light of the blessings the Christian has received through his union with Christ, he should seek to glorify God (I Cor. 10:31; Eph. 1:12; Phil. 1:11) and please Him (Eph. 5:10; Col. 1:10; I Thess. 2:4; 4:1). The grace of God is an expression of His love, and the love of God for Paul was both ideal and motive, aim and incentive. It is the love

---

[61] Dodd, *The Meaning of Paul for To-day*, p. 137.
[62] Cave, p. 79.

of Christ, not our love for Christ, that constrains, controls, or presses us in on every side (II Cor. 5:14).

Paul also used the example of Jesus as a motive. He introduced or at least utilized the Incarnation of Christ to make an appeal to the Philippians for ethical living. The brief and yet full exposition of the Incarnation is preceded and followed by ethical exhortations—preceded, in the main, by what might be considered some basic moral concepts and followed by some very practical appeals to moral living. Sitting in the midst is the following appeal and statement:

> Have this mind among yourselves, which you have in Christ Jesus, who, though he was in the form of God, did not count equality with God a thing to be grasped, but emptied himself, taking the form of a servant, being born in the likeness of men. And being found in human form he humbled himself and became obedient unto death, even death on a cross [Phil. 2:5–8].

Preceding this wonderful statement Paul had appealed to the Philippians for unity of spirit, unselfishness, and humility. Immediately preceding the statement Paul says, "Let each of you look not only to his own interests, but also to the interests of others" (v. 4). Why should they do this? Because Christ looked after the interest of others; He emptied Himself. The Philippians are further admonished to work out their own salvation with fear and trembling (v. 12). They should "do all things without grumbling or questioning," that they might "be blameless and innocent, children of God without blemish in the midst of a crooked and perverse generation," among whom they "shine as lights in the world" (vv. 14–15).

Paul exhorted the Colossians "to lead a life worthy of the Lord" (Col. 1:10) and to forgive one another as the Lord had forgiven them (Col. 3:13; cf. Eph. 4:32). Christ was cited as an example of love for the Ephesians (5:2) and of humility to the Philippians (2:4–8). Paul appealed to the Corinthians to be imitators of him as he was of Christ (I Cor. 11:1; cf. I Thess. 1:6). He used the example of Jesus to appeal for a liberal offering for the saints at Jerusalem (II Cor. 8:1–9) and for the strong "to bear with the failings of the weak" (Rom. 15:1–3). Paul believed that Christians should live in such intimate and responsive union with Christ that naturally and inevitably some of His spirit and character would be revealed in and through them. As Alexander so aptly says, "Christ . . . is the Alpha and Omega of Paul's whole conception of the Christian life. He is at once end, norm and motive."[63]

There is even some place in Paul's ethic for an appeal to fear (Rom. 2:5; 8:13; I Cor. 5:5; 10:8; Gal. 5:21; Eph. 5:5–6) and to the hope for reward (Rom. 6:23; I Thess. 2:12; II Thess. 1:5). Fear and reward are frequently closely related to the eschatological in Paul. Many of his moral exhortations are grounded upon and hence motivated by certain aspects of his eschatology. For example, the exhortation to keep awake and be sober (I Thess. 5:6) is based on the fact that "the day of the Lord," which was evidently an early Christian watchword, "will come like a thief in the night" (I Thess. 5:2). In his lengthy discussion of the resurrection he says, "If the dead are not raised, 'Let us eat and drink, for tomorrow we die' " (I Cor. 15:32). He ends this passage with the glorious climax: "Thanks be to God, who gives us the victory through our Lord Jesus Christ." There follows an equally glorious exhortation: "Therefore, my beloved brethren, be steadfast, immovable, always abounding in the work of the Lord, knowing that in the Lord your labor is not in vain" (I Cor. 15:58). Another example of the relation of the eschatological and the ethical is found in the Roman letter. Paul reminded them that "the night is far gone, the day is at hand" (Rom. 13:12) and then proceeds to exhort them to "cast off the works of darkness": reveling, drunkenness, debauchery, licentiousness, quarreling, and jealousy. He concludes by saying, "Put on the Lord Jesus Christ, and make no provision for the flesh, to gratify its desires."

Regardless of the motives Paul appeals to, he is at his best in his persuasions. In the main, his severity of argument is laid aside. There is a note of tenderness that breathes through his words of personal appeal.

63 Alexander, p. 171.

Vices and Virtues

This study of Paul's ethic would not be complete without at least a brief statement concerning the place of vices and virtues in his epistles. In general, Paul admonished his converts to let their lives "be worthy of the gospel of Christ" (Phil. 1:27) or "to lead a life worthy of the Lord" (Col. 1:10). Since Paul was dealing almost exclusively with immature Gentile converts, he did not restrict himself to generalities. He spelled out quite specifically his and the Lord's expectations.

1. Lists of vices and virtues.

The spelling out of his expectations along with the balancing of the negative and positive, so typical of Paul, are seen in some of the lists of vices and virtues.[64] This is particularly true in Galatians 5 and Colossians 3. In the former, Paul sets forth in a specific way the works of the flesh and the fruit of the Spirit (Gal. 5:16–23). In the Colossian passage, he says that those who have been raised with Christ are to "put to death" what was earthly in them, and he enumerates some of the things that are earthly. He further says that they are to "put off the old nature with its practices." In contrast, they are to "put on the new nature," with the qualities of this new nature spelled out (Col. 3:5–14; cf. Eph. 4:22, 24). There is enough in these two passages to challenge the sincere Christian to the end of life's journey. It is well to remember, however, that it is "the fruit of the *Spirit*" and that the new nature, with its virtues, results from one's resurrection with Christ. It is through the indwelling Christ that our lives become increasingly fruitful for Him. In other words, we do not live the Christian life in our own strength but in His strength. This is our hope, this is the glory of the life we live in fellowship with Him.[65]

---

[64] Similar lists were quite common in the days of Paul.

[65] For additional, more or less well-defined lists of vices or virtues see: Romans 1:28–31—the conduct of those God has given up; I Corinthians 6:9–10—those who cannot inherit the kingdom of God; II Corinthians 6:4–10—Paul vindicates himself; Ephesians 4:1–3—a life worthy of the Lord; Ephesians 4:22–32—a mingling of the negative and the positive; and Ephesians 6:10–18—the armor of God.

2. *"Theological virtues."*

The so-called theological virtues (so labeled by Aquinas and many others since his day)—faith, hope, and love—are quite prevalent in the Pauline epistles. One author claims that these "are the three most pregnant words of Christian ethics," and that "they continually merge into each other."[66] They are inward dispositions that provide the base or foundation for the outward expression of the Christian life.

As a triad, they are frequently grouped together in Paul's epistles. The most familiar example is in the verse that closes the superlative love chapter: "So faith, hope, love abide, these three; but the greatest of these is love" (I Cor. 13:13). In the Roman epistle Paul says, "We are justified by faith," "rejoice in our hope of sharing the glory of God," and the latter does not disappoint us "because God's love has been poured into our hearts" (Rom. 5:1-5). The relation of the three is underscored in a particularly clear way in the following statement: "We have heard of your faith in Christ Jesus and of the love which you have for all the saints, because of the hope laid up for you in heaven" (Col. 1:4-5), which suggests an eschatological motivation. Paul thanked the Lord for the "work of faith and labor of love and steadfastness of hope" of the Thessalonians (I Thess. 1:3). He was grateful that their faith was growing and their love increasing (II Thess. 1:3). There are times when he simply joins faith and love with an "and." For example, he admonished the Thessalonians to "put on the breastplate of faith and love, and for a helmet the hope of salvation" (I Thess. 5:8; cf. I Tim. 1:14; II Tim. 1:13).

Paul says that love believes all things and hopes all things (I Cor. 13:7); nevertheless, faith and hope are distinct from love as Christian virtues. The former may be subsidiary to the latter. They are certainly closely interrelated. The love the Christian has is really not his but the love of God expressed through him. Our response to God's love for us is our faith in Him. Through this faith we have come into a vital relationship with the real source of the love that partakes of the divine quality (*agape*). In turn,

---

[66] Kenneth E. Kirk, *Some Principles of Moral Theology* (London: Longmans, Green, 1920), p. 43.

through faith we become a channel for His love to others—faith works through love (Gal. 5:6), is "active in love" (NEB), or "expresses itself in love" (Phillips). This love, in turn, is the ground or source of all the virtues that characterize the truly Christian life. Love is the greatest of the virtues not only because it is the source of all others, but also because it is from God and can be and is equated with God (I John 4:8, 16).

Some might contend that while "love" is "ethical," this is not true of faith and hope. There might be some basis for a question regarding hope but not faith, when the latter is properly understood. Paul uses the term in more than one sense. In general, however, faith for him "is at once a confession and a life renewed in obedience to Christ."[67] It involves commitment to the way of Christ as well as trust in Christ. Marshall concludes that "in all genuine faith there are three elements and in each of these elements there is an ethical motif. The elements are—*belief, trust, loyalty.*"[68] Faith is a dynamic factor in moral living—second only to love in its importance. In Paul's writings it frequently is joined with or stands side by side with love or *agape* (see Eph. 1:15; 3:17; 6:23; I Thess. 3:6; 5:8; II Thess. 1:3; Philem. 5).

3. The crowning virtue.

"Faith, hope, love abide . . . but the greatest of these is love [*agape*]" (I Cor. 13:13). Faith and hope might pass away but *agape* "never ends" or fails (I Cor. 13:8). "Faith without love is cold, and hope without love is grim. Love is the fire which kindles faith and love is the light which burns hope into certainty."[69] It is a love that is not jealous or boastful, arrogant or rude, irritable or resentful. It does not insist on its own right or rejoice at wrong. It is patient and kind, bears, believes, hopes, and endures all things (I Cor. 13:4-7). Such a love never ends because it is derived from and belongs to the very nature of God. It could not end any more than He could come to an end. Like God, it has

[67] Ph.-H. Menoud, "Faith," *A Companion to the Bible,* ed. Von Allmen, p. 107.

[68] Marshall, p. 271.

[69] William Barclay, *The Letters to the Corinthians,* 2nd ed. (Philadelphia: Westminster Press, 1965), p. 140.

existed from eternity and will last through eternity. As the fruit of the Spirit in the human person (Gal. 5:22) it proceeds normally, naturally, and even inevitably from the Christian's union with the resurrected Christ. As Paul says in another place, we are "taught by God to love one another" (I Thess. 4:9). Instruction from any other source is not needed.

Love (*agape*) has been called the supreme, the all-embracing, the transcendent virtue, the queen of the virtues, and "the golden chain of all the virtues" (Col. 3:14, Phillips). It has been described as "the dominant principle of Paul's ethic" and "the master-key" of his morals.[70] Paul himself spoke of *agape* as the "more excellent way" (I Cor. 12:31), "the highest way of all" (Phillips), "the best way of all" (NEB), or "a way that is better by far" (Williams).

Many scholars believe that *agape*, which is used almost exclusively by Paul for love and which was born in the bosom of revealed religion, should not have been translated. Hunter suggests that it is "notoriously difficult to translate,"[71] while Dodd says that it is "strictly untranslatable," although he says that it carries the idea of "energetic and beneficient good will."[72] Barclay similarly says that it involves *"unconquerable benevolence, invincible good will."*[73]

While Paul does not attempt to define *agape*, he does describe it and sets forth its significance for the Christian life and the Christian community. It is not for him "a virtue among other virtues." Rather, "it is that total attitude which is brought about by exposure to the love of God."[74] Paul says that "God's love has been poured into our hearts ["has flooded our inmost heart," NEB] through the Holy Spirit which has been given to us" (Rom. 5:5). This love which has been poured into our hearts (and this is the only possible source for the *agape* type or quality of love) flows through us to bless the lives of others. We are capable of love because we have first been its objects.

[70] Hunter, *Interpreting Paul's Gospel*, p. 47.
[71] *Ibid.*, p. 119.
[72] Dodd, *Gospel and Law*, p. 42.
[73] William Barclay, *More New Testament Words* (London: SCM Press, 1958), p. 16.
[74] Dodd, *Gospel and Law*, p. 4.

This love which flows through the life of the Christian is all-inclusive. It finds expression in personal relations such as the family (Eph. 5:25, 28, 33), expands to the Christian community, and ultimately to all people (Rom. 13:9; Gal. 5:14; I Thess. 3:12). As described by Paul, it is genuine (Rom. 12:9; II Cor. 6:6; 8:8), forbearing (Eph. 4:2), forgiving (II Cor. 2:7–8), and is associated with gentleness (I Cor. 4:21). It controls or regulates liberty (Rom. 14:15; Gal. 5:13) and truth (Eph. 4:15), and is the source of the unity of the Christian community (Phil. 2:2; Col. 2:2). *Agape* builds up or edifies (I Cor. 8:1), "binds everything together in perfect harmony" (Col. 3:14), is the fulfillment of the law (Rom. 13:8–10; Gal. 5:14), and is the first mentioned and the most basic fruit of the Spirit (Gal. 5:22).

No wonder Paul admonished the Romans to owe no man anything but to love him (Rom. 13:8), encouraged the Corinthians to make love their aim or to "put love first" (I Cor. 14:1, NEB), and exhorted the Ephesians to "walk in love" (Eph. 5:2; cf. Rom. 14:15). He prayed for the Philippians that their love might abound more and more (Phil. 1:9) and for the Thessalonians that their love might increase and abound "to one another and to all men" (I Thess. 3:12). Paul believed that everything within the Christian fellowship should be done in love (I Cor. 16:14).

Paul's ethic is basically an experiential ethic. The various aspects of his ethical teachings are related in some way and to some degree to his own personal experience. This is true although his letters, in the main, were written to particular churches to meet particular needs. He was quite explicit at times in the application of his teachings to specific situations. Some of these applications are largely if not entirely irrelevant for the contemporary period. This is true, although the basic teachings underlying the applications may be abidingly relevant. The relation of the basic and the applied in Paul's epistles is comparable to the relation of the principles taught by Jesus and His illustrations or the application of those principles; the principles are continuously relevant and valid while the illustrations or applications are largely passing and irrelevant.

It is Paul's basic ethic that stems from his personal experience and gives unity to his applied ethic. The central event in his experience was his confrontation with the resurrected Christ on the Damascus road. There he was brought into a vital life-changing union with the living Christ. He learned there a lesson which was a constantly deepening one that if any man is in Christ he is a new creation. Paul interpreted all of life from the perspective of his encounter with Christ and his expanding experience in fellowship with Christ. The indwelling Christ became for him both the goal of the Christian life and the motivation or inner drive to attain that goal. His ethic, as was true of his theology, was Christocentric.

The main features of Paul's experience with Christ were considered by him to be the norm for all Christians. His personal ministry, in the main, was given to confronting individuals with the claims of Christ and bringing those individuals into a Christian community or fellowship. Most of his letters were written to those communities or churches. The predominant purpose of the letters was to lead the churches and those who were a part of their company to a deepening fellowship with the resurrected Christ and an expanding understanding of His expectations of them. In other words, he was concerned, in the main, in his epistles with Christian maturity. This inevitably meant that the ethical or the moral had a very important place in his writings.

CHAPTER VII

THE JOHANNINE LITERATURE

Book titles rather than topics will be used for the main headings in this and the succeeding chapter. One reason for this method in the present chapter on Johannine literature[1] is the contrast in approach and emphasis in the Gospel, the Epistles, and the Revelation or Apocalypse. For example, the last is so distinct that its content can not be correlated effectively with the

---

[1] There are many critical problems regarding the Johannine writings. Some of these stem from the striking similarities and yet the sharp dissimilarities of the various writings attributed to John in the ordinary versions of the Bible. Concerning similarities, Alan Richardson says, "There is a surprising number of real affinities of thought and outlook, and even of vocabulary" (*The Gospel According to Saint John: Introduction and Commentary* [London: SCM Press, 1959], p. 11). Another writer says that it seems that "all five books originated in the same circle," although "the Apocalypse stands apart" (W. F. Howard, *Christianity According to St. John* [Philadelphia: Westminster Press, 1946], p. 15). Most scholars agree that the "circle" that produced the literature centered in Ephesus. There is a wide divergence of opinion about the author or authors. For an excellent digest of the conclusions of relatively recent scholarship concerning the Johannine writings, see A. M. Hunter, *Interpreting the New Testament, 1900-1950* (London: SCM Press, 1951), pp. 78-123. What Hunter says concerning the Gospel could be said for the other writings. His statement is, "Happily, the spiritual value of the Fourth Gospel does not stand or fall with the conclusion of the critics" (p. 92).

other writings. Even the Gospel and the Epistles differ notice-
ably, although they contain some common concepts.

Preliminary Considerations

Before discussing the ethical content of the various writings,
there are a few preliminary matters that should be briefly considered.

1. The Gospel of John and the synoptics.

No attempt will be made to compare, in general, the synoptics
and John's Gospel.[2] Our concern will be restricted to a comparison of the ethical content of the synoptics and John's Gospel. It is
quite evident that the latter is not as concerned as the synoptics
with the ethical teachings of Jesus. It has only a secondary and
somewhat indirect and incidental place for the ethical. The lack
of emphasis on the ethical might have stemmed from an assumption by the writer that those to whom he was writing were well

[2] The relation of the Fourth Gospel to the synoptics is another
major critical problem in the area of Johannine literature. For many years
scholars rather generally agreed that the author of the Fourth Gospel had
available and made some use of the synoptics, particularly Mark. One of the
earliest books that challenged that position was P. Gardner-Smith's *Saint
John and the Synoptic Gospels* (Cambridge: University Press, 1938). The author concluded that "when all the facts are taken into consideration, it becomes difficult to believe that the author of the Fourth Gospel was familiar
with those Gospels which are generally thought to have been written and
given to the Church before he undertook his task" (p. 88). Some years later
A. J. B. Higgins in *The Historicity of the Fourth Gospel* (London: Lutterworth Press, 1960) concluded that "John is independent of all the Synoptic
Gospels" (p. 82). For a much more comprehensive and technical volume than
either of the preceding, see C. H. Dodd, *Historical Tradition in the Fourth
Gospel* (Cambridge: University Press, 1963). After a careful comparison of the
Fourth Gospel and the synoptics, Dodd concludes that "behind the Fourth
Gospel lies an ancient tradition independent of the other gospels." He further
says that this tradition merits "serious consideration as a contribution to our
knowledge of the historical facts concerning Jesus Christ" (p. 423). Two addi-
tional books that will be of interest to those who want to do some further
study are: B. H. Streeter, *The Four Gospels: A Study of Origins*, 8th imp.
(London: Macmillan, 1953) and W. F. Howard, *The Fourth Gospel in Recent
Criticism and Interpretation*, revised by C. K. Barrett, 4th rev. ed. (London:
Epworth Press, 1955).

acquainted with the teachings of Jesus. Furthermore, a major emphasis on the ethical would not have fitted in with the purpose for the writing of the Gospel. The author states the purpose as follows: "Now Jesus did many other signs . . . but these are written that you may believe that Jesus is the Christ, the Son of God, and that believing you may have life in his name" (John 20:30–31). The preceding does not mean that there was no place for the ethical in John's Gospel. As we shall see, it contains considerable ethical content and what is there is of major importance.

The ethical teachings found in John's Gospel differ from the synoptics. Jesus, according to the synoptics, set forth largely general principles or concepts. John presents his ethical teachings primarily in broad abstract terms such as "life," "light," "love," and "truth." There is also a difference in the method of moral teaching in John and the synoptics. In the latter Jesus used the parable as a major teaching instrument, some of his greatest moral lessons being expressed in or illustrated by parables. The story of the Good Samaritan is an example. In contrast, John's Gospel contains some marvelously rich allegories (shepherd and sheep, vine and the branches) but few parables, unless "parable" is used in a relatively broad sense.[3]

2. John and Paul.

Paul and John were both mystics. The idea contained in Paul's expression "in Christ" is quite prevalent in the Johannine writings, particularly in the Gospel and I John. This largely explains the fact that the ethic of both was basically theological and inner, with outer conduct a natural expression of an inner relationship. Theirs was a "radical inwardness." Similarities in their theological perspective and in their ethical thought do not necessarily mean that either borrowed from the other. They had a common inheritance of a vital faith that centered in the work and person of Jesus Christ. His presence within them determined the nature of their Christian experience and hence, in the main, the nature and content of their basic ethic.

Although their general ethical perspective is strikingly similar,

---

[3] *See,* Dodd, *Historical Tradition in the Fourth Gospel,* pp. 366–87, for a discussion of "Parabolic Norms" in the Fourth Gospel.

there is considerable contrast in content. For example, Paul is more specific than John. This stemmed, to a degree, from the fact that Paul wrote most of his epistles to particular churches with particular problems.[4] Some of those problems grew out of the recent conversion of many of the members of the churches, most of whom were Gentiles. They needed not only to know the basic concepts of the Christian way of life; they also needed to see the application of those concepts to their lives, their churches, and their culture. John, evidently writing somewhat later than Paul, wrote to those who were more mature in the faith, to those who were possibly acquainted with the teachings of Jesus and Paul. Whatever may have been the reason, John did not think it was necessary for him to spell out as specifically as Paul the application of his basic ethical concepts. Furthermore, one purpose of his writing was obviously to combat certain aspects of Gnosticism. The latter helps to explain his emphasis on knowledge and on the commandments in both the Gospel and particularly I John.

The preceding is one reason why John, in ethics as well as in theology, does not cover as broad an area as Paul. He seems satisfied to set forth a few ideas and repeat them over and over again. While he lacked the breadth of Paul, he did not lack his depth. "It is doubtful that anyone penetrates more deeply into the wonders of spiritual experience,"[5] or into the basic nature of the Christian life than John.

One area in which both the similarity and the contrast between Paul and John is revealed quite clearly is in their concept of love. For Paul, love and the other Christian virtues result from the Christian's union with Christ. For John this union is with the One who is Love. Love is not so much a result as an integral part of the Christian's experience with Christ. This idea is implicit in Paul, explicit in John. For the latter, Christian morality could be summed up as likeness to Christ or likeness to God, and since God is equated with light and love, the Christian is to walk in the way of light and love. For John love was not simply the

---

4 Ephesians and Galatians were possible exceptions, but even these were addressed to churches of a particular area with some distinctive problems.

5 W. T. Conner, *The Epistles of John*, rev. ed. (Nashville: Broadman Press, 1957), p. 5.

crowning virtue of the Christian life, it was the inclusive virtue, a concept that is not entirely lacking in Paul (see Rom. 13:8–10; Gal. 5:14).

3. The Gospel and the Epistles.

The Gospel and the Epistles of John reveal striking similarities as well as divergencies. Typical Johannine concepts and words such as life, light, love, and truth are prevalent in both. If there is an order of dependence it seems that the Epistles are dependent on the Gospel. At least, I John is full of echoes of the Gospel; one writer goes so far as to say that "no idea emerges in the Epistle which has not its text in the Gospel,"[6] while another author calls the Epistle "the earliest commentary" on the Fourth Gospel.[7] It has also been suggested that the Epistle applies "the main thoughts of the Gospel to the practical needs of the churches."[8] The ethical is more central in the Epistles, particularly I John, than in the Gospel. What is largely implied in the Gospel is expanded and made more explicit in the Epistle.

4. General characteristics of Johannine ethics.

Before discussing the ethical teachings of the Gospel, the Epistles, and the Apocalypse let us briefly set forth, at the risk of some repetition, some of the general characteristics of the ethic of John's writings. Similar to Jewish ethics in general, the Johannine ethic is non-systematic. Also, in common with the teachings of Jesus in the synoptics and the Pauline epistles, John's ethic is non-legalistic. It "is not a new legalism but the natural outcome of a new relationship."[9]

For John the Christian ethic is a faith ethic; faith for him had a moral quality. Its outer expression spontaneously springs from an inner condition and relationship. There is also a sense in which his is a dualistic ethic. At least the lines are sharply drawn

---

6 Walter Lowrie, *The Doctrine of Saint John* (London: Longmans, Green, and Co., 1899), p. 157. This excellent old book is largely reproduced in Edwin Kenneth Lee's *The Religious Thought of St. John* (London: S.P.C.K., 1950).

7 Howard, *Christianity According to Saint John,* p. 20.

8 *Ibid.,* p. 18.

9 *Ibid.,* p. 177.

between good and evil, life and death, light and darkness, love and hate. For him there is no half-way house.

Furthermore, John's ethic, as was true of the Jewish perspective in general, is basically theological. In this regard he is closely akin to the Old Testament and to the other writers of the New Testament. One author goes so far as to say that "with no other writer in the New Testament is the relation of theology to life so transparent, so immediate, and so necessary."[10] His ethic evolves more or less naturally from his theology. This close relationship is seen, at least to some degree, in the structure of the Gospel. In the first twelve chapters, which cover the public ministry of Jesus, the emphasis is on believing in Christ, with a minimum of attention to Christian living. The emphasis on the latter is found in the closing chapters that record the conversations of Jesus with His disciples immediately preceding His crucifixion. As Glasson says, "It is when men have first come to Christ in faith and have received him that they are ready for instruction in righteousness."[11] John's order, it should be noted, is the same as Paul's, at least in most of his major epistles, first the predominantly theological followed by the ethical.

One evidence of the theological nature of John's ethic is the fact that it is theocentric. For John, God is righteous and the one who knows Him will be righteous. God is Light, His child will walk in the light rather than in the darkness. God is Love, the one who is in the Christian fellowship will not only love God but also the children of God. The relation of John's concept of God to his ethic is seen nowhere more clearly than in his teachings concerning love, a subject to which we shall return. Love is central in the ethic of John, because love is central in the character of God. When one is brought into the family of God, into fellowship with the Father in the community of God, he is brought into union or fellowship with love. It is this that makes love the comprehensive and inclusive virtue. It is the germ which produces every form of Christian service. For John, love comprises "the

10 Lowrie, p. 195.
11 T. Francis Glasson, *Moses in the Fourth Gospel* (London: SCM Press, 1963), p. 94.

whole conception of Christian morality."[12] While love is prevalent in the synoptics and Paul, it more nearly dominates the thought of John. This is pointed up by the frequency of the use by John of "love" as compared to the synoptics. For example, the noun *agape* and the verb *agapaō* are found more frequently in John's Gospel than in all of the synoptics combined, and considerably more frequently in I John than in any of Paul's epistles. Even *phileō*, another word translated love, is found more than twice as often in the Fourth Gospel as in the other three Gospels. John's ethic can properly be labelled an ethic of love.

The Gospel

The Fourth Gospel claims as its author "the disciple whom Jesus loved" (13:32; 19:26; 20:2; 21:7, 20, 24).[13] Whoever was its author, and we have no problem personally with its apostolic authorship, the writing of the Gospel "was one of the great events of history."[14] It "is in many ways the crown of the Scriptures. It is the simplest and at the same time the most profound book in the New Testament."[15] Furthermore, the author "stands out as a religious genius of the first order, like the apostle Paul and the unnamed author of the Epistle to the Hebrews."[16] The Gospel is prized by most Christians because of its mystical and devotional

[12] Lowrie, p. 205.

[13] Some modern scholars question if they do not deny that the Apostle John is the author of the Fourth Gospel. Floyd V. Filson, in *Current Issues in New Testament Interpretation,* ed. William Klassen and Graydon F. Snyder (New York: Harper, 1962), pp. 119–23, makes out an interesting case for Lazarus as "the beloved disciple" and hence the author of the Fourth Gospel. For the external and internal evidence for the apostolic authorship see H. P. V. Nunn, *The Authorship of the Fourth Gospel* (London: Alden and Blackwell, 1952). A rather compact survey of the same evidence will be found in Samuel A. Cartledge, *A Conservative Introduction to the New Testament,* 6th ed. (Grand Rapids: Zondervan, 1951), pp. 181–98. Higgins concludes (p. 19) that the historical value of the book is not dependent on the knowledge of the name of the author.

[14] Floyd V. Filson, *Opening the New Testament* (Philadelphia: Westminster Press, 1952), p. 68.

[15] Howard, *Interpreter's Bible,* VIII, 437.

[16] *Ibid.,* p. 441.

tone. Although it contains less ethical content than the synoptics or Paul's epistles, it has more emphasis on ethics than many people realize.

1. Eternal life.[17]

The word "life," particularly with the prefix "eternal," is one of the key words in the Johannine writings. In the Gospel it is a constant and recurring emphasis from the prologue to the statement of the purpose of the Gospel near the close (20:31). Filson calls John "the Gospel of Life."[18] Life is the theme of "the little gospel" (3:16), which is possibly the most frequently quoted verse of the Bible. It was Jesus who said: "The Father has life in himself, so he has granted the Son also to have life in himself" (5:26). He who had life in Himself came that His sheep might have life (10:18, 28). In some of the "I am" statements[19] by Jesus, He revealed that He is the bread of life (6:48), the resurrection and the life (11:25), the way, the truth, and the life (14:6). The water that He gives will become in one "a spring of water welling up to eternal life" (4:14). In His high priestly prayer He said: "And this is eternal life, that they know thee the only true God, and Jesus Christ whom thou hast sent" (17:3). Those who know Him have life through a mystical union with Him (6:54). This union with Christ, whatever may be its basic nature, provides the dynamic or motivation for an outreach of service on the behalf of the indwelling Christ, an outreach in the Christian community and in the world.

The expression "eternal life" is found in the synoptics but it is much more common in John. If there is such a thing as a *summum bonum* in Christian ethics, then for John it was eternal life. As such the expression is comparable to the kingdom of God in the synoptics. And as is true of the kingdom concept in the latter, "eternal life" is both a present possession and a future

17 See chapter three of W. H. Rigg, *The Fourth Gospel and Its Message for To-day* (London: Lutterworth Press, 1952), for a helpful discussion of "Eternal Life, Now and Hereafter."

18 Klassen and Snyder, p. 113.

19 The use of "I am" is strikingly characteristic of John. For some additional "I am" references see John 6:35, 51; 8:12, 23; 10:7, 9, 11, 14; 15:1, 5.

hope in the Johannine literature (3:36; 5:24). Really, for John eternal life is timeless. Westcott's frequently quoted statement is: "It is not an endless duration of being in time, but being of which time is not a measure."[20] The emphasis is on "a present quality of life that is above time."[21] How could it be otherwise when this eternal life results from one's union with *The* Eternal Person, who is the eternal or abiding I AM. Rigg sums the matter up by saying that eternal life is "union with the Father and the Son of God, within time and beyond time."[22] It is a mutual indwelling—Christ in the believer and the believer in Him.

This conception of eternal life as a present possession has important ethical significance. This is particularly true when we remember the kind of Person with whom we have been brought into union and the further fact that the life we have in Him is not only to be lived in union with Him but also in fellowship with His children. In this fellowship and in the world in general the child of God is to let the indwelling Eternal Person live in him and express Himself through him. In this way He can reveal most clearly what it means to have eternal life as a present possession. It is this that will give to eternal life what some one has called its "social character." Ethical conduct is the result or the fruit of union with the Eternal Person.

2. The fruitful life.

To the disciples shortly before his crucifixion Jesus said: "You did not choose me, but I chose you and appointed you that you should go and bear fruit and that your fruit should abide" (John 15:16). Notice that He and not they had done the choosing—the "you" and "I" are emphatic. Whether this referred to His selection of them as Apostles or simply as disciples, He had done the choosing. This He continues to do. How glorious is His grace that He has chosen us, unworthy as we are, to be with Him and to represent Him in the world.

[20] Brooks Foss Westcott, *The Epistles of St. John*, 3rd ed. (London: Macmillan, 1892), p. 215. Subsequent references to this commentary will be in parentheses (Westcott) in the body of the material.

[21] Edward W. Bauman, *An Introduction to the New Testament* (Philadelphia: Westminster Press, 1961), p. 159.

[22] Rigg, p. 87.

Notice also that Jesus revealed the purpose of the choosing, which is a continuing purpose. He had chosen them that they might keep on going, keep on bearing fruit, and that their fruit might keep on abiding: "not a mere spurt, but permanent growth and fruit-bearing" (WP). "The bearing of fruit is simply living the life of a Christian disciple (see vv. 5, 8); perhaps especially the practice of mutual love (v. 12)."[23] The fruit Jesus was talking about is the fruit of a good life, a life like the one He lived while He walked among men. He was going away from them. He had chosen them to be with Him that He might prepare them for the time when He would leave them. Now He would live in them and bear fruit through them.

They were to bear fruit in His place, but their fruit bearing was conditioned on their vital relationship to Him. The verse referred to above (15:16) is preceded by and is an integral part of the famous vine and branches passage. This is one of the great symbols or allegor   in John's Gospel. This allegory is introduced with one of the "I am" sayings of Jesus. He says, "I am the true [or genuine] vine" (15:1),[24] which is repeated later with the addition: "You are the branches" (v. 5). He encourages them to abide in Him (or "remain in union with Him," Williams) and says, "As the branch cannot bear fruit by itself, unless it abides in the vine ["remains united to the vine," Williams], neither can you, unless you abide in me" (v. 4). It is the disciple who abides in Him who bears much fruit, for apart from Him we can do nothing (v. 5). A vital, continuing union with the resurrected Christ is the secret to the fruitful life for Him. The branches draw their sustenance from the vine. They can only bear fruit as they remain a part of the vine. Fruit is normal and natural for the branches.

In verse 8 Jesus says, "By this my Father is glorified, that you bear much fruit, and so prove to be my disciples." It is possible as Robertson suggests that the "herein" or "by this" points both backward and forward (WP). It may refer both to the vital union

23 C. K. Barrett, *The Gospel According to St. John* (London: S.P.C.K., 1955), p. 395.
24 The "vine" is a metaphor that was rather common in Jewish thought (see Ps. 80:8–16; Isa. 5:1–7; Ezek. 15:1–8; 19:10–14), being a recognized symbol for the Messiah.

of the branches with the vine and to the fruit that comes as a result of that union. It is by living a fruitful life that glorifies God that we prove that we are disciples of Christ. There is a sense in which the discipleship as is true of the abiding in Him and the bearing of fruit for Him is a continuing and a deepening experience. This is also true of the Christian's experience in prayer. He will mature in prayer as he lives a fruitful life, a life that glorifies God, and as he grows in his union with Christ. His prayers will be increasingly answered since he will increasingly abide in Christ and hence pray in His name (v. 16; cf. 14:13; 15:7).

3. "A new commandment."

In one of those intimate conversations with His disciples the night before His Crucifixion Jesus said to them, "A new commandment I give to you, that you love one another; even as I have loved you, that you also love one another" (John 13:34). Why would He say that love was a new commandment? It was certainly not the first time He had mentioned the commandment of love.

It may help us to interpret correctly the statement by Jesus if we understand that there is more than one word translated "new" in our New Testament. One is a word (*neos*) that means young in contrast to old, the word being translated "young" much more frequently than "new." Another word (*kainos*) translated "new" means fresh as opposed to worn out. It is the latter word that is used in John 13:34.[25] In other words, the commandment to love one another may be an old commandment, but Jesus breathed new life into it.

Before suggesting ways that the commandment to love was new, let us notice that it was a commandment. There are very few ethical precepts attributed to Jesus in John's Gospel. In contrast, He rather frequently is reported to have made the general statement that His disciples should keep His commandments. He does not spell out these commandments except the commandment to love. On the surface it may sound like moving in a circle, but one proves his love for Christ by keeping His commandments: love

25 Both words are used in Matthew 9:17, which is translated in the Revised Standard Version: "But new wine is put into fresh wineskins."

entails obedience (14:15, 21, 23–24), and yet his one specifically stated commandment is to love. It should be noted, however, that the commandment to the disciples is not to love Him but to love one another (15:12, 17).

How was this a "new" commandment? How did Jesus breathe new life into an old commandment? There is a sense in which the commandment was new (1) in its source: "I give to you." He is not quoting from the Old Testament or from any other source; He is speaking His own authoritative word. It was also a new commandment (2) in motive: "as I have loved you" (cf. 15:12). The natural response of the disciple to the love of Christ is to love Him. But if we love Him, we shall keep His commandments, and His commandment is that we love one another. The commandment is also new, at least to a degree, (3) in its nature. It is not a lew legalism, but an obedience that naturally evolves from a new relationship. It does not set forth the law of the Christian community but rather the spirit that should permeate the community.

Furthermore, it is a new commandment (4) in its dimensions. It involves a peculiar and distinctive love for those within the Christian community. Certainly the Christian is to love all men, but just as he has a special affection for the members of his own family so he has a special love for those within the Christian family. There is also in the commandment a new depth. This new depth evolves from the quality of life Christ lived and the fact that He loved enough to give His life. The disciples were to love one another as He had loved them. This statement by Jesus possibly looked in two directions: back to His washing of their feet: love (*agape*) will render the humblest service; forward to His death on the cross: love (*agape*) will make any sacrifice. Following the words "as I have loved you" in 15:12 is the statement: "Greater love has no man than this, that a man lay down his life for his friends" (v. 13). Christ was going to do this, it is the measure of the disciples' love for one another. The "as" in the previous statement not only carries the idea of comparison but also of conformity, i.e., our love for one another is to have the same quality as His love for us.

There are also some glorious if not entirely new results that will flow from the keeping of this new commandment of love. Jesus stated one of those results as follows: "By this everybody will know that you are my disciples if you keep on showing love for one another" (13:35, Williams). Also, obedience to this and His commandments in general will make us friends of His (15:14). He and the Father "will come in face-to-face fellowship" with us and will make Their "special dwelling place" with us (14:23, Williams).

4. The will of God.

The ethic of Christianity is so deep and meaningful that many terms are required to describe it adequately. This is seen in the Fourth Gospel. Its author has been correctly called the apostle of love and his ethic an ethic of love. His ethic could also be called an ethic of the will of God, an ethic of self-denial, an ethic of the cross; all of which are closely interrelated. The emphasis on the will of God in John is seen more in what Jesus said concerning Himself than in what He said regarding His disciples. But Jesus taught as much by the life He lived as by what He said.

He said of Himself: "I have come down from heaven, not to do my own will, but the will of him who sent me" (6:38). Again He said: "I seek not my own will but the will of him who sent me" (5:30). His statement to the wondering disciples at Jacob's well was: "My food is to do the will of him who sent me, and to accomplish his work" (4:34). He had a deep awareness of having been sent,[26] sent to do the Father's will. Doing the will of the Father meant self-denial and ultimately death on the cross (see 12:24–25, 32–33). He did not complete the will of God for His life among men until on the cross He said, "It is finished" (19:30).

The resurrected Christ appeared to the little group of disciples and said to them: "As the Father has sent me, even so I send you" (20:21; cf. 17:23). This was the commission of Christ just as much as the one on the mountain in Galilee (Matt. 28:16–20) or the one on the Mount of Olives (Luke 24:44–51; Acts 1:3–11), and is

---

[26] Howard, *The Interpreter's Bible*, VIII, 438, says that Jesus used "he who sent me" twenty-six times and a synonymous verb eighteen times in John's Gospel. It represents another key idea in John, comparable to "life," "light," and "love."

followed by the words: "He breathed on them, and said to them, 'Receive the Holy Spirit'" (20:22). Here is both the commissioning and the enduement or empowerment—an anticipation of Pentecost. What did He mean by the statement, "As the Father . . ."? He had a deep consciousness of having been sent not to do His own will but the will of the Father; they likewise were sent not to do their will but His. He had been sent into the world to reveal God and to redeem man; He was sending them into the world to reveal Him and to be a redeeming influence among men. Really, they were to carry on His mission in the world. He was sending them to do what the Father had sent Him to do. It was one mission, not two. And just as He could not do the will of His Father, could not reveal God, and could not redeem man without going to the cross; so they and we cannot do the will of God, cannot reveal Christ, and cannot be a redeeming influence among men without denying self and taking up a cross to follow Him. To the degree that we have a deep consciousness of having been sent to do His will, to that degree there will be in our lives a sense of holy urgency, which characterized His life. On one occasion He said: "We must work the works of him who sent me, while it is day; night comes, when no one can work" (9:4).

The Epistles[27]

The First Epistle of John is a gold mine of ethical instruction, with the emphasis primarily on basic ethics as contrasted to social or applied ethics. To a considerable degree, it is an expansion of the fundamental concepts of the Gospel, particularly the concept of love. The epistle sets forth "the specific ethical demands of the Gospel's deeper religious principles. Taken together, the Gospel and First John constitute one of the richest deposits of spiritual truth in the Christian religion."[28]

27 The second and third epistles of John are so brief and contain so little distinctive material that they will be referred to only incidentally a time or two.
28 Bauman, p. 167.

1. The purpose.

Some scholars suggest that one purpose of the Epistle, as was true of the Gospel, although not stated specifically, was to meet the challenge of Gnosticism. Other scholars strongly contend that this is not true, some suggesting that the Gnostic movement made use of certain things found in the writings of Paul and John.[29]

While Gnosticism may provide a background for an understanding of the Epistle, John more specifically states one or more other purposes for the writing of the letter. It is generally agreed that his dominant purpose is found in the statement: "I write this to you who believe in the name of the Son of God, that you may know that you have eternal life" (5:13), "a knowledge final and certain" (Westcott). The Gospel was written that those who read it might "believe that Jesus is the Christ" and that believing they might "have life in his name" (John 20:31). The Epistle was written to give assurance to those who had believed.[30]

When the Epistle is read with 5:13 in mind as its purpose it comes to life in an unusual way. We see that the rich ethical teachings of the Epistle provide the tests[31] of whether or not one has eternal life. These tests or proofs can be applied by the individual child of God or by others to him. Several of these tests or proofs are introduced with the words "By this we know," or "By this we can be sure." For example, John says, "By this we may be sure that we know him" (2:3) and "are in him" (2:5). He further says, "By this we know that he abides in us" (3:24), "that we abide

29 The following will be helpful for those who want to do some general reading on Gnosticism: R. M. Grant, *Gnosticism and Early Christianity* (New York: Columbia University Press, 1959) and another volume edited by Grant, *Gnosticism* (New York: Harper, 1961), Hans Jonas, *The Gnostic Religion* (Boston: Beacon Press, 1958), and R. McL. Wilson, *The Gnostic Problem* (London: A. R. Mowbray, and Co., 1958). Grant also has an article on Gnosticism in *The Interpreter's Dictionary of the Bible* (New York: Abingdon, 1962).

30 Other possible purposes for the writing of the Epistle are "that the joy of us all may be complete" (1:4, NEB); "that you may not sin" (2:1); and "I write this to you about those who would deceive you" (2:26). The latter may refer to the Gnostics.

31 An old but standard commentary on I John by Robert Law is entitled *The Tests of Life* (Edinburgh: T. & T. Clark, 1909).

in him and he in us" (4:13). There are also statements such as the following: "By this we know love" (3:16), "By this we know the spirit of truth and the spirit of error" (4:6), and "By this we know that we love the children of God" (5:2). The Christian's knowledge is based primarily on personal experience. To know God means to have fellowship with Him, to be responsive to Him, and to strive "after conformity with Him" (Westcott). The tests or proofs of this relationship and hence of eternal life can be grouped under three or four major headings. These will provide the basis for most of the remainder of this section on the Epistle.

2. *Righteousness and sin.*

How can one "be quite sure that, here and now he possesses eternal life" (Phillips)? One test that John gives is one's relation to sin and righteousness. He says that we are to acknowledge and confess our sins, possibly another thrust at some of the Gnostics who denied the reality of sin. If we confess our sins we can know that God "will forgive our sins and cleanse us from all unrighteousness" (1:8–9). On the other hand, John says that one who abides in Him and hence has eternal life will have the victory over sin (3:6; 5:18). He will not sin because "God's nature abides in him, and he cannot sin because he is born of God" (3:9). On the surface there seems to be a conflict between this statement and the earlier one in the first chapter. Quite evidently John does not mean that one who has eternal life never sins. There are several ways of avoiding the seeming contradiction. It is claimed by some that John in Chapter 3 is stating the Christian ideal and as is typical of him he states it in an extreme form. Others suggest that the Christian life in its essence is a life of perfect righteousness. Westcott, for example, says, "As long as the relationship with God is real . . . sinful acts . . . do not touch the essence of the man's being." The New English Bible avoids, at least to a degree, the problem by translating 3:6a as follows: "No man therefore who dwells in him is a sinner" (cf. 3:9). Other translations such as Phillips and Williams suggest continuous or habitual action. For example, Williams translates 3:6 as follows: "No one who continues to live in union with Him practices sin. No one who practices sin has ever seen Him or come to know Him." Phillips similarly says, "The man who lives 'in Christ' does not habitually sin. The regular sinner has never seen or known Him." David Smith says, "The believer may fall into sin but he will not walk in it" (Ex. G). The translation or interpretation of Williams, Phillips, and Smith seems to be the most satisfactory. One does not have eternal life if he lives habitually in sin.

As one would expect, there is a comparable emphasis on righteousness. Sin and righteousness cannot dwell together; it is a moral impossibility. Typical of John's sharp way of expressing things, there are two classes of people: those who practice righteousness and those who commit sin, children of God and children of the devil. In harmony with the interpretation of the preceding paragraph, one can know that he has eternal life as a present possession by the direction or movement of his life regarding sin and righteousness. If he has been brought into union with the Eternal Person, who gives life, the movement will be away from sin and toward righteousness.

The emphasis in John on righteousness is on actual or personal righteousness in contrast to righteousness as "acquittal." which is so prevalent in Paul. Paul, when he speaks of righteousness, is usually concerned with the initial Christian experience when one is made right with God. John applies "righteousness" primarily to the life of the maturing child of God. For him the forgiven sinner has been brought into union or fellowship with the righteous God, or one who is morally consistent and upright. There has been implanted within the child of God a new moral nature or disposition. This, which has its source in a righteous God, predisposes His child away from sin and toward righteousness.

In his typically plain and pointed way John says, "If you know that he is righteous, you may be sure that every one who does right is born of him" (2:29): the words "does right" suggest that righteousness for John is primarily active rather than passive. Again he says, "He who does right is righteous, as he is righteous" (3:7); it reveals the character of the individual. Still again he says, "Whoever does not do right is not of God, nor he who does not love his brother" (3:10). Note the relating, in the last quotation, of righteousness and love. John seems to treat them practically as equivalent, which Lowrie considers a peculiarity of his ethic.[32] Robert Law suggests that in I John the "whole moral activity of the Divine Life proceeds" from righteousness and love.[33]

3. Light and darkness.

The discussion of light and darkness could have been included in the section on "righteousness and sin." They are, in the main, two ways of looking at the same thing. A separate section has been devoted to them, however, because of the prominence of "light" and "darkness" in the epistle as well as in the Johannine literature in general. In the Gospel Christ is revealed as "the true light" (John 1:9; cf. 1:4–5). Jesus Himself said that He was the light of the world (8:12; cf. 12:46); through belief in Him as the light men could "become sons of light" (2:36). In the Epistle the statement that "God is light" (I John 1:5) provides the background if not the theme for the first portion of the Epistle as "God is love" does for the latter portion.[34] And "light" for John contains an ethical element. It is used as a symbol of goodness, while darkness is a symbol of moral evil. He suggests that one can know whether or not he has eternal life as a present possession by his relation to light and darkness.

The full statement of the verse referred to above (1:5) is as follows: "This is the message we have heard from him and proclaim to you, that God is light and in him is no darkness at all." Notice that John claims that he had this message from Christ, and evidently he means to suggest that this is a summary of the basic revelation of God in and through his Son. "Light" refers primarily to revelation, but the revelation is inclusive of the nature and character of God. Since He is an ethical or moral being, the concept of "light" naturally and inevitably moves into the ethical

[32] Lowrie, p. 200.

[33] Law, p. 67. For a careful analysis of the relation of these two qualities in the character of God, see Law, pp. 67–88.

[34] John more than any other biblical writer tells us what God *is*, in contrast to what He *does*. God is revealed as spirit (John 4:24), light (I John 1:5), love (I John 4:8, 16). These are not mere attributes of God, they are His very essence.

area. Thus it seems that when John speaks of God as light, he means to include all moral perfection.[35]

The statement by John in 1:5 is immediately followed with the typically sharp statement: "If we say we have fellowship with him while we walk in darkness, we lie and do not live according to the truth" (1:6). For John there is no twilight zone. It is impossible for those who walk in darkness to have fellowship with God, who is Light. Light and darkness cannot dwell together. One dispels the other. On the other hand, "if we walk in the light, as he is in the light," we not only walk with Him but "we have fellowship with one another" (1:7). The latter is the visible evidence and proof of fellowship with God. To walk in darkness is to walk in the way of moral evil or sin. To walk in the light is to walk with the One who is Light and in union with Him to walk in the way of goodness. "This fellowship that John is talking about is a moral fellowship; it depends on moral conditions and issues in moral results."[36]

John also implies a close relation between light and love as he does between righteousness and love. This close relation should be expected since "light" and "love" are united in God. One cannot walk in light without at the same time walking in love. John specifically says, "He who says he is in the light and hates his brother is in the darkness still" (2:9). This is immediately followed with the opposite statement, a method or technique quite common in the Epistle. The statement is: "He who loves his brother abides in the light, and in it there is no cause for stumbling" (2:10). Again he says, "He who hates his brother is in the darkness and walks in the darkness, and does not know where he is going, because the darkness has blinded his eyes" (2:11). Such a one certainly lacks assurance. He does not have the evidence in his life that he has eternal life.

4. Love and hate.

Love (*agape*) has been called "the very key word in NT ethics,"[37] and "the positive element in the Christian ethic."[38] In

---

35 Conner, p. 15.
36 *Ibid.*, p. 19.
37 Barclay, *More New Testament Words*, p. 13.
38 Law, p. 231.

both Testaments there is considerable emphasis on God's love for man, on man's responsive love for God, and on man's love for his fellowman. Man's love for God and his fellowman are two aspects of a single virtue, "the two *agapes* . . . are as convex is to concave."[39] However, in John, as suggested earlier, the emphasis is almost exclusively on love for those within the Christian fellowship. For example, in I John, he says, "We [emphatic] know that we have passed out of death into life, because we love the brethren" (3:14; cf. John 5:24). The love of the brethren is a proof or test and not the ground of assurance. He states the negative as well as the positive aspects of the truth and states it in extremes; there is no middle ground between love and life on the one hand and hate and death on the other hand. If one does not love he remains in death: "To love is to live."[40] If one hates his brother, and to hate is to have no love (*agape*) for him, he is a murderer, and "no murderer has eternal life abiding in him" (3:15).

There is a sense in which John made love very inclusive. It is "the one commandment which includes all others, being repeated . . . with magnificent monotony."[41] He related love in a special way to the other tests or proofs of eternal life. It is closely related to if not inclusive of light: "He who loves his brother abides in the light" (2:10), and to righteousness: "whoever does not do right is not of God, nor he who loves not his brother" (3:10). He also closely relates love to belief or faith (3:23). Law suggests that the relation of love to righteousness and belief "is that of the test to the thing tested." For him "love is the test."[42] It seems that in II John the author would equate "following the truth" with following the commandments, and the one commandment they had heard from the beginning was to "follow love" (II John 4–6).

Love is a commandment, but what is the source for the love of the brethren? The question is answered in specific ways in 4:7–21, where the Epistle rises to its sublimest heights. Love (*agape*) in its deepest and most meaningful sense is the spontaneous fruit of a vital relationship with a God, who is Love (*agape*) (4:8, 16). Love

39 Dewar, *An Outline of New Testament Ethics*, p. 203.
40 Law, p. 240.
41 Stauffer, "Love," Kittel's *Bible Key Words*, I, 63.
42 Law, p. 248.

is the very essence of God's being; His love is life's ultimate reality. God is the source of all *agape*, of love that partakes of the divine quality (4:7): "love originates with God" (Williams).[43] One who does not love does not know God since God is Love (4:8). He may know, like the Gnostics, some things about God, but he does not know God. Furthermore, since God is Love, one "who abides in love abides in God, and God abides in him" (4:16). "The nature of the believer must be conformed to the nature of God" (Westcott). "We love, because he first loved us" (4:19). The latter is not as the old version says, "We love him, because he first loved us." It is a glorious truth that we respond in love to His love for us, but it is a greater truth that love characterizes our lives because He first loved us. "Our love is the light kindled by the love of God" (Westcott). Our response to His love is not only love for Him but we make ourselves a channel for His love for others. John sets forth this relationship by saying, "Every one who loves the parent loves the child" (5:1); God is the parent, a fellow Christian is the child.

The motivation for our love for one another is grounded in God's love for us. He loved us enough that He sent His Son, "so that we might live through him" (4:9). The Son was sent to be "the expiation ["remedy," NEB; "the atoning sacrifice," Williams] for our sins" (4:10). John concludes, "Beloved, if God so loved us, we also ought to love one another" (4:11). Earlier he had said, "By this we know love ["have come to know and still know," WP], that he laid down his life for us" (3:16). Christ on the cross is the one perfect or full embodiment of love or *agape*. Christ giving Himself is contrasted with Cain, who murdered his brother (3:12). John concludes that since Christ laid down His life for us, that "we ought to lay down our lives for the brethren" (3:16). There follows what might be considered John's one pointed practical application of the principle of love. He says, "But if anyone has the world's goods and sees his brother in need, yet closes his heart [locks his heart, or slams "the door of his com-

---

[43] Law suggests that *agape* "is virtually a coinage of Christianity" (p. 70), and that in its noun form it had been comparatively unused, seemingly "providentially reserved to express that purely ethical love the conception of which Christianity first made current among men" (p. 71).

passion," WP] against him, how does God's love abide in him?"
(3:17). Notice that it does not say, "How does the love of his
neighbor or brother abide in him," but "How does God's love
abide in him"—love for God or possibly better love that comes
from God.

Let us state again that love, particularly love for the brethren,
is a test if not the one comprehensive test of eternal life as a
present possession. If we love one another, God, the Eternal Person who gives eternal life, abides in us (4:12, 16). On the other
hand, if one says that he loves God, "and hates ["habitually
hates," Williams] his brother, he is a liar; for he who does not
love his brother whom he has seen, cannot love God whom he
has not seen" (4:20). And certainly if he does not love God he
does not have eternal life.

5. Life and death.

Life and death represent another pair of opposing concepts
that is present in the Epistle, although not as clearly drawn as the
three preceding ones: righteousness and sin, light and darkness,
love and hate. The Epistle opens and closes with an emphasis on
life. This is the theme that ties it together. The eternal life concerning which John was writing was in the Father and had been
made manifest in His Son (1:2–3). This truth, stated in the introduction or prologue of the Epistle, is recapitulated and enlarged
on in a very emphatic way in the last chapter. John says that
eternal life is a gift of God, given to us in His Son (5:11; cf. John
3:16). It is a gift, but it cannot be separated from the Giver; the
life is in God. It involves self-communication. Eternal life comes
through a vital union with the Eternal Person. John plainly says,
"He who has the Son has life; he who has not the Son has not
life" (5:12; cf. John 10:10). In the Gospel Jesus had said that He
was the bread from heaven that gave "life to the world" (John
6:33), and that He was the resurrection and the life (John 11:25).

The Christian religion, for John, is described most fully as
abiding in or having fellowship with God and with His Son, and
in them there is life (see John 5:26). There are two general conditions that must be met to have that fellowship and hence to
have eternal life. One is a right belief about Christ and the other

is ethical living for Christ. The combination of these is seen with particular clarity in his statement that the commandment of God is "that we should believe in the name of his Son Jesus Christ and love one another" (3:23; cf. 5:1). Faith or doctrine is for John so closely related to morals that faith "is always fundamentally a moral attitude."[44] For him theology and ethics form a unity. Faith in Christ and a life fashioned by Him are vitally and inescapably united. Faith is the response of one's "entire moral and spiritual nature. . . . It . . . revolutionizes one's moral nature and makes him a child of God."[45]

The faith that gives life through union or fellowship with God and His Son will also give victory over the world (5:4–5). This victory is an evidence that one has eternal life. The initial victory is in the initial experience when one becomes a child of God. This victory is the assurance of continuing victories.

John closes the Epistle with a thrice repeated emphatic, "We know," which possibly reveals again the Gnostic influence on the Epistle. Here at the close he states some divine certainties. As a part of the last "we know" he says, "We know that . . . we are in him who is true, in his Son Jesus Christ. This is the true God and eternal life" (5:20).

6. Conclusion: the way of the Lord.

In one of those marvelously rich discourses just before His crucifixion, Jesus said to his disciples, "I am the way . . . no one comes to the Father, but by me" (John 14:6). Jesus does not point out the way, neither is He the guide to or along the way; He *is* the way. This mean, among other things, that Christian morality is the natural expression or outgrowth of one's relation to the One, who is the way. This outgrowth is so natural that it becomes a proof of the relationship. A closely related and supplementary statement to the one above is found in I John: "He who says he abides in him ought to walk in the same way in which he walked" (I John 2:6). Christ is not only the way *to* the Father; He is also the way *of* the Father. His disciples ought to walk in that way; "ought," the key word of Christian ethics, carries the

44 Conner, p. 96.
45 *Ibid.*, p. 113.

idea of an obligation or a debt. To walk in the way of the Lord means to walk in fellowship with Him, which in turn means to walk in the light, in righteousness, and in love. The supreme test of the Christian's life is whether or not he exhibits in his life these and other qualities that belong essentially to the character of God as revealed in His Son.

The preceding means that the standard of conduct for the child of God is not in a code, but in a Person. That Person, however, has given some commandments, and to know Him and to walk in His way entails obedience to those commandments, and incidentally, contrary to what the Gnostics might say, we cannot know Him experientially or really without walking in obedience with Him. For example, John says that "we may be sure that we know him, if we keep ["keep on keeping," WP] his commandments" (2:3). We get to be sure of our knowledge of Him through our obedience. On the other hand, one who says that he knows Him and does not keep His commandments "is a liar and the truth is not in him" (2:3-4; cf. 3:24). As we have stated previously, the one commandment specifically stated is the commandment to love (3:23; 4:21; II John 5), but in turn "this is love, that we follow his commandments" (II John 6). John suggests that the commandments of God are not burdensome (5:3). This does not mean that their demands are light, that they are easily kept. They are not burdensome because they are best for us, and also because as we are obedient to them we have a deepening fellowship with the One who gave them. This fellowship gives us the lift of spirit, the drive, the dynamic to do the best we can to keep His commandments, which means to live the kind of life we know He wants us to live.

Let us suggest again, however, that to live the Christian life is to walk in the way of the Lord. This is the supreme, the inclusive proof of eternal life as a present possession. John spells this out in various ways. For example, he says that we should "walk in the light, as he is in the light" (1:7). Again he says that every one who "hopes in him purifies himself as he is pure" (3:3). Furthermore, we are to be righteous as He is righteous (3:7). The measure of our love is His love for us (3:16; 4:11).

The Revelation

The opening words of the book are: "The revelation of ["by," Williams; "from," Phillips] Jesus Christ, which God gave him to show to his servants" (1:1). The first word in the statement is *apocalypsis* which means "unveiling" or "uncovering." Many things are unveiled in the book, but primarily it unveils or reveals Jesus Christ. We find in the book "the unveiled Person, the unveiled program of His purpose, and the unveiled power."[46]

Typical of apocalyptic literature[47] the unveiling was accomplished largely through the use of symbolic images and numbers. The symbols used were familiar to those to whom the book was written.[48] They were acquainted with other apocalyptic literature such as Daniel in the Old Testament and books of the Apocrypha and Pseudepigrapha, some of which were apocalyptic. Such literature was particularly prevalent from 200 B.C. to A.D. 100. An apocalyptic element is present, to a limited degree, in some of the other New Testament writings, Mark 13:3-27 (Matt. 24:3-36; Luke 21:7-36) frequently being referred to as "the little apocalypse" (see also II Thess. 2:1-12). Revelation, however, is considered "the finest example of an apocalypse in existence,"[49] far surpassing "the whole range of pseudonymous works which stand

46 Donald W. Richardson, *The Revelation of Jesus Christ* (Richmond: John Knox Press, 1939), p. 36.

47 In contrast to the typical apocalypse which was usually pseudonymous, Revelation in the prologue (1:1, 4, 9) and in the epilogue (22:8) claims to have been written by John. The scholars do not agree on which John: the son of Zebedee, the Elder or Seer, or another John. As D. T. Niles says, "Happily . . . neither the interpretation nor the authority of the book are dependent on solving this problem of authorship" (*On Seeing the Invisible* [New York: Harper, 1961], p. 21). Most scholars date it near the end of the reign of Domitian (95–96), while a few date it earlier, either during the reign of Nero (about 68) or of Vespasian (about 77).

48 The possible meaning of a few of the major symbols is as follows: the woman "clothed with the sun" = Mary, Israel, or the Christian Church; the male child = Christ; the dragon = Satan; the beast = the Roman emperor, the Lamb = the redeeming Christ; the sickle = eternal judgment. For a discussion of the symbolism of numbers see Henry Barclay Swete, *The Apocalypse of St. John* (Grand Rapids: Eerdmans, 1954), pp. cxxxv–cxxxix.

49 Martin Rist, "The Revelation of St. John the Divine," *The Interpreter's Bible*, XII, 347.

between the Book of Daniel and itself."[50] There is a sense in which it is the logical climax and provides a glorious, triumphant ending to the New Testament. In it we hear "the final note . . . from the trumpets of heaven," with the "Hallelujah Chorus" by the "multitude of the redeemed in the presence of God and the Lamb."[51] The book is addressed "to the seven churches that are in Asia" (1:4) or Asia Minor and was written at a time of severe persecution. It was "a tract for hard times."

1. The place of ethics.

The Revelation has been called "a stirring and exhilarating dramatic symphony on a cosmic scale."[52] If it is a drama, God is the central figure. If it is a symphony, He is the conductor. The book is thoroughly theocentric. The God revealed there is a moral or ethical Person. He is holy (15:4; cf. 3:7; 4:8; 6:10), just (15:3; 16:5, 7), and true (6:10; 15:3; cf. 19:2, 11). The Apocalypse does not stress the love and fatherhood of God, yet the spirit of love is evident in God's concern for His saints (see 1:5, 6; 2:27; 3:5, 9, 19, 21; 14:1). As an apocalyptist, the author thought of God primarily as the sovereign God of the universe, whose Will must prevail.

It seems on the surface that ethics has a comparatively minor place in Revelation. Furthermore, what we find there does not seem to measure up to what is found elsewhere in the New Testament. There is little if any emphasis on the moral qualities that are considered most distinctly Christian such as love, humility, and forgiveness. We do not find much of the spirit expressed by Jesus: "Father, forgive them; for they know not what they do" (Luke 23:34), or of Stephen: "Lord, do not hold this sin against them" (Acts 7:60).

In contrast, the souls of the martyrs under the altar "cried out with a loud voice, 'O Sovereign Lord, holy and true, how long before thou wilt judge and avenge our blood on those who dwell

[50] H. H. Rowley, *The Relevance of Apocalyptic,* new and rev. ed. (New York: Association Press, 1963), p. 138.

[51] A. M. Hunter, *Introducing the New Testament* (Philadelphia: Westminster Press, 1946), p. 106.

[52] Donald T. Rowlingson, *Introduction to New Testament Study* (New York: Macmillan, 1956), p. 170.

upon the earth?' " (Rev. 6:10; for a similar spirit see 16:6 and 18:6–8). How are we to interpret this cry? Is it a cry for personal vengeance? One commentator suggests that it is "a protest of righteousness against iniquity," a cry "for just judgment . . . for the speedy coming of the kingdom."[53] Would we agree that this paragraph (6:9–11) "reflects the moral necessity for judgment" and that "wrath against sin is an essential part of the righteousness of God"?[54] Is it possible that the cry here, as elsewhere, was not so much against the sinner as a person as it was against sin?

What can we say in general about the place of ethics in the book? To appraise properly its ethical content we must remember that it was an apocalypse, and as such it was not a theological or moral treatise. Rather, it was "a book for a crisis." Its one dominant purpose was to strengthen and encourage Christians. This it did by setting forth the triumph of God and righteousness. It was beyond the purpose of the author to suggest a system of morals for Christians in a normal situation.

The preceding does not mean, however, that there is no significant ethical content in the Apocalypse. A brief look at the use of the word "works" in the book will reveal, in a preliminary way, something of the ethical emphasis in Revelation. The word is quite prominent in the book, the letter to five of the seven churches being introduced with the statement: "I know your works" (2:2, 19; 3:1, 8, 15), works good and bad. To the church in Thyatira the word was, "I will give to each of you as your works deserve" (2:23). Later in the book it says that the works or deeds of those who die in the Lord will follow them (14:13). The dead will be judged "according to their works" (20:12, 13, KJV; cf. 22:12), or "by what they had done." However, we should not expect and will not find as much emphasis on the ethical in Revelation as we do in the Sermon on the Mount, the epistles of Paul, or the other Johannine literature.

How much of the ethical one finds and particularly the value he attaches to what he finds will be determined, to a considerable

---

53 Isbon T. Beckwith, *The Apocalypse of John* (New York: Macmillan, 1919), p. 526.

54 Ray Summers, *Worthy Is the Lamb: An Interpretation of Revelation* (Nashville: Broadman Press, 1951), p. 142.

degree, by the method he uses to interpret the book. Its abiding moral and theological values depend upon what its symbols meant to the people to whom it was written, i.e., the members of the churches in Asia Minor in a time of persecution. It loses much of its real significance if we are literalistic and highly imaginative in applying its symbols to the present or the future.[55]

2. The State.

The major ethical emphases in the Apocalypse stem largely from the problems Christians and churches were having with a hostile State. John insists, at least by implication, as does no other New Testament writer that "there can be no divergence between the moral laws binding on the individual and those incumbent on the State."[56]

There appears, at least on the surface, to be a marked contrast between John's view of the State and that of other New Testament writers. For example, Paul in speaking of government as such says, "There is no authority except from God, and those that exist have been instituted by God" (Rom. 13:1). In contrast, for John, the Roman Empire was the beast, which had received its authority and power from the dragon (Satan) (Rev. 13:1-2). It might relieve the apparent conflict, to a limited degree, if we recognized that Paul was speaking of constituted authority in general, while John was faced with a particular formulation of that authority—the Roman Empire. Paul also set forth what should be true of the State; it should restrain the evil and approve the good. This was definitely not true of the Empire in Domitian's

[55] The major methods of interpreting the Revelation are: (1) the futuristic: a description primarily for events that immediately precede the end of the world; (2) the preterist: practically all of the book has been fulfilled, primarily in the early days of the struggle of the church with the Roman Empire; (3) the continuous-historical: a forecast of the history of the church from John's time to the close of time; (4) the symbolic: "the external principles of the prophecies should be deduced and then applied to the ongoing issues of life" (Charles M. Laymon, *The Book of Revelation* [New York: Abingdon Press, 1960], p. 8). For a discussion of various methods of interpretation, see Summers, *Worthy Is the Lamb*, pp. 27-51. For a historical sketch of methods of interpretation, see R. H. Charles, *Studies in the Apocalypse*, 2nd ed. (Edinburgh: T. & T. Clark, 1915), pp. 1-78.

[56] R. H. Charles, *The Revelation of St. John* in *The International Critical Commentary* (New York: Scribner's, 1920), I, xv.

day. Paul lived and carried on much of his work under the protective, if not friendly, arm of Rome. John had apparently been exiled to Patmos "on account of the word of God and the testimony of Jesus" (1:9). He faced the challenge of a state that claimed for itself not only what belonged to Caesar but also what belonged to God. This usurpation of authority John and his fellow Christians could not accept. Doubtlessly Paul would have taken the same position under similar conditions. He would have said with Peter and the Apostles and Christian heroes and martyrs through the centuries, "We must obey God rather than men" (Acts 5:29), whether those men represented religious authorities or political powers. In other words, John's position was basically in harmony with the rest of the New Testament.

As intense as is the hostility to the Roman Empire, there is not the least hint of rebellion. As Moffatt says, "The Apocalypse is a call to arms, but the arms are only patience and loyalty to conviction."[57] Resistance was encouraged but it was passive or "suffering" resistance. This may be the main lesson or truth in 13:10:

> If any one is to be taken captive,
> to captivity he goes;
> if any one slays with the sword,
> with the sword must he be slain.

Some commentators would apply both portions of this statement to the persecuted Christians. For example, Swete says, "The whole is a warning against any attempt on the part of the church to resist its persecutors. If a Christian is condemned to exile, he is to regard exile as his allotted portion, and to go readily; if he is sentenced to death, he is not to lift his hand against the tyrant; to do so would be to deserve his punishment." Other commentators would make the last half of the statement apply to their persecutors. It would be a source of encouragement to the persecuted, "Remember that those who use the sword against you shall themselves perish by the sword." Whichever interpretation is correct, there is no suggestion of rebellion. The way of victory for the Christian and the Church is "the way of the Cross."

[57] James Moffatt, "Revelation of St. John the Divine" in *The Expositor's Greek Testament*, V, 313.

The Church is to be a source of strength and encouragement to its members, but in relation to the State it is to serve as a watchman. It is to warn the State against the transgression of its legitimate limits. This warning is found more in Revelation than any other book of the New Testament. Emperor worship was the characteristic of the State in John's day in which it exceeded most specifically and seriously its proper limits. And "as the State remains within its limits or transgresses them, the Christian will describe it as the servant of God or as the instrument of the Devil."[58] There is no question about how it is described by the author of the Apocalypse.

3. Philosophy of history.

Niles suggests that in the Apocalypse "God is unveiled as the Author and Finisher of the course of human history, the Initiator and Fulfiller of the course of world redemption, the Beginning and the Ending of the course of divine judgment."[59] In common with the biblical perspective in general, God is revealed as the chief character in history.[60] In portraying this perspective John paints on a broad canvas. His is a world view, including the world to come as well as the world of his day.

His perspective or "philosophy of history" might be summarized as follows: (1) There is a real struggle in history between the good and the evil. (2) This struggle is finally and basically spiritual; it is a struggle between God and Satan—a conflict over sovereignty. (3) The Roman Empire was the instrument of Satan. (4) God was in control of history and ultimately would be victorious within history. His would be the last word. This assured those who were suffering persecution that they lived in a moral universe under the control of a God who would right their wrongs.

It might be that the beast was allowed to make war on the

58 Oscar Cullmann, *The State in the New Testament* (New York: Scribner's, 1956), p. 86.
59 Niles, p. 27.
60 See Laymon (pp. 42–43) for a brief statement concerning four views of history: the cyclic, the evolutionary, the economic-deterministic, and the apocalyptic.

saints and to conquer them (11:7), but near the end of what some consider to be the first apocalypse (1–11) the Christian's word of victory was, "The kingdom of the world has become the kingdom of our Lord and of his Christ, and he shall reign for ever and ever" (11:15; cf. 12:5). The divine conquest is so vivid and real that it is celebrated "as though already achieved,"[61] which is "the crowning lesson of the Apocalypse" (WP). Or as Laymon says, the supreme message of Revelation "is its assurance that Christ will emerge in history at long last as King of kings and Lord of lords." Laymon further suggests that the victory of Christ "will be the victory of all who place their trust in him."[62]

The tempo of the book picks up in a noticeable way beginning with Chapter 12. "In climactic sequence judgment on Rome is followed by judgment on all evil. Finally the conflict emerges into complete victory for God and the forces of righteousness."[63] The triumphant word is, "Hallelujah! For the Lord our God the Almighty reigns" (19:6). Finally there will come the new heaven and the new earth—the New Jerusalem. In it there shall be no pain, no death, no mourning "for the former things have passed away" (21:1–4). This note of victory, which provides an undertone for everything in the book, makes that which was written for first-century Christians meaningful for Christians of every century. The child of God can know that however dark may be the clouds that overshadow him the sun still shines. This is a truth of considerable ethical as well as religious significance.

4. Miscellaneous emphases.

In addition to the major themes that have been discussed, there are a number of secondary emphases. Although the emphasis in the Apocalypse is on social rather than personal ethics, the latter is not entirely absent. This is evident particularly in the vices condemned and the virtues commended. Most of the vices are found in one list (21:8) that is repeated with one addition in another list (22:15). Listed are cowardice, faithlessness, pollution or defilement, murder, fornication (cf. 2:14, 20; 17:2; 18:3, 9), sor-

---

61 Charles, *The Revelation of St. John*, I, 293.
62 Laymon, p. 9.
63 Summers, *Worthy Is the Lamb*, p. 169.

cery (cf. 9:21), idolatry, and lying (cf. 2:2; 3:9; 14:5; 21:27). The addition in 22:15 is "dogs," a term of deep contempt, possibly meaning those who were morally unclean, "those who had been defiled by long contact with the foul vices which honeycombed pagan society" (Swete). Notice that standing first in the list of vices (21:8) is cowardice, not found in any other list of vices in the New Testament, followed by unfaithfulness. These two were related in a particular way to those who were suffering persecution. There was no greater sin, from the perspective of the Apocalypse, than for one to fail under pressure of persecution.

On the other hand, "patient endurance" or "fortitude" (NEB) was considered *a* chief virtue if not *the* chief virtue for the Christian or the Church. This emphasis is found, to some degree, throughout the book, but it is particularly prevalent in the letters to the seven churches. The "patient endurance" of three of those churches is specifically commended (2:2–3, 19; 3:10), while another is admonished to be faithful unto death (2:10). There is lacking in the Revelation, except in a very minor way, the "tender virtues" prevalent elsewhere in the New Testament. There is nothing comparable to the fruit of the Spirit of Paul (Gal 5:22–23). It may be that John assumed that "patient endurance" or fidelity to Christ was inclusive of other Christian virtues. At least we know that he related endurance for Christ with the keeping of the commandments of God (14:12). If we tend to be critical of the author of the Apocalypse for his rather limited references to the Christian virtues, we should remember that he wrote for a particular purpose. His message was not for normal times, unless persecution by an unfriendly world is considered normal for the child of God and the Church of God.

The fact that John was writing for a particular situation may help to explain a statement that disturbs some people. In speaking of the 144,000 who stood with the Lamb on Mount Zion it is said, "It is these who have not defiled themselves with women, for they are chaste ["celibate," Phillips]" (14:4; for another reference see 7:4–8). Regardless of whether this refers to a special class of the redeemed or is a symbolic number for all of the redeemed, what is the meaning of "defiled" and "chaste"? Does John here exalt celibacy above marriage, or does he suggest that it is advantageous for the situation in his day? If the latter is correct it would be somewhat comparable to Paul in I Corinthians 7. This seems the preferable interpretation if the statement is to be taken literally.

There are, however, a number of interpretations that relieve if they do not eliminate the problem. Beckwith suggests that the reference is to adultery or fornication. On the other hand, Swete and others would somewhat spiritualize the whole matter. For example, Swete says that the statement "must be taken metaphorically, as the symbolic character of the Book suggests." Similarly, Rist says that it is "a symbol of the 'spotless' character of the martyrs who had not participated in idolatry, which is frequently compared with immorality and fornication" (IB). Whether it is symbolic or not, to evaluate it properly one needs to compare the statement with the beautiful imagery in Chapter 21 where the New Jerusalem is compared to "a bride adorned for her husband" (21:2), who is the Lamb (21:9).

There are in the book other more or less incidental teachings. One of these is the danger of riches, particularly evident in the letter to the church at Laodicea. The latter was a banking and business center, and the church and its members had evidently become proud, arrogant, and felt that they needed nothing (3:17). These are some of the abiding dangers of riches to an individual, a church, or a community.

Still another emphasis, common to the biblical perspective, is that God is no respecter of persons. The Lamb had ransomed men for God "from every tribe and tongue and people and nation" (5:9). Similarly, the great multitude that the seer saw, which no man could number, were "from all tribes and peoples and tongues" (7:9; cf. 14:6).

What can we conclude concerning the ethic of the Apocalypse? What is its basic nature? How valid is it? Is it abidingly relevant? First, the fundamental question of an apocalyptic ethic is not what is the good or what is the right. Neither is it how can one attain the good or know and do the right. In an apocalypse the end is given, it is inevitable, it is in the hands of God. The question is, "What can one do in the light of the inevitable?" Or, possibly more specifically ethical in emphasis, "Why be good or why should one seek to do the right?" The answer basically is that God controls things, that He as the Sovereign will triumph over His enemies. He will care for His own. Here is motive for Christian living in any age and under any conditions. In other words, the central message of Revelation is abidingly relevant. Niles suggests that "this is not simply a letter of John to the Christians in Asia; it is a communication from the Lord to the Christians of all lands and every generation."[64]

[64] Niles, p. 11.

CHAPTER VIII

OTHER NEW TESTAMENT WRITINGS

In this chapter we shall discuss all the New Testament books that have not been considered in previous chapters: Acts, Hebrews, James, I and II Peter, and Jude. Each of these has some ethical content, although the amount and value varies widely.

Acts

There is some difference of opinion about Luke's purpose in writing Acts.[1] It is possible he wrote the book, which has been called "the key book in the formation of the New Testament canon,"[2] to defend Christianity against the charge of sedition, or to prove to Rome that she had nothing to fear from the Christian movement. The chief purpose, however, seems to have been Luke's desire to prove the universality of the Christian movement. As Stagg so aptly says, Luke "writes to show . . . the expansion of a concept, the liberation of the gospel as it breaks through

[1] There is general agreement that Luke, the physician-companion of Paul on some of his journeys, wrote the third gospel and the book of Acts. Some scholars suggest that the gospel and Acts really constitute one two-part book.

[2] Filson, *Three Crucial Decades*, p. 115.

barriers that are religious, racial, and national."[3] This dominant purpose has tremendous ethical as well as religious implications. It also explains Luke's concentration on the work of Peter and Paul; they were the ones who were primarily used of the Lord to expand the work of Christ from Jew to Gentile, from Jerusalem to Rome.

The book of Acts, being history, is rather limited in its ethical content and perspective. Also, the ethical content is of a rather general nature, although some is of major significance.

1. An ethic of the Holy Spirit.

The "Spirit" or the "Holy Spirit" is specifically referred to approximately sixty times in the book of Acts, much more frequently than in any other book in the New Testament. The influence of the Holy Spirit is quite evident in the ethical teachings of Acts.[4] For example, from the negative perspective the Spirit is specifically related to sin or wrongdoing. This is plainly seen in the story of Ananias and Sapphira. When others were selling what they had and bringing the proceeds to the Apostles that distribution might be made to those in need, Ananias and his wife sold "a piece of property" but "kept back some of the proceeds" (5:1-2). They evidently pretended to bring it all. Peter asked Ananias the searching question: "Why has Satan filled your heart to lie to the Holy Spirit . . . ?" (5:3; cf. 5:4). The love of money or material things may have been the root of the sin of Ananias and Sapphira, but their basic sin was against the Holy Spirit.

The Spirit is also associated specifically in Acts with certain virtues, such as "good repute," "wisdom" (6:3), "faith" (5:5; cf. 11:24), "peace" (9:31), and "joy" (13:52). (Paul includes the last two in his fruit of the Spirit—Gal. 5:22.)

The work of the Spirit is apparent in the important conference of the Church at Jerusalem. Paul and Barnabas had been plagued by the Judaizers, who claimed that the Gentile converts must keep the Mosaic Law; that they must be circumcised. The matter

[3] Frank Stagg, *The Book of Acts* (Nashville: Broadman Press, 1955), p. 12.

[4] Dewar in *An Outline of New Testament Ethics*, as suggested previously, calls his chapter on Acts "The Ethic of the Holy Spirit."

was carried to the Apostles and Elders and the assembly of the Church at Jerusalem. Under the leadership of Peter and James, the brother of Jesus, and with the assistance of the testimony of Paul and Barnabas, the Church agreed that the Gentiles did not need to be circumcised. The message to the Gentile Christians included the following: " 'It is the decision of the Holy Spirit, and our decision, to lay no further burden upon you beyond these essentials. You are to abstain from meat that has been offered to idols, from blood, from anything that has been strangled, and from fornication. If you keep yourselves free from these things you will be doing right. Farewell' " (15:28–29, NEB; cf. 15:20; 21:25). Notice that the Church claimed the guidance and authority of the Holy Spirit. Notice also that there were four things the Gentile Christians were admonished not to do and that three of these are more or less ritualistic, while the other (fornication) is ethical.

There is another sense, however, in which the communication or exhortation of the council, at least by implication, had and has considerable ethical significance. The things the Gentile Christians were asked to abstain from were not essential for their salvation; they did seem to be necessary for peaceful relations with some Jewish Christians. They were relatively minor burdens if by bearing them they could maintain and enrich the fellowship within the Christian community. These "burdens," at least in one or two cases, represented a compromise, but such compromises are frequently necessary for the best human relations. And let us not forget that the Spirit was given as an authority for the compromise or accommodation, and the Holy Spirit will not approve a compromise on things that are basic or essential. It is possible that the action of the Jerusalem church was the background for Paul's instructions regarding the eating of meat offered to idols (see particularly Rom. 14 and I Cor. 8), instructions that involve accommodation but also instructions that provide helpful guidance for Christians in every age.

2. A fellowship ethic.

Paul and John had a prominent place in their writings for an ethic of the Christian community. A distinctive emphasis on this aspect of the Christian life is found in Acts. This is seen particularly in the first chapters of the book and in a special way in chapters 2 and 4. There was present in the Jerusalem church a depth of fellowship that has seldom been duplicated by any Christian group. This fellowship was revealed not so much by what was said as by what these early Christians did. Their fellowship was so meaningful that they shared with one another in a way and to a degree that has perplexed and at times frustrated Christians through the intervening centuries. We should remember, however, that their sharing resulted from the fact that "they devoted themselves to . . . fellowship [*koinonia*]," (2:42), and that they "were of one heart and soul" (4:32). The latter are the most characteristic words in the early chapters of Acts and a Hebrew expression for complete harmony or accord. Their sharing was an outer manifestation of their inner unity. Their fellowship partook of the family spirit. It was also an inclusive fellowship: the well-to-do and the poor, the educated and the uneducated, the Palestinian Jew and the Hellenistic Jew. Within this family the strong served the weak, those who had naturally shared with those who did not. Their fellowship was a continuation of the fellowship some of them had had with Jesus while He walked among them. Within that fellowship they had shared with Him from the common purse. Now their fellowship was with one another in union with the Risen Christ.

There is inherent in the idea of the Christian fellowship or *koinonia,* as suggested formerly, the concept of sharing. The sharing within the Jerusalem Christian community is spelled out in various ways. It is said that they "had all things in common; and they sold ["continued to sell," Williams] their possessions and goods and distributed them to all, as any had need ["as any one had special need," Williams]" (2:44–45). Later, possibly as an introduction in part for Barnabas and for the story of Ananias and Sapphira, Luke says that in the Jerusalem fellowship "no one said that any of the things which he possessed was his own, but they had everything in common" (4:32). He further says that "there was not a needy person among them," i.e., there were no beggars among the believers. Why? "For as many as were possessors of lands or houses sold them, and brought ["continued to bring," Williams] the proceeds of what was sold and laid it at the apostles' feet; and distribution was made ["was continuously made," Williams] to each as any had need" (4:34–35). The verb forms throughout this statement express the iterative—what occurred from time to time. With such unity and such practical demonstration of Christian fellowship it was natural if not inevitable that the Apostles would bear "witness with great power to the resurrection of the Lord Jesus," and that "they were all held in high esteem" (4:33, NEB).

So far as we know, sharing, such as was practiced in the Jerusalem fellowship, was not repeated in other New Testament churches. This fact implies that there were special reasons for the sharing in the Jerusalem Christian community. Some scholars suggest that the expected early return of the Lord was a factor. It is doubtful if this could have been a major factor, since other Christian communities with the same messianic expectations did not follow the pattern of the Jerusalem church. It seems that the nature and the extent of the sharing must have stemmed from some unusual circumstances present at Jerusalem but not prevalent elsewhere. It may be that some who were visitors in Jerusalem and were converted on the Day of Pentecost and the days immediately following remained behind after their conversion. Their supplies were soon exhausted. It is also possible that some who lived in the city lost their jobs when they became Christians. Whatever may have been the situation that called forth the rather drastic expression of Christian fellowship, it must have continued for some time since Paul took offerings for the saints at Jerusalem (see Acts 11:29–30; 24:17; Rom. 15:25–27; I Cor. 16:1–4; II Cor. 8:1–4; 9:1–2, 12; Gal. 2:10).

A special need might help to explain the "Jerusalem experiment," but need alone fails to explain fully the generosity of those who had possessions. The extent of the sharing by the latter can be explained only by their depth of commitment to the Risen Christ and to those who were their brothers in Christ. The motive for their giving sets this experience sharply apart from contemporary communism. Their sharing was voluntary. There was no compulsion, except the inner compulsion of love. This is clearly brought out in Peter's statement to Ananias: "While it remained unsold, did it not remain your own? And after it was sold, was it not at your disposal?" (5:4). It is also evident that some Jerusalem Christians such as Mary, the mother of Mark, retained their homes (12:12). It seems that these Jerusalem Christians considered their possessions a trust; they were held in trust not only for God but also for the Christian fellowship. If they were needed by the fellowship they were to be shared.

Regardless of the reason or reasons for the "Jerusalem experiment," there is revealed through the experience some abidingly relevant principles or ideals. For example, if a real need arises within any Christian group, the members of the group should share with one another. If one's immediate family cannot or will not provide the needed assistance, the Christian should not have to look outside of his Church family. One wonders if the Christian movement has not lost considerably in its impact on the world by shifting its emphasis from caring for the members of the fellowship to the promotion of a program.

3. An inclusive ethic.

The fellowship so prominent in Acts is an inclusive fellowship. This idea of inclusiveness, which is *a* if not *the* major purpose of the book, has considerable moral as well as spiritual significance. It is possible that it was the main reason for the rejection of Jesus by the Jews. They saw that His movement ultimately would eventuate in a world Christian brotherhood.

The framework for the inclusiveness of Acts is seen in the statement by the Risen Christ, which might be considered Luke's form of the "Great Commission." It is as follows: "You shall receive power when the Holy Spirit has come upon you; and you shall be my witnesses in Jerusalem and in all Judea and Samaria and to the end of the earth" (1:8). The book develops, in general, in harmony with this commission. The enlarging of the circle began in the brief but spectacular ministry of Stephen. The first notable movement of the Spirit outside of Jerusalem was the revival in Samaria under Philip, one of the seven (Chapter 8). There then follows the conversion of Saul, of whom the Lord said, "He is a chosen instrument of mine to carry my name before the Gentiles" (9:15). Then comes Peter's vision and his proclamation of the gospel to Cornelius and his household (Chapters 10 and 11), followed by the scattering of the disciples because of persecution (Chapters 11 and 12), and the concentration on the ministry of Paul to the Gentiles beginning with Chapter 13.

Luke obviously considered the experience of Peter and Cornelius unusually important, since he gives all of one chapter to the incident and most of another chapter to Peter's defense before the Jerusalem Christian group. The story opens with the vision of Cornelius, followed by a record of Peter's thrice-repeated vision. The main point from the viewpoint of Christian ethics about the vision is the following statement made to Peter: "What God has cleansed, you must not call common" (10:15). Peter, under the impact of the Holy Spirit, had an expanding understanding of the meaning of this statement. For example, in the house of Cornelius he said, "God has shown me that I should not call any man common or unclean ["vulgar or ceremonially unclean," Williams]" (10:28). Originally he saw in the sheet let down from heaven "all kinds of animals" (10:12)—clean and unclean. Now he sees in that sheet all kinds of men—Jews and Gentiles.

It was more or less natural that the first words of Peter's sermon in the house of Cornelius would be: "Truly I perceive [I am catching on[5]] that God shows no partiality, but in every nation any one who fears him and does what is right is acceptable to him" (10:34–35). God shows no favorites. He is no accepter of faces or persons. He looks on or in the heart rather than on the face or the outer circumstances of life. What is true of God should be true of His children.

This whole episode and particularly the first words of Peter's sermon have tremendous significance for human relations. It is true that some people claim that the statement that God shows no partiality or is not a respecter of persons applies exclusively to the spiritual realm. They say that all men of all races and cultures are under condemnation for sin, and that the way of salvation by faith is available to all. They deny that either the statement or Peter's vision has any social significance.

Peter's reaction is sufficient answer to this contention. When he came into the house of Cornelius he said to him and the others:

5 Stagg, p. 120.

"You yourselves know how unlawful it is for a Jew to associate with or to visit any one of another nation; but God has shown me that I should not call any man common or unclean" (10:28). It is even possible that he remained as a guest of Cornelius for several days (10:48). Furthermore, when he went up to Jerusalem, those of the circumcision party pointedly asked him, "Why did you go to uncircumcised men and eat with them?" (11:2–3). Their real problem was not his preaching to Cornelius and other non-Jews but his eating with them, which was a violation of the cere-monial law or rather the common Jewish interpretation of the law. As A. T. Robertson says, "There is nothing more binding on the average person than social custom" (WP). This was cer-tainly true of the critics of Peter.

The latter did not answer directly the question of his critics. Rather, he told them about his vision and his response to it. His clinching statement was: "As I began to speak, the Holy Spirit fell on them just as on us at the beginning" (11:15; cf. 15:7–11). Here was the final proof that God was no respecter of persons. Peter closed his statement by asking his questioners a question: "Who was I that I could withstand God?" (11:17). The record then simply says, "When they heard this they were silenced" (11:18).

Notice that the Jerusalem brethren never said that it was all right to ignore or violate any of the Jewish customs. The Church was very slow to learn this lesson. Really, has the Church learned even yet that God does not look on the color of the skin or the class or culture one comes from? Have we learned yet that He shows no partiality, that He is not a respecter of persons?

One reason for the inclusiveness of the Christian gospel and ethic is the fact that all men come from one source; they are a part of one human family. This is revealed pointedly and clearly in Paul's sermon, or the brief of his sermon, on Mars' Hill. Among other things, he said, "And he [God] made from one ["of one stock," NEB; "from one forefather," Phillips and Williams] every nation of men to live on all the face of the earth" (17:26). Paul's sermon that day stressed the oneness and sovereignty of God and the unity of mankind. The proud Athenians, the Jews, and all other peoples were from one common source. There was no valid basis for those of any group to feel superior to those belonging to any other group.

4. Miscellaneous matters.

There is revealed in Acts a deep respect for constituted authority but also a recognition of its limitations. Paul, for example, was proud of his Roman citizenship. On several occasions he claimed the privileges and protection that that citzenship provided for him (16:37; 22:25–29). The Roman authorities, on one occasion, rescued him from an angry Jewish mob which would have doubtlessly killed him (21:27–31; 22:22–24). There were times when Rome helped rather than hindered him in his work (18:12–17). It is no wonder that he appealed to Caesar rather than return to Jerusalem for trial (25:9–12).

It is clear, however, in Acts that the disciples of Christ must obey God rather than men (4:19–20; 5:29), whether those men are Jewish or Roman officials. On the other hand, there is not the least hint of active resistance or rebellion. Theirs was a passive resistance, a quiet suffering except for the singing of hymns and the preaching of the gospel. The only point of conflict seemingly between the authorities and the disciples was over the right to witness or preach.

There are also mentioned in Acts some specific vices and virtues. Among the former are lying (5:3), covetousness by implication (20:33), and wickedness in general (3:26). In addition, Peter exhorted the people on the day of Pentecost to save themselves from the crooked or perverted generation or age (2:40). Simon the Sorcerer was described as one who was "in the gall of bitterness and in the bond of iniquity ["a bitter weed and a bundle of crookedness," Williams]" (8:23).

Among the virtues that are specifically mentioned or exemplified are forgiveness—Stephen (7:60), humility—Paul (20:19), purity (21:25; cf. 15:20, 29), unselfishness (20:24), justice and self-control (24:25), and good works or generosity, which was a recurring emphasis in the book (9:36; 10:2, 4).

Hebrews

This epistle—"a finely written and closely reasoned tract"[6]—by an unknown author to an unknown group of Hebrew Christians, who were in danger of falling away, is possibly the most exclusively theological book in the New Testament. It was written primarily to defend, or to argue for the superiority of Christianity. It has been called "The First Apology for Christianity."[7] At first glance it may appear "to be a speculative discourse on the person of Jesus" but "every speculative flight of imagination issues in a 'therefore' with respect to faith and conduct."[8] It may contain less ethical material than any other book of comparable length in the New Testament, but what it contains is of considerable significance.

1. The superiority of Jesus.

Jesus is the central unifying figure in Hebrews. His superiority is the theme of the book. Naturally, this superiority includes the ethical or moral. He is "the very stamp," "flawless expression" (Phillips), or "exact imprint" (Williams, marg.) of God's nature (1:3), and God is consistently revealed in the Scriptures as a moral person.

The writer of Hebrews says that Jesus "learned obedience through what He suffered ["in the school of suffering," NEB]" (5:8) and was made "perfect through suffering" (2:10). He is revealed as a merciful and faithful high priest (2:17). He is able "to sympathize with our weaknesses," since He "in every respect has been tempted as we are, yet without sinning." Because this is true we can keep on drawing near with confidence (courage or boldness), knowing that from Him we will "receive mercy and find grace to help in time of need" (4:15–16). Similar to Melchizedek (see Gen. 14:17–20; Ps. 110:4), He is "king of righteousness" (7:2), but He is also "a high priest, holy, blameless, unstained

---

[6] Hunter, *Introducing the New Testament,* p. 90.

[7] The subtitle of A. B. Bruce's *The Epistle to the Hebrews* (Edinburgh: T. & T. Clark, 1899).

[8] Rowlingson, *Introduction to New Testament Study,* pp. 152–53.

["undefiled," NEB], separated from sinners ["beyond the very reach of sin," Phillips], exalted above the heavens" (7:26). Robertson, commenting on "unstained" or "undefiled," says this does not refer to mere "ritual purity (Lev. 21:10–15), but real ethical cleanness" (WP). Christ has no need like earthly high priests to make sacrifices for Himself; He is "a Son who has been made perfect for ever" (7:27–28). He is not only the high priest but also the offering, an offering "without blemish" (9:14). Furthermore, He is the mediator of a new and inner covenant (12:24; cf. 8:8–13).

2. Exhortations.

This epistle, similar to several of Paul's epistles, closes with a hortatory section. However, as is also true of Paul's epistles, there are some exhortations in the earlier, more theological chapters of the epistle. Hunter suggests that the author "has a trick of digressing in order to exhort his readers."[9] There are repeated exhortations to confidence, boldness, or fearlessness, depending on the translation (3:6; 4:16; 10:19, 35). There is a warning concerning "the deceitfulness ["delusive glamour," Phillips] of sin" (3:13), and also warnings against disobedience (4:11), dullness of hearing (5:11), and sluggishness, laziness (NEB), or carelessness (Williams) (6:12).

The author remonstrated with those to whom he wrote about their immaturity. They should now be teachers of others, rather than needing someone to instruct them in the first principles of their faith. They should be ready for solid food. Milk is for the "unskilled in the word of righteousness." On the other hand, "solid food is for the mature, for those who have their faculties trained by practice to distinguish good from evil" (5:11–14). This is followed with the general exhortation: "Let us . . . go on to maturity" (6:1), or "let us advance toward maturity" (6:3, NEB).

There is a considerable hortatory section in Chapter 10, introduced with a "therefore" ("so now," NEB, or "since then," Williams) with the basis of the "therefore" following rather than preceding it. The statement is, "Therefore, brethren, since we have confidence to enter the sanctuary by the blood of Jesus"

9 Hunter, *Introducing the New Testament*, p. 92.

(10:19), which is followed with a thrice-repeated "Let us." They are: (1) "Let us draw near with a true heart ["in sincerity of heart," NEB] in full assurance of faith"; (2) "Let us hold fast the confession of our hope without wavering"; (3) "Let us consider how to stir up ["to sharpen, to stimulate, to incite," WP] one another to love and good works ["active goodness," NEB]" (10:22–24). Notice in the preceding the great trilogy, rather common in the Pauline epistles, of faith, hope, and love. The author of Hebrews spells out and illustrates the first of these—faith—in the next chapter. He starts with a definition of faith as "the assurance of things hoped for, the conviction of things not seen" (11:1). He also says that "without faith it is impossible to please" God (11:6). It was by or through faith that Moses chose "rather to share ill-treatment ["to suffer hardship," NEB] with the people of God than to enjoy the fleeting ["transient," NEB; "passing," Williams] pleasures of sin" (11:25).

The most exclusively hortatory section of the epistle is in chapters 12 and 13. This section is also introduced with a "therefore." The word translated "therefore" literally means "consequently and us" which the New English Bible translates "and what of ourselves?" Regardless of how the word is translated, it refers back to the great faith chapter. Notice that the author includes himself in his exhortation. He says, "Therefore, since we are surrounded by so great a cloud of witnesses, let us also lay aside every weight ["encumbrance," NEB], and sin which clings so closely ["every sin to which we cling," NEB], and let us run ["let us keep on running," WP] with perseverance ["resolution," NEB] the race that is set before us ["for which we are entered," NEB], looking to Jesus the pioneer ["source," Phillips] and perfecter ["goal," Phillips] of our faith ["the perfect leader and example of faith," Williams]" (12:1–2).

This is followed with a considerable section on chastening, instruction, or discipline. The author pleads with his readers not to "regard lightly the discipline of the Lord" nor to lose courage when it comes. After all, "the Lord disciplines him whom he loves." When discipline comes, they can be assured that God is treating them as sons. In the following words he contrasts the discipline of earthly fathers with the discipline of the Heavenly

Father: "They disciplined us for a short time at their pleasure, but he disciplines us for our good ["true welfare," NEB], that we may share his holiness." All discipline may seem painful, but "later it yields the peaceful fruit ["harvest," NEB] of righteousness ["an honest life," NEB] to those who have been trained by it" (12:5–11).

The author admonishes his hearers or readers to "strive for ["aim at," NEB] peace with all men, and for the holiness without which no one will see the Lord" (12:14). They are warned against bitterness (12:15) and immorality (12:16). They are to "let brotherly love continue" (13:1) and not to "neglect to show hospitality to strangers, for thereby some have entertained angels unawares" (13:2), doubtlessly a reference to Abraham and Lot (Gen. 18:1f; 19:1f.). Then he pointedly says, "Let marriage be held in honor among all ["marriage is honourable; let us all keep it so," NEB], and let the marriage bed be undefiled; for God will judge the immoral and adulterous" (13:4). He then says, "Keep your life free from love of money ["Do not live for money," NEB], and be content with what you have," which is followed with a reason for such an admonition or a basis for such contentment. It is: "For he has said, 'I will never fail you nor forsake you'" (13:5). They are also admonished to remember, obey, and submit ("defer," NEB) joyfully to their spiritual leaders (13:7, 17). There is also the general exhortation, "Do not neglect to do good ["never forget to show kindness," NEB] and to share what you have, for such sacrifices are pleasing to God" (13:16). There is even a word of implied exhortation in the benediction: "Now may the God of peace . . . equip you with everything good ["make you perfect in all goodness," NEB] that you may do his will" (13:20–21).

James

Although it is impossible to know for sure about the author of the book, the traditional view has been that it was the brother of Jesus and a leader in the Jerusalem church. He was evidently writing to Christians in general but primarily to Jewish Christians. There are numerous reflections in the book of the Sermon on the Mount and of Jewish wisdom literature. Rather than a letter, the book is more of a series of exhortations without a sustained or unifying theme, such as is so clearly evident in Hebrews.

The book has been called "a tract on moral issues"[10] written "for the special purpose of recalling Christians to the *agenda* of their faith."[11] It has also been called "an ethical scrapbook"[12] and "a coat of many colors . . . a manual of instruction . . . a Christian homily."[13] It is the most exclusively practical and ethical book in the New Testament. And since "the New Testament has a place for stubborn practical sense,"[14] there is a place for James in the New Testament canon. That place, from the perspective of Christian ethics, is a particularly important one.

Since the book is so exclusively practical we cannot comment on every specific teaching. This would require an analysis of almost every verse. We shall restrict our discussion, in the main, to passages of at least several verses with a central theme.

1. Doers and hearers (1:22–25).

The author admonishes those to whom he wrote to be quick to hear or to listen (1:19), which James Moffatt says "was a common ethical maxim" (MC). They were warned, however, not to be hearers only but to show themselves more and more to be doers of the word (1:22), somewhat reminiscent of the teachings of Jesus (Matt. 7:21, 24–27). Moffatt, modernizing the exhortation, says, "When the sermon is done, it is not done; something remains to be done by the hearers in life" (MC). The word translated "doers" (*poiētēs*) occurs four times in the Epistle and only twice elsewhere in the New Testament (Acts 17:28, where it is translated "poets," and Rom. 2:13). It is typical of the continuing emphasis in James on Christian living. Anyone who merely hears and does not do anything about what he hears deceives, deludes, or misleads himself (1:22); he does not deceive anyone else.

10 Rowlingson, p. 176.
11 James Moffatt, *The General Epistles* in *The Moffatt New Testament Commentary* (London: Hodder & Stoughton, 1928), p. 1.
12 Hunter, *Introducing the New Testament*, p. 96.
13 Bauman, *An Introduction to the New Testament*, p. 147.
14 Filson, *Opening the New Testament*, p. 186.

One who "listens to the message but never acts upon it" (NEB) or "without obeying it" (Williams) is compared to a man who "observes his natural face [literally, "the face of his birth," NASB, marg.] in a mirror . . . and at once forgets what he was like" (1:23–24). Mayor suggests that the imperfect knowledge gained through reflection in the mirror contrasts with the perfect knowledge of reality.[15] It is possible, of course, that a good look in the mirror would not only reveal the superficial appearances of the natural face but also one's moral needs as reflected in the ugly traces of sin on his face.

In contrast to the one who looks at himself in a mirror, possibly in a rather casual way, is the one who bends over or stoops down to look carefully or to fix his gaze (cf. John 20:5–11) on "the perfect law, the law of liberty" (1:25). He who perseveres or makes it a habit to look on the perfect law in the above fashion will not be "a hearer that forgets" but "a doer that acts."

What is this perfect ("flawless," Williams) law which James calls "the law of liberty"? Evidently he was not referring to the Old Testament Law or Torah. It seems rather that he identifies the perfect law with the law of love (see 2:8, 12), which is the fulfillment of all of the law (Matt. 22:40; Rom. 13:10; Gal. 5:14). This explains why the perfect law can be equated with the law of liberty. The law of love is not and cannot be enforced by external compulsion. It "is a law of constraint rather than of restraint."[16] It moves from within outward. It is a law, but a law to which one will respond spontaneously if he has been brought into union with the One who is love. As Moffatt so succinctly says, "The ethical hope of the age . . . was," and still is, "in the obedience of the inward life to the law of divine duty" (MC). The section in the Epistle on doing rather than just hearing is closed with the second of the author's beatitudes: "He shall be blessed in his doing" (1:25, cf. 1:12).

---

15 Joseph B. Mayor, *The Epistle of St. James* (Grand Rapids: Zondervan Publishing House, 1954), p. 71. This is a reprint of this classic commentary, using the revised third edition, published in 1913. Subsequent references to this commentary will be in the body of the material.

16 R. J. Knowling, *The Epistle of St. James* (London: Methuen, 1904), p. 33.

2. Partiality and the law (2:1–13).

This passage on respect of persons, partiality, or snobbery is one of the most abidingly challenging and relevant sections of James. It not only challenges but poses a threat to race- and culture-conscious contemporary Christians and Churches.

The section opens with an exhortation. Phillips translates the exhortation as follows: "Don't ever attempt, my brothers, to combine snobbery with faith in our Lord Jesus Christ." Mayor similarly says, "Do not you, who call yourselves believers in Christ, disgrace your faith by exhibitions of partiality." Moffatt sums up the matter by saying, "Belief in Christ is incompatible with any social favoritism" (MC).

James applies his no-partiality doctrine to one particular area: the treatment of the rich and poor in the assembly of Christians. He doubtlessly had observed such partiality in some Christian groups. He says that if a rich man and a poor man, evidently neither a regular worshiper, come to their meeting, possibly in a home, and the rich man is directed to a seat while the poor man is told to stand or to sit on the floor, they are showing partiality. Notice the contrasts in the passage: "fine clothing" versus "shabby clothing," "pay attention to" versus simply "say to," "have a seat" versus "stand" or "sit at my feet," "here" versus "there." James very pointedly asks if such treatment does not "prove that you are making class distinctions in your mind, and setting yourself up to assess a man's quality?—a very bad thing" (2:4, Phillips).

James says that God is impartial. His impartiality is revealed by His choosing those who are poor, from the perspective of the world, to be "rich in faith" or "rich because of their faith" (WP) and "heirs of the kingdom." This does not mean that the poor are inevitably and universally men of faith and inheritors of the Kingdom. The emphasis is not that poverty is advantageous, but that God is no respecter of persons and that His people should not be. In the purpose and plan of God, rich spiritual blessings are available to the poor as well as to other men. The poor man, who was created in the image of God and who has the potential of rich spiritual experiences, is dishonored, "insulted" (NEB), or "humiliated" (Williams), when he is not treated with the same respect as the rich man.

Why should those of the Christian group treat a rich man with particular respect? Was it not the rich who oppressed them, dragging them (a word suggesting violent treatment—see Acts 16:19; 21:30) into court? Was it not the rich "who blaspheme that honorable ["beautiful," WP] name"—the name of the One to whom they belonged?

James then proceeds to relate "partiality" to the "royal law" ("sovereign law," NEB) (see Lev. 19:18); a law that applied to rich and poor. It was the "royal law" because it was given by God and was "fit to guide a king, or such as a king would choose, or even the king of laws" (WP). In the light of what Jesus (Matt. 22:40) and Paul (Rom. 13:8–10; Gal. 5:13–14) said, it seems that the last of the preceding viewpoints would be the preferable interpretation: it is the royal, the sovereign, the supreme law; the essence or summary of the entire moral law. Partiality violates this law and is sin. Those who practice partiality "are convicted by the law as transgressors," as those who have stepped or crossed over the line which marks the way in which they should walk.

Partiality or respect of persons not only violates "the royal law"; it is a violation of all the law. One who fails or stumbles in one point of the law "has become guilty of all of it." One cannot choose the laws he wants to obey. The unity of the law is grounded in the unity of God, the Law-giver. The law is an expression of one Will. Sin, basically, is disobedience to that Will. And since God's Will is an expression of His nature, any violation of any law of His is a sin against Him. Partiality is such a sin. For James "the Law was the embodiment of the divine will summed up in the supreme ethical principle of love to one's neighbors" (MC).

James appeals to his readers to "so speak and so act as those who are to be judged under the law of liberty" (2:12). This law "is not laxity but a strict ethical rule of God, and we shall be judged by our adherence to its supreme principle of brotherly love or mercy" (MC). This law of liberty involves not so much external statutes as inner virtues.

While James applies the no-partiality doctrine or principle

only to the treatment of rich and poor, the principle itself is general and universally applicable. Insofar as individual Christians or churches show partiality in their treatment of those of different classes, cultures, or races, they are not measuring up to the expectations of their Lord, who showed no partiality. One reason why partiality or the making of distinctions is bad is that it destroys the unity of the Christian group.

3. Faith and works (2:14–26).

More logically and smoothly than usual, James moves from his emphasis on no partiality in the faith to the relation of faith and works or good deeds. James opens the section with two closely related questions: (1) "What does it profit, my brethren, if a man says ["if one keeps on saying," WP] he has faith but has not works?"; (2) "Can his faith save him," or "Can that faith save him" (NEB)? The form of the last question suggests that a negative answer was expected.

Through illustrations and summary statements James proceeds to answer his own questions. He first gives the illustration of a "brother or sister" who is ill-clad and hungry. James was possibly still thinking of the poor man who was slighted in the congregation. He assumes that one of them turned aside such a needy brother or sister by saying, "Go in peace, be warmed and filled," without giving the things that were needed. He then asks, "What does it profit?" and concludes that similarly "faith by itself, if it has no works, is dead." Or, as Mayor suggests, "just as a compassion that expends itself in words only is counterfeit" so is a faith that is fruitless. The New English Bible suggests that faith, "if it does not lead to action . . . is in itself a lifeless thing"; "it is not merely outwardly inoperative but inwardly dead" (Mayor).

James then enters into a conversation or argument with an imaginary opponent. To this one James says, "Show me your faith apart from your works, and I by my works will show you my faith." As an evidence that "faith apart from works is barren," idle, or unproductive, he cites the cases of Abraham and Rahab. Abraham, for example, proved his faith in God by the offering of Isaac his son. Thus Abraham's "faith was active along with his works, and faith was completed by works," or "faith was at work in his actions, and . . . by these actions the integrity of his faith was fully proved" (NEB). Faith ripens or matures in obedience to God. Faith and works or good deeds are a unity in one's relation to and experience with God. James, concluding his use of Abraham as an illustration, summarizes the relation of faith and works as follows: "You see that a man is justified by works and not by faith alone."

There follows a brief illustration of Rahab, who would be farthest removed in many ways from Abraham, but like Abraham her faith was proved genuine by what she did.

The personal conclusion of James to the entire discussion is as follows: "As the body is dead when there is no breath left in it, so faith divorced from deeds is lifeless as a corpse" (NEB). James is not belittling faith; he is insisting that it be a real faith. Faith is not real if it does not have enough life and vitality to produce fruit. James "remains as a needed warning against every attempt to make religion a substitute for goodness."[17]

Possibly a brief statement should be made about the seeming conflict between Paul and James regarding faith and works. Paul, for example, uses Abraham to prove that one is justified by faith apart from works (Rom. 4:1–25), while James uses him to prove that "a man is justified by works and not by faith alone" (James 2:24). Both of them quote the statement about Abraham that he "believed the Lord; and he reckoned it to him as righteousness" (Gen. 15:6; cf. Rom. 4:3; James 2:23). A reading of Romans and James will reveal, however, that they were using Abraham for different purposes. Paul was producing proof that "a man is justified by faith apart from works of law" (Rom. 3:28). He suggests specifically that circumcision had nothing to do with the justification of Abraham.

In contrast, James was not concerned with the works of the Law but works or good deeds in general. Also, he suggests that the offering of Isaac was the proof of the validity of Abraham's justification by faith, which took place some years before. Notice that James says that Abraham's "faith was completed by works, and the scripture was fulfilled which says, 'Abraham believed God . . .'" (2:22–23). The primary concern of James is with

---

[17] Cave, *The Christian Way*, p. 90.

sanctification and not justification. Progress in the former is evidence of the latter. In other words, for James the only kind of faith that saves or justifies is a faith that is meaningful enough to produce fruit or good deeds. There is no contradiction between James and Paul. Paul uses the word "works" to refer to "conduct required by the Jewish law"; when James used the word he referred to the conduct "demanded by Christian ethics" (ICC).

4. Use and abuse of the tongue (3:1–12).

James, in a somewhat epigrammatic way, had previously spoken of the tongue. The brethren should be "quick to hear, slow to speak" (1:19). James had also said: "A man may think he is religious, but if he has no control over his tongue, he is deceiving himself" (1:26, NEB). It is in Chapter Three, however, that he discusses most fully the tongue.

He opens this section with the general admonition: "Let not many of you become teachers . . . for you know that we who teach shall be judged with greater strictness." He follows this with a confession, in which he again includes himself: "We all make many mistakes." This, in turn, is followed with the statement: "If any one makes no mistakes in what he says he is a perfect man, able to bridle the whole body also." The bit in the mouth of a horse is used to guide the entire body of the horse. The implication is that the tongue, in like manner, controls the whole body of man: "It is with men as with horses: control their mouth and you are master of all their action" (ICC).

The tongue is also compared to the rudder of a ship. The rudder is quite small, but it is used by the pilot to guide the ship, although the latter may be large and the winds may be strong. "So the tongue is a little member," but it can control the whole man. It can boast "of great things."

Next, James compares the tongue to a fire. He says, "How great a forest is set ablaze by a small fire?" He then adds, "and the tongue is a fire" (cf. Prov. 16:27; 26:18–22), it sets "on fire the cycle of nature" and is "set on fire by hell." The latter portion of this expression is translated in a particularly graphic way in the New English Bible. It is as follows: "It keeps the wheel of our existence red-hot, and its flames are fed by hell." The tongue is also called "an unrighteous world among our members" which stains or pollutes our whole being or body. It is a "restless evil, full of deadly poison," and cannot be tamed by any human being, although we may properly conclude that it can be tamed by God.

How tragically true, as James says, that the tongue is used to bless or sing the praises of "the Lord and Father"—the highest function of the tongue—and also to curse men, "who are made in the likeness of God." James tersely concludes, "My brethren this ought not to be so." This statement is followed with some rhetorical questions that close the section. These questions point out that it is just as inconsistent and inconceivable that the tongue should be used both to bless and curse as it is for both "fresh water and brackish" ("bitter," Phillips) to flow from the same spring or for a fig tree to bear olives or a grapevine figs (cf. Matt. 7:16). Also, it is just as inconsistent as it would be for salt water to yield fresh water. "It is a moral incongruity for blessing and cursing to come out of the same mouth" (WP).

5. Wisdom and the good life (3:13–18).

This is a brief but very rich passage. James introduces the new topic with a question, a technique which he frequently uses. The question is: "Who is wise and understanding, skilled, or expert among you?" The question was possibly addressed directly to the teachers or would-be teachers among them. Wisdom is an important part of a teacher's equipment. Boasting about one's wisdom, however, would prove that he did not have real wisdom, the wisdom that comes from God. Just as faith must prove itself by good works, so the wise man, teacher or otherwise, will show or prove his wisdom or possibly, better, "his meekness" (ICC) by "his good life." As Robertson says, "Actions speak louder than words even in the case of the professional wise man" (WP).

Typical of James, his interest in wisdom is practical and not theoretical or intellectual. This is seen in his discussion of both earthly and heavenly wisdom. There is a wisdom that is earthly, unspiritual, and even devilish or demonical. This wisdom is characterized by "bitter jealousy and selfish ambition" and the boastful spirit. The presence of these qualities produce or at least imply the presence of "disorder and every vile practice" or "evil of every kind" (NEB).

On the other hand, there is a wisdom that comes from above. That wisdom produces and is evidenced by the good life. James, in what one author calls "the moral 'pearl of great price,' "[18] spells out some of the matchless qualities of the wisdom that comes from above. This wisdom "is first pure": "first in rank and time" (WP). It is first pure because of the close relation of purity to God. It is the man with "clean hands and a pure heart," who shall "ascend the hill of the Lord" and "stand in his holy place" (Ps. 24:3–4). It was Jesus who said that it is the pure in heart who shall see God (Matt. 5:8). No wonder James said "first pure." There follows six or seven more qualities of the "good life," all of which emanate from purity. They describe the kind of life that proves that one has the wisdom from above. Such wisdom is peaceable; it is not self-assertive and argumentative. The one who has this wisdom is gentle or forbearing, without the pugnacious spirit. He is "open to reason," is "approachable" (Phillips), or "willing to yield" (Williams): "the opposite of stiff and unbending" (MC). This wisdom and hence the man who possesses it is also "full of mercy and good fruits." Finally, the one who has the wisdom from above is "without uncertainty or insecurity"—no hypocrisy or pretense.

In closing this section James suggests, at least by implication, another contrast between earthly and heavenly wisdom. Righteousness and peace are products of the wisdom from above. This is in contrast to the jealousy and selfish ambition of earthly wisdom, which result in disorder and every vile practice. Teachers, or others, who have the wisdom from above will sow in peace and will be instruments of peace. This will be one aspect of the good life, which will show or prove that they have the heavenly wisdom.

6. *Rich and poor (5:1–6).*

James apparently had an aversion for wealth and the wealthy. He gave recurring attention to the rich and, to a lesser degree, to the poor. For example, if the rich man boasted, it

[18] Dewar, p. 263.

should be "in his humiliation," because he will pass away in the midst of his pursuits like the grass, which is withered by the scorching heat, and the flower, whose beauty fades or perishes (1:9–11). As discussed previously, James warned against preferential treatment of the rich man in the congregation or assembly. Also, he reminded the tradesman of the uncertainties of life, telling him that he is "a mist that appears for a little time and then vanishes" (4:13–16).

The latter warning provides the immediate background for the most pointed and fullest statement by James concerning the rich. His opening words are: "Next a word to you who have great possessions. Weep and wail over the miserable fate descending on you" (NEB). He spells out, to some degree, the nature of their "impending miseries." Typical of the prophet of God, the judgment was so real that James says, "Your riches *have* rotted and your garments *are* moth-eaten" (cf. Matt. 6:19). The rust from their gold and silver, which they had obtained unjustly and hoarded selfishly, will be evidence or a witness against them. They have become so identified with their wealth that James says that the rust from their wealth will eat their flesh like fire. They have laid up treasures, but they have laid them up for the last days. The coming of the Lord (5:8) and the judgment are just around the corner.

The rich are condemned by James not only because they have hoarded their wealth; they had also been unjust in getting their wealth. They had withheld or "kept back by fraud" the wages of the laborers who had mowed their fields.[19] Those wages cried out against them. Also the cries of the laborers or harvesters had "reached the ears of the Lord of hosts"; he "hears the cries of the oppressed workmen even if the employers are deaf" (WP).

Still another charge against the rich is that they lived "in wanton luxury" (NEB) or "in luxury and self-indulgence" (Williams). They had fattened themselves "like cattle" (NEB), and,

---

[19] The Old Testament law says, "You shall not oppress a hired servant who is poor and needy, . . . you shall give him his hire on the day he earns it, before the sun goes down. . . ; lest he cry against you to the Lord, and it be sin in you" (Deut. 24:14–15).

just as was true of fatted cattle, "the day for slaughter" had come (NEB).

A closing thrust is that the rich had condemned and killed the -righteous, who offered no resistance. The implication is that God knows and that He will judge. This is suggested by the following verses: "Be patient, therefore, brethren, until the coming of the Lord. . . . Establish your hearts, for the coming of the Lord is at hand" (5:7-8). James, in common with Paul (Rom. 13:11-12; I Cor. 7:29), Peter (I Peter 4:7), and John (I John 2:18), lived in the expectation of the coming of the Lord. The culmination of the Kingdom for them was imminent.

7. *Additional admonitions.*

Chapters 2 and 3 have been discussed in their entirety in the preceding sections. The "additional admonitions" in this section will be gathered from Chapter 4 and from the portions of Chapters 1 and 5 that have not been discussed.

The practical nature of James is evident in two summary statements found in the book. The first of these, which is possibly the most familiar verse in the book, is as follows: "Pure religion and undefiled before God and the Father is this, To visit the fatherless and widows in their affliction, and to keep himself unspotted from the world" (1:27, KJV). Moffatt says, "A *pure, unsoiled religion* expresses itself in acts of charity and in chastity—which impressed the contemporary world" (MC). Another verse which might be considered a summary statement is as follows: "Whoever knows what is right to do and fails to do it, for him it is sin" (4:17).

James admonished his readers to rejoice when they met "various trials." They could know through their own experiences that the testing of their faith produces steadfastness or "breeds fortitude" (NEB). In addition, when this steadfastness or fortitude is permitted to do its work, it will move them toward perfection or "will go on to complete a balanced character that will fall short in nothing" (NEB) 1:2-4; cf. 5:11). Again, he says that the man is blessed or happy who endures trial, "for when he has stood the test he will receive the crown [the victory wreath] of life which God has promised to those who love him" (1:12).

The readers were challenged not only to be "slow to anger" (1:19) but also to "put away all filthiness and rank growth of wickedness" or "all that is sordid, and the malice that hurries to excess" (NEB) (1:21). They were not to covet (4:2) nor to speak evil against a brother or to judge their neighbor (4:11–12). Neither were they to "grumble . . . against one another" or blame their "troubles on one another" (5:9, NEB), a continuing human weakness. "Above all" they were not to swear or "use oaths" (NEB). James says, "When you say yes and no, let it be plain 'Yes' or 'No' " (5:12, NEB; cf. Matt. 5:33–37). They were to cleanse their hands and purify their hearts (4:8). They were to humble themselves, remembering that God "gives grace to the humble" (4:6) and exalts them (4:10, cf. Matt. 23:12; Luke 14:11; 18:14).

James warns those to whom he writes about wars and fightings among themselves (4:1). Mayor suggests that war "denotes any lasting resentment" and fightings "any outburst of passion." James also warns them against "friendship with the world" (4:4). Such friendship or "love" of the world is "enmity to God"— "whoever chooses to be the world's friend makes himself God's enemy" (4:4, NEB). Such a one is an unfaithful creature or an adulterer. How can the preceding be made compatible with the fact that God loves the world? There is a sense in which God's child not only can but should love the world, but it must be a love that stems from and is similar in kind to God's redemptive love for the world. The love or friendship condemned by James is a love for the things of the world, a friendship that means compromise for the Christian and unfaithfulness to God.

In the closing chapter, in addition to the things previously mentioned, James appealed to his readers to be patient, long-suffering, or literally long-tempered "until the coming of the Lord" (5:7). He cited as examples of patience the farmer (5:7) and the prophet (5:10). The closing exhortations, all of which have some ethical overtones, are to pray over and anoint the sick (5:14), to confess their sins (5:16), and to restore wanderers to the faith (5:19–20).

I Peter

This letter by Peter, with Silvanus or Silas serving as amanuensis—who doubtlessly left his imprint on the style and possibly, to some degree, on the content—was addressed "to the exiles of the dispersion" ("God's scattered people," NEB) in certain provinces of Asia Minor. Wand calls it a "gallant and high-hearted exhortation" and says that it "breathes a spirit of undaunted courage and exhibits as noble a type of piety as can be found in any writing of the New Testament outside the gospels."[20]

The key to this epistle of courage and hope is the statement, "If one suffers as a Christian" (4:16). It was written to encourage those who suffered persecution or testing as Christians. Practically everything in the epistle is related to this basic purpose. The testing or persecution was evidently unofficial. At least it was still considered proper to counsel loyalty to the State. Selwyn says, "The trials besetting the readers of I Peter were spasmodic and particular rather than organized on a universal scale, a matter of incidents rather than of policy."[21]

1. Therefore . . ."

I Peter has been called "a teaching Epistle," teaching which embraced "not only what is commonly called doctrine but also ethics or principles and canons of conduct governing the practical life of Christians in the Church and in the world."[22] The latter emphasis is seen in the lists of vices (2:1; 4:3, 15) and at least one list of virtues (3:8-9) in the book.[23] Most of its ethical content is found, however, in a few sections introduced with "therefore" and in the rather extensive discussion of submission or subjection to authorities.

20 J. W. C. Wand, *The General Epistles of St. Peter and St. Jude* (London: Methuen, 1934), p. 1.

21 Edward Gordon Selwyn, *The First Epistle of Peter*, 2nd ed. (London: Macmillan, 1946), p. 55.

22 *Ibid.*, p. 64. References other than to the lengthy introduction (115 pages) will be in the body of the material.

23 See Dewar (pp. 230-41) for a discussion of the virtues and vices in I Peter.

I Peter, as is true of the New Testament in general, contains a "therefore morality" or ethic. Its moral exhortations, in the main, follow and are based upon theological premises. "Christian ethics follow from divine grace."[24] On the other hand, theological precepts find their fulfillment in moral exhortations. "Truth for the apostolic writers is always 'truth in order to goodness.' "[25] "Therefore" is frequently used by Peter, as is true in Paul's epistles, to make the transition from theology to ethics, from principle or premise to exhortation. Where a "therefore" is not found, the "therefore" perspective is present. One evidence of the latter is the frequent use in I Peter of such words as "since," "because," "forasmuch," and "for." We shall have to restrict ourselves, however, in this section to a rather general examination of three of the major "therefore" passages.

The first of these "therefore" or hortatory passages is in the first chapter. Peter had set forth some of the blessings that had come to his readers because of the "living hope" that was theirs "through the resurrection of Jesus Christ from the dead" (1:3–12). Using a "therefore," he proceeds to remind them of the responsibilities that evolve from those blessings (1:13–22). "The emphasis throughout the passage is on the ethical demands which follow from the Christian faith" (Selwyn). Peter admonished his readers to gird up their minds, an oriental metaphor meaning to get ready for action ("be like men stripped for action," NEB). They were to be sober or "perfectly self-controlled" (NEB). They were also to set or fix their hope "upon the grace that is coming" when Christ is revealed. As obedient children they were not to be conformed (cf. Rom. 12:2) to the passions or desires that were theirs before they became Christians.

One commentator (Cranfield) compares verses 12–23 to a piece of weaving. He suggests that the warp "describes the nature of the Christian life, while the woof indicates its motives." The warp consists of obedience to God, holiness, fear of God, and love

---

[24] C. E. B. Cranfield, *I and II Peter and Jude* (London: SCM Press, 1960), p. 46. Any subsequent references will be in the body of the material.

[25] A. M. Hunter, *The First Epistle of Peter* in *The Interpreter's Bible*, XII, 99.

of the brethren. The separate threads of the woof, indicating motives, are (1) God is holy and you belong to Him; (2) you address the impartial judge of all men by the intimate name of Father; (3) you have been redeemed by the precious blood of Christ; and (4) you have been begotten again by the eternal Word of God. The close intertwining of motive and exhortation reveals that the "therefore" perspective or psychology is a continuing theme.

The second "therefore" passage that we shall discuss (2:1-10) is introduced in the Revised Standard Version by the word "so." However, the same word (*oun*) is translated "therefore" in 4:7 and 5:6, which is by far the most common translation of the word. Wand summarizes these verses with their background (1:22-25) as follows: "The new birth with its recognition of the ideal of brotherly love among Christians involves the laying aside of all unsocial traits and the cultivation of that simple sincerity which is alone able to insure spiritual growth" (WC). The new life in Christ demands a new way of life before men. This means the putting away of "all malice" or "ill-feeling," "all guile" or "deceit" (NEB), "insincerity" or pretense, "envy" and "all slander." Notice in this list of things to put away that all are primarily inner except the last. This is in harmony with the general emphasis in the ethics of original Christianity. Notice also the threefold use of "all," which expresses something of the vehemence with which these sins are condemned, sins that were hardly recognized as sins previous to the Christian movement.

Our statement concerning this passage would not be complete without calling attention to the positive as well as the negative emphasis in the passage. Like newborn babes, they should long— a verb which expresses urgency or intensity—for the pure, unadulterated, or uncontaminated spiritual or natural milk, that by it they might "grow up to salvation" or might thrive upon it to their "soul's health" (NEB). There follow several verses that have as a theme the Church or the people of God—a New Israel. Central in these verses is an emphasis on holiness: "a holy priesthood" (v. 5) and "a holy nation, God's own people" (v. 9).

The third and last "therefore" passage we shall use[26] is in Chapter 4 (4:7-11). It opens with the striking statement: "The end of all things is at hand; therefore. . . ." Here is the sound of reveille. The conclusion or the culmination of history, depending on one's perspective, is just around the corner. In the light of this, Peter says, "Keep sane and sober for your prayers" or "Be calm, self-controlled men of prayer" (Phillips). There follows the rather striking statement: "Above all hold unfailing your love [*agape*] for one another" ("keep your love for one another at full strength," NEB). *Agape* is a love that gives, that cares. This kind of love "covers a multitude of sins": sins of the one who is loved or of the one who loves, but possibly primarily the latter (see Prov. 10:12; Luke 7:47).

There follows an exhortation for a practical expression of love. "Practice hospitality ungrudgingly ["without complaining," NEB] to one another" ("complaint spoils hospitality," WP). Hospitality was quite important in the society of that day and became particularly important for the missionary outreach of the Christian movement.[27] Moreover, what gifts they may have are to be employed or used "in service to one another" (NEB), "as good stewards of God's varied grace." An evidence of the varied, manifold, or many-colored nature of that grace is the gifts of the Spirit. Christians are stewards of that grace and of the gifts they have received through that grace. They are responsible unto God and to their fellowman. This is true whether it is the grace of hospitality or the gift to preach. All is to be done that "God may be glorified through Jesus Christ." This whole passage contains what has been called, "ethics for the crisis"—the crisis referring to the return of the Lord and the winding up of things.

2. Subjection to authorities.

The opening words of this rather lengthy section (2:13-3:9) are as follows: "Be subject . . . to every human institution." The verses immediately preceding provide an introduction and back-

[26] For another brief "therefore" passage, in which the main thrust is on humility, with some attention to sobriety and watchfulness, see 5:6-8.
[27] Selwyn (p. 218) would make this refer to "house-churches."

ground for Peter's exhortation. He appealed to his readers "as aliens and exiles" ("as strangers and temporary residents," Phillips) "to keep on abstaining from the evil desires" of their lower nature (Williams) and to "maintain good conduct among the Gentiles." Here we see movement from the inner (evil desires) to the outer (good conduct), which is so typical throughout the New Testament. One motive for their good conduct was that those who considered them wrongdoers might see their good deeds and glorify God (cf. Matt. 5:16).

One way for them to convince those who accused them was to be subject to or submit themselves to every human or "fundamental social" (Selwyn) institution. Peter applies this basic principle of submission to three specific areas: the relation of the citizen to the State, the servant to his master, and the wife to her husband. In each case he emphasizes duties that belong to the "humbler side" of the relationship. He also restricts himself to general statements without considering possible exceptions.

Peter says that they were to live as free men but also as servants or slaves of God. In other words, the freedom that they had, which is so central in the Christian experience, is a freedom coupled with servitude. When this is properly understood, it saves Christian liberty from its two greatest temptations: insubordination to civil authorities and antinomianism in morals, dealt with particularly in II Peter and Jude but also touched upon here in I Peter. Peter said that his readers were not to use their freedom as a pretext or cloak for misconduct or evil. On the other hand, because they were servants of God they were to be submissive to the emperor or to governors "sent by him to punish those who do wrong and to praise those who do right" (cf. Rom. 13:1-7). "Religious freedom (1:18) must never be made an excuse for moral or social anarchy" (MC). Peter's statement on the relation of the citizen to the civil authority closes with an appropriate summary for the section: "Honor all men. Love the brotherhood. Fear God. Honor the emperor."

There follows a rather lengthy section (2:18-25) regarding the submission of household servants to their masters (cf. Eph. 6:5-7; Col. 3:22-25; I Tim. 6:1-2; Titus 2:9-10). They were to be submissive not only "to the kind and gentle but also to the overbearing ["difficult," Phillips]." If they suffered unjustly, let them remember Christ who had suffered for them. "When he was reviled ["abused," NEB], he did not revile in return; when he suffered, he did not threaten; but he trusted to him who judges justly." He left an example for them to follow.

The last of Peter's applications of the general principle of submission is to the relation of wives to their husbands (cf. Eph. 5:21-33; Col. 3:18-19). The freedom the Christians had might tend to make some wives as well as slaves self-assertive and restless. Peter says that Christian wives are to be submissive to their husbands even if the latter are pagan. They are to live chaste and reverent lives before them. Their beauty, he says, "should reside, not in outward adornment . . . but in the inmost centre" of their being, "with its imperishable ornament, a gentle, quiet spirit, which is of high value in the sight of God" (NEB). Inner moral beauty in contrast to outer adornment is imperishable; it never fades or wears out. Peter closes the statement to wives with some striking words: "And you are now her [Sarah's] children if you do right and let nothing terrify you"—"keep calm and courageous, even when a pagan husband threatens you with violence" (MC).

Peter then inserts a brief but significant word to Christian husbands. They are to live "considerately" with their wives, possibly referring to the sexual aspects of marriage, remembering that wives are weaker physically. But at the same time they should remember that the wife is a joint heir with her husband of the grace of God. Furthermore, the husband is to be considerate of his wife in order that their prayers might not be hindered or interrupted. "God will not hear prayers from a home when the man bullies and overbears the woman" (MC).

Let us notice that in the general statement of the principle of submission and in the three illustrations or applications, Peter gives in each case a motive for the exhortation. They are admonished to be submissive to every human institution "for the Lord's sake"—because of what Christ (the Lord) taught (Luke 20:22-25), because of the example He set, or preferably simply for the sake of His cause. The motive for submission to governmental authorities is "that by doing right you should put to silence the ignorance of foolish men." Concerning "put to silence," Selwyn says,

"The simple sense of 'muzzle' need not be excluded, for it is better to prevent an ass from braying than to stop it when it has brayed." Servants should submit to masters that they might have the approval of God and follow the example of Jesus. Christian wives should be submissive even to pagan husbands "so that some . . . may be won . . . by the behavior of their wives."

Peter closes this most lengthy unified section of his epistle with a general appeal: "Finally ["to sum up," NEB], all of you, have unity of spirit, sympathy, love of the brethren, a tender heart and a humble mind." The "all of you" included masters and slaves, husbands and wives, rich and poor. They are not to return evil for evil, not to revile but to bless that they may obtain a blessing. He then quotes from Psalm 34 (vv. 12–16), a passage that has considerable ethical emphasis. He who "would love life and see good days" must "keep his tongue from evil . . . his lips from speaking guile"; he must "turn away from evil and do right; . . . seek peace and pursue it."

II Peter and Jude[28]

These two general epistles are discussed together because they are so strikingly similar. Most of Jude is incorporated into II Peter (see 2:1–18; 3:1–3), although it is not quoted verbatim. One writer suggests that II Peter is essentially Jude expanded and given a preface and an appendix (WC). They had one common, dominant purpose: to combat the heretical idea that daily living was of little consequence for the Christian life; that a truly religious or spiritual man was exempt from the moral law. Jude (v. 4) suggests that some who held this heretical idea had secretly gained admission into the Christian group (cf. II Pet. 2:1). From the perspective of both Jude and Peter this antinomianism, which

---

28 Most scholars agree that the author of Jude was the half-brother of Jesus. There are comparatively few scholars who believe that the apostle Peter was the author of II Peter. Cartledge, a conservative, concludes that "probably most Conservatives will continue to hold rather tentatively to the Petrine authorship." (*A Conservative Introduction to the New Testament*, p. 174.)

may have been an expression of certain forms of Gnosticism, was a threat to Christianity. It is possible that the antinomian emphasis or movement stemmed, to a degree, from a misinterpretation of Paul's doctrine of justification by faith (see II Peter 3:15–16). Whatever the source of the heretical doctrine, Jude and II Peter drove home "the truth that upright moral living is an essential part of the Christian life."[29]

Peter, in common with Jude, warns against "scoffers" (Jude 18; II Pet. 3:3) but spells out more specifically the subject of their scoffing or scorn. They scornfully ask, "Where is the promise of his coming?" The author reminds these scoffers, who "live self-indulgent lives" (II Pet. 3:3, NEB), and his readers in general that with the Lord one day is as a thousand years and a thousand years as a day (3:8). He further adds that "the day of the Lord will come like a thief" (3:10). He reminds his readers that in the light of the day of the Lord and the dissolving of the earth they should live lives of holiness and godliness, waiting for the day of the Lord and the coming of a new heaven and a new earth "in which righteousness dwells" (3:11–13).

1. A ladder of Christian virtues.

In the first chapter of II Peter, before we come to the material common with Jude, there is the wonderful ladder of Christian virtues (1:5–9). The exhortation, as is usual in the New Testament, looks back or is based on something previously said. In other words, the "therefore" perspective is present. The statement opens with the words: "For this very reason ["With all this in view," NEB]." What had been said? The author had suggested that his readers had escaped "from the corruption that is in the world" and had "become partakers of the divine nature" (1:4). Because this was true they should "make every effort ["try your hardest," NEB]" to supplement their faith with virtue ("real goodness," Phillips; "moral character," Williams), "and virtue with knowledge, and knowledge with self-control, and self-control with steadfastness ["patient endurance," Williams; "fortitude," NEB], and steadfastness with godliness ["piety," NEB], and godliness with brotherly affection, and brotherly affection with love."

[29] Filson, *Opening the New Testament*, p. 205.

Notice two or three things about this ladder of Christian virtues. The expression "supplement your faith with virtue" could properly be translated "in your faith supply virtue." Wand suggests that "the 'in' so often repeated implies that each quality is a kind of soil in which the next one grows." There is a sense in which faith is the soil that produces all of the others. It is the basis or ground for all Christian virtues. At least it is the first rung on the ladder. Notice also that the last rung of the ladder is love (*agape*). Love as such or in general stands above love of the brethren (*philadelphia*). *Agape* may be cultivated within and evolve from the Christian fellowship, but it cannot be restricted or limited to that fellowship. Its very nature demands that it reach out to all men.

Then notice what is said after the catalogue of virtues. Phillips' translation is particularly graphic at this point. It says,

> If you have these qualities existing and growing in you then it means that knowing our Lord Jesus Christ has not made your lives either complacent or unproductive. The man whose life fails to exhibit these qualities is short-sighted--he can no longer see the reason why he was cleansed from his former sins.
>
> Set your minds, then, on endorsing by your conduct the fact that God has called and chosen you [1:8–10].

2. Sins of the heretics.

Much of the ethical content of II Peter and Jude is negative in emphasis. This stems from the fact that they were attempting to meet the challenge of heretics or "false teachers," who had secretly brought in "destructive heresies" (II Pet. 2:1). These teachers were licentious (2:2; Jude 4), indulging "in the lust of defiling passion" (2:10; Jude 16, 18), with "eyes full of adultery, insatiable for sin" (2:14). They were greedy (2:3), having "hearts trained in greed" (2:14; cf. 2:15, Jude 11), despised authority (2:10; Jude 8) (possibly the authority of God or Christ), were "bold and wilful," and reviled "the glorious ones" (2:10)—perhaps angels. They even counted "it pleasure to revel in the daytime" (2:13), and were blemishes on the love feasts, "as they boldly carouse together" (Jude 12; cf. II Pet. 2:13). They were boastful

(2:18; Jude 16), grumblers, malcontents, loud-mouthed, flatterers of people to gain advantage (Jude 16), worldly, and "devoid of the Spirit" (Jude 19).

These false teachers "utter big, empty words, and make of sensual lusts and debauchery a bait to catch those who have barely begun to escape from their heathen environment" (2:18, NEB). Those who are caught by the bait are the "unsteady souls" (2:14), recent immature converts. The false teachers promise them freedom, possibly from the moral law, but they themselves are slaves of corruption, "for a man is the slave of whatever has mastered him" (2:19, NEB). One who had once escaped the defilements of the world and returned to them, to use a couple of common proverbs, were like dogs that returned to their vomit or sows that having been washed wallowed again in the mire (2:19–22). In this passage the author "reiterates that Christianity is a revelation which involved moral enterprise and moral obedience" (MC).

The authors of II Peter and Jude use some rather colorful language to describe the false teachers. Jude says, "They are clouds carried away in the wind without giving rain, trees that in season bear no fruit, dead twice over and pulled up by the roots. They are fierce waves of the sea, foaming shameful deeds; they are stars that have wandered from their course, and the place for ever reserved for them is blackest darkness" (Jude 12–13, NEB; cf. II Pet. 2:17). They are "like irrational animals, creatures of instinct, born to be caught and killed" (II Pet. 2:12; cf. Jude 10). As animals are led to their destruction by their appetite, so the false teachers are led to destruction through their lusts. Like animals they follow their natural desires rather than control those desires. This means enslavement and destruction.

3. Conclusions.

Both books have rather impressive closings with some ethical significance. As suggested previously, II Peter mentions the day of the Lord and the dissolving of the earth, followed by the statement: "Since the whole universe is to break up in this way, think what sort of people you ought to be, what devout and dedicated lives you should live!" (3:11, NEB). They "wait for new heavens and a new earth in which righteousness dwells" (3:13). There follows a "therefore" passage: "Therefore, beloved, since you wait for these, be zealous to be found by him [when he comes] without spot or blemish, and at peace ["in serene assurance," Moffatt]" (3:14). Moffatt suggests that "the deep thought" in this statement "is that the Christian hope ought to produce a moral and spiritual quickening of conscience" (MC). He further says, "For the writer it was impossible to give up the hope of the Advent without ethical deterioration." The readers are also admonished not to be carried away by "the error of lawless men" and thus lose their stability, but to grow "in the grace and knowledge of our Lord and Saviour Jesus Christ" (3:17–18).

Jude, in his conclusion, says, "But you, beloved, build yourself up on your most holy faith; pray in the Holy Spirit; keep yourselves in the love of God; wait for the mercy of our Lord Jesus Christ unto eternal life" (Jude 20–21). Notice here the great triology, prominent elsewhere in the New Testament, of faith, hope, and love. Notice particularly the beautiful statement: "Keep yourselves in the love of God," His love is a protecting shield or sphere around one; abide in His love and you are safe from all harm.

Jude further says, "There are some doubting souls who need your pity; snatch them from the flames and save them. There are others for whom your pity must be mixed with fear; hate the very clothing that is contaminated with sensuality" (Jude 22–23, NEB).

CHAPTER IX

CONCLUSION

There have been concluding paragraphs at the end of some of the preceding chapters, with a more extended conclusion at the close of the last chapter on the Old Testament (Chap. III). The present chapter in a summary way will state some personal conclusions concerning the ethical content of the entire Bible.

1. *Ethics has a very important place in both the Old Testament and the New Testament.* The ethical is a significant phase of practically every book of both testaments and is the central theme or dominant interest of a number of the books. It is clearly evident that ethics is an integral part of the biblical revelation. The Scriptures reveal primarily a way of life rather than a theory about life. This way is to be followed by those who claim to know the One who not only points out the way but who is the Way.

2. *Biblical ethics has been neglected in a great deal of Bible study.* This includes many books that have been written on the theology of the Bible and on its teachings in general. The approach has tended to be too exclusively historical and theological. No study of the Bible is complete without a consideration of its ethics.

3. *God is as central in the ethics of the Bible as He is in its theology.* He is the God not only of the sanctuary but also of the marketplace. In other words, the sovereign God of the universe is revealed as one who is interested in and has a will for the totality of the life of the individual, the nation, and the world. Furthermore, the God who is the central character of the Bible is revealed as a moral Person. This is true whether He is Yahweh, the God of the Hebrews, or the God fully revealed in Christ. Since God is a moral Person, it is natural that the ethical should have an important place in His revelation of His will and purpose for man.

4. *The dominant ethical appeal in the Bible is for the people of God to be like Him.* This kinship motive or appeal is prominent in both testaments. This is the nearest thing we have in biblical ethics to one unifying theme or motif. This means, among other things, that the nature and content of the biblical ethic evolves from the nature of God. For example, in the Old Testament certain qualities, such as holiness, justice, and righteousness, are particularly prominent in the character of God and, in turn, in His expectations of His people. In the New Testament, in the light of the revelation of God in Christ there is a more central place for love, although this emphasis is present in some Old Testament books, such as Deuteronomy and Hosea.

5. *Religion and ethics are thoroughly integrated in the Bible.* This is natural since the ethical content of the Bible is derived primarily from the nature of God. The close relation of religion, strictly speaking, and ethics is particularly noticeable in the great summaries of the basic requirements of our faith, such as the Ten Commandments and the central messages of the Prophets. Similarly, right relations to God and man are thoroughly integrated in the New Testament. For example, salvation comes through faith and faith alone, but the purpose of that salvation is good works or a life of goodness (Eph. 2:8–10; cf. Matt. 5:14–16; John 15:16), and the proof of the faith that saves is the quality of life that is lived (Matt. 7:15–23; Rom. 6:1–4; James 2:14–16; I John 2:3–6). Love for God and man belong together and are the fulfillment of the Law and the Prophets (Matt. 22:34–40; Rom. 13:8–10; Gal. 5:14). The love of our fellowman, which is the

proof of our relation to and love for God (I John 3:14–15; 4:7–8, 16, 19, 20–21), will express itself in helpful service (Luke 10:25–37; John 21:15–17; I John 3:11–18). Furthermore, we cannot have the forgiveness of our heavenly Father unless we forgive those who have sinned against us (Matt. 6:12–15; 18:21–35). In other words, it is clearly revealed in both Old Testament and New Testament that one cannot be right with God unless he is right with his fellowman. The prophets cried out against the sins of a people who thought they would be acceptable to God if they were faithful to the formalities of their faith. Jesus faced the same problem with the Pharisees. His word to them and to all who err in the same direction was and is "These you ought to have done, without neglecting the others," and "the others" referred to "the weightier matters of the law, justice and mercy and faith" (Matt. 23:23).

6. *Theology and ethics belong together.* There is no evidence in the Bible of a purely speculative theology, a type of theology that crept into the Christian movement through its contact with certain aspects of Greek thought. It is recognized that a separation of theology and ethics for study purposes may be justified, but it will be most unfortunate for both if it is not recognized that they are simply two ways of looking at a unified revelation of God and His way and will for man. Theology in the Bible is used primarily as a basis for exhortations that men live for God and their fellowmen.

7. *There is a rather remarkable unity in the midst of diversity in the ethical content of the Bible as well as in the Bible as a whole.* There tends to be unity of over-all purpose while there is diversity in approach and emphasis. The unity and diversity so prominent in the Bible stem to a considerable degree from its divine-human nature. Broadly speaking, its unity is derived from its divine nature, and its diversity from its human nature. For example, God had to use as the recipients of, or channels for, His self-disclosure men who were limited by their finiteness and, to some degree, by the historical situations surrounding them. In turn, the recipients of the revelation passed on what they, by inspiration, had been able to comprehend to people who were limited in their capacity to understand, accept, and apply the

revelation. For example, Jesus said that Moses, because of the hardness of heart or the perversity of life of the people, permitted them to put away their wives, which was contrary to the original purpose of God. The preceding means, among other things, that the unity in the ethical content as well as in the Bible as a whole is not static but, to use a recurring expression of H. H. Rowley, it is "a dynamic unity" or a "unity of growth."

8. *The developmental nature of the unity within the Old Testament is climaxed in the ministry and messages of the great eighth-century prophets.* For the prophets the ethical was supremely important. They spoke out in particular, as prophets have in every age, in defense of the oppressed and underprivileged. This was true because they believed that God was especially concerned about the widow, the orphan, the stranger, the social and moral outcast of society.

9. *The movement or progress in the Scriptures is particularly clear when one moves from the Old Testament to the New Testament.* The climax of God's revelation of Himself and also of His attitude toward and His will and purpose for man is in Christ. The latter is God's final and full word to man. It is the writer of Hebrews who says, "When in former times God spoke to our forefathers, he spoke in fragmentary and varied fashion through the prophets. But in this the final age he has spoken to us in the Son" (Heb. 1:1–2, NEB). Jesus Himself said, "You have heard that it was said. . . . But I say to you. . . ." Here is the voice of authority.

10. The fact that God's revelation of His will for man is climaxed in Christ means that *the Old Testament should be interpreted and particularly evaluated in the light of the fuller revelation in the New Testament.* As Rowley, an Old Testament scholar, says, "The New Testament must be finally normative for the Christian understanding of the Old."[1] Unfortunately, many Christians do not understand that this is true and they become what might be termed Old Testament Christians. They derive their standards of daily living primarily from the Old Testament rather than from the fuller light that is in Christ. The preceding does not mean that the Old Testament is not a legitimate part

[1] H. H. Rowley, *The Rediscovery of the Old Testatment*, p. 14.

of the Christian Bible. It forms an over-all unity with the New Testament, but let us repeat that it is a unity of progress and movement. One can properly be considered the seed or the germ, and the other, the fruit. Rowley[2] compares the relation of the Old Testament and the New Testament to parts of a musical cadence or sonata. He suggests that the New Testament is the final movement, but that the Old Testament belongs as a part of the sonata. The close relation of the two and their movement is clearly evident in biblical ethics. Sometimes the movement is nothing more than a matter of emphasis. For example, the emphasis in the New Testament is more on principle and less on law or precept than is true in the Old Testament. Also the emphasis is greater on the inner and less on the outer in the New Testament than in the Old Testament. Likewise, love is more central and has a deeper meaning in the former than in the latter.

11. While the climax of biblical ethics is reached in the life and teachings of Jesus, *there is a sense in which the biblical ethic attains its most significant stage in the post-resurrection period.* This is particularly true of the emphasis that daily Christian living is a natural outgrowth of a vital, life-changing union with the resurrected Christ. This perspective is particularly prominent in the epistles of Paul and in I John. The movement from within the Christian experience outward is such a natural expression of the vital relationship with the resurrected Christ that the outer expression, in turn, becomes a proof of the inner relationship.

12. Another way of stating what we have been saying is to suggest that *the ethical teachings of the Bible are not on a plain, but are a part of a path.* That path, however, does not always move smoothly or upward. There are valleys as well as mountain peaks. Whatever upward movement there is results from a clearer insight into the revelation of the character and will of God. While it may be correct to say that man has been on a constant search for God and for a fuller understanding of His way and will, the Bible also reveals that God has been seeking at the same time to reveal Himself and His will more fully to man. It is even possible that man's seeking is a result of God's seeking.

2 H. H. Rowley, *The Relevance of the Bible* (New York: Macmillan, 1944), pp. 82–83.

13. *The biblical perspective concerning history is an important factor and really an integral phase of biblical ethics.* There is clearly evident in the Bible a theology of history. The general view is that the sovereign God of the universe is in control of history and that He will ultimately achieve His purposes within or over history. This perspective is prevalent throughout the Old Testament but it is also evident in the New Testament, particularly in the book of the Revelation.

14. *Eschatology,* which represents a particular aspect or view of history, *is rather closely related to ethics in the Bible.* The biblical ethic can properly be called an eschatological ethic, if one understands that this is simply one of many ways to describe it. The eschatological has a prominent place in the teachings of the prophets and in the ministry and message of Jesus. It is present as a motive and used as a basis for an appeal for daily Christian living by Paul, Peter, John, and James. The eschatological is particularly important in the Revelation or the Apocalypse.

15. As implied above and also in previous chapters, *the biblical ethic is so deep and broad,* as is true of the Christian life in general, *that it cannot be described adequately by the use of any one term.* One does violence to the material found in the Bible if he attempts to force everything under one descriptive term. Many terms may be used and still the depths of the biblical ethic will not be fully fathomed. It has been indicated at various stages in our study that the biblical ethic could be properly called "a covenant ethic," "a *koinonia* ethic," "a love ethic," "a will of God ethic," "a kingdom of God ethic," "an eschatological ethic," "a perfectionistic ethic," "a disciples' ethic," "a Holy Spirit ethic" which may be the New Testament equivalent of "a holiness ethic" in the Old Testament, and "an ethic of the cross" which in a sense is the central unifying symbol of the divine revelation and of the Christian life. Some of these concepts are more prevalent in the Bible than others. For example, no one idea is more pervasive of the Old Testament ethic than the covenant concept. The idea of *koinonia* which is closely related to the covenant concept is implicit throughout the Bible, but is particularly evident after the formation of the Church. The will of God or the way of the Lord has a prominent place in both Testaments. Love,

which is central in a couple of books in the Old Testament (Deuteronomy and Hosea), permeates thoroughly the New Testament, being revealed as the crowning virtue of the Christian life. The most distinctive New Testament concept, which has much more significance for ethics than is generally supposed, is the cross. While the cross is much more than a symbol, it is the unifying symbol of the Christian life.

16. *Much of the biblical ethic is just as relevant today as it was in the days in which the books of the Bible were written.* A leading English scholar says that the Bible is "urgently relevant" to our age[3] and it could be added that it is distressingly relevant in some areas. As indicated previously, the Bible is not relevant in the sense that it is a rule book to which we can go for a chapter and verse answer to every question—for a solution for every problem. There are some instructions in the Bible that are so thoroughly historically conditioned that they do not apply to our world. However, behind and sometimes permeating even these instructions there are basic principles that are relevant for every day. This correctly implies, as has been stated previously, that the most relevant portions of the Bible are its principles or ideals and, contrary to the view of many, the most constantly relevant ideals are its ideals of perfection. These ideals or principles are above and beyond history, eternally transcendent but also, and for that reason, eternally relevant. They are the ideals that create the dynamic tension at the heart of our Christian faith which is the secret to its creativity.

17. *My conviction that the Bible is authoritative has been strengthened* as this study has progressed. A recognized American biblical scholar speaks of the Bible as "the indispensable and incomparable book which speaks an urgently authoritative word to every generation."[4] But wherein rests the authority of the Bible? While many of its precepts and principles are authoritative, its authority does not rest primarily in them, but in the God who is back of those principles and precepts. In other words, the Bible does not possess any authority independent of God. Its

---

3 Rowley, *The Relevance of the Bible,* p. vii.
4 Floyd V. Filson, *Which Books Belong in the Bible?* (Philadelphia: Westminster Press, 1957), p. 17.

authority stems from the fact that it is a product of and contains God's word to man.

18. *There is a very real sense in which the authority is Christ's,* since He is the climax of the revelation of God. The Scriptures can lead us to Christ, but as sacred as they are, they cannot take the place of Christ. He is the Word made flesh. To Him the printed page of the Bible bears record. When properly understood, this does not detract from the authority of the Bible; it clarifies and deepens it. Back of the Bible is the divine Person who gave birth to the Bible, whose authority is prior to the Bible but also is expressed through the Bible. God will speak through the Bible to our age, as well as every other age, if we have ears to hear and hearts that are willing to listen to His voice and to walk in His way.

SUGGESTIONS FOR ADDITIONAL STUDY

It is hoped, as indicated in the preface, that these suggestions will be helpful to laymen and ministers. We recognize, however, that they will be used more generally by teachers who may want to use one or more of the following as special assignments. The suggestions have been arranged in what seems to be a logical order: the exegetical first, followed by the topical, and then by a study of a book or books. Some teachers may prefer to have at least two exegetical studies and cover the topical material in class lectures. These supplementary studies can provide rich and rewarding experiences for serious minded students.

I. Exegetical.
Using several commentaries, make a thorough exegesis of one of the following:
    1. General or basic ethic
        (1) Leviticus 19:9–18: the requirements of a holy God.
        (2) Job 31:1–15, 16–28, *or* 29–40: no greater statement of ethical religion in the Old Testament.
        (3) Psalm 15:1–5: a summary of the requirements of an ethical religion.
        (4) Isaiah 1:10–17: righteousness preferred to ritualistic faithfulness.
        (5) Amos 5:10–27: God's punishment for sins against one's fellowman.
        (6) Micah 6:6–15: the basic demands of true religion.
        (7) Matthew 22:34–40: love, the greatest of the commandments.
        (8) John 15:1–17: the fruitful life.
        (9) Galatians 5:16–26: the fruit of the Spirit.

  (10) Ephesians 5:1–17: the Christian walk.

  (11) Colossians 3:1–14: the resurrected life.

  (12) I Thessalonians 4:3–12: the sanctified life.

  (13) James 2:14–26: faith and works.

  (14) I Peter 1:13–22: the holy life.

  (15) I John 4:7–21: the centrality of love.

 2. Specific or applied ethic

  (1) Deuteronomy 24:1–4: the law regulating divorce.

  (2) Proverbs 23:29–35: "Look not thou upon the wine."

  (3) Malachi 2:11–16: mixed marriages and divorce.

  (4) Matthew 6:19–34: the disciple and material possessions.

  (5) Matthew 19:3–12: marriage and divorce.

  (6) Matthew 20:20–28: greatness in the kingdom.

  (7) Mark 10:23–31: the rich man, the camel, and the needle's eye.

  (8) Luke 20:19–26: things that are Caesar's.

  (9) Romans 13:1–7: the Christian and the powers that be.

  (10) I Corinthians 7:1–16: family relations.

  (11) Ephesians 5:22—6:4: relations in the home.

  (12) I Timothy 3:1–13: qualifications of bishops and deacons.

  (13) Philemon: slavery.

  (14) James 2:1–13: respect of persons within the church.

  (15) I Peter 2:13—3:9: subjection "for the Lord's sake."

II. Topical.

 1. Basic

Outline the ethical content and implications of one of the following as found in the Bible:

  (1) The covenant concept.

  (2) Holiness.

  (3) Righteousness.

  (4) Justice.

(5) Love.

(6) Perfection.

(7) Freedom or liberty.

(8) Will of God.

(9) The work of the Holy Spirit.

(10) The cross and self-denial.

(11) "The way of the Lord."

(12) Eschatology.

(13) Relation of individual and community.

(14) *Koinonia,* community, or fellowship concept.

(15) Relation of precept, principle, and relationship in biblical perspective.

2. Social or applied

Outline the teachings of the Bible on one of the following:

(1) The individual and his worth.

(2) The body and health.

(3) Impartiality or no respecter of persons.

(4) Widows, orphans, and underprivileged in general.

(5) Motivation for ethical living.

(6) Marriage and divorce.

(7) Relations within the home.

(8) Sex and sexual ethics.

(9) Wine and strong drink.

(10) Economic life and relations.

(11) Poverty and wealth.

(12) Government and the state.

(13) Crime and the punishment of crime.

(14) Race and race relations.

(15) War and the use of force.

III. Book or Books.

Prepare a detailed topical outline of the social and ethical teachings of one of the following:

(1) Exodus.

(2) Deuteronomy.

(3) Proverbs.

(4) Isaiah, Hosea, Amos, and Micah.

(5) Matthew.

(6) Luke.
(7) Romans and Galatians.
(8) I and II Corinthians.
(9) Remainder of Paul's epistles.
(10) The General Epistles (Hebrews through Jude).

INDEX OF SCRIPTURE

This index includes only those passages that receive some interpretation or comment in the text.

INDEX OF SUBJECTS